Strategy to Reality

What leaders and change makers are saying about Whynde Kuehn and Strategy to Reality…

One word: Powerful! In *Strategy to Reality*, globally recognized strategy execution and business architecture expert, Whynde Kuehn, has bottled the secret sauce necessary to enable the transmutation of big ideas into operating reality. Her timely and practical *how-to* guide is based on decades of hands-on experiences enabling organizations around the world to successfully execute transformational ideas that have materially impacted the top and bottom lines.

Mark I. Johnson, Editorial Board Chair, Chief Data Officer Magazine and Regional Vice President & Executive Leader, Strategic Data Management and Analytics, Fusion Alliance

Whynde Kuehn filters the noise in the space of digital business transformation practices. She provides invaluable firsthand knowledge and advice that can greatly benefit both individuals and corporations in not only comprehending how to best drive change but also gives the techniques that can be readily applied as solutions to real-life scenarios.

Suleiman Barada, Senior Advisor, Union of Arab Banks

There is no voice more astute on the importance of and the proper execution of business architecture than Whynde Kuehn. Having worked alongside her for several years, I saw firsthand the impact she has on organizational transformation and strategy. The discipline of business architecture is needed in any modern and progressive organization and her perspectives and techniques in this space are essential.

Toby O'Rourke, President & CEO, Kampgrounds of America, Inc.

Successful strategy implementation is vital for any business leader or organization. Whynde Kuehn has an exceptional understanding of not only the challenges but also the methodology which has already helped business leaders across the world in this very complicated discipline. *Strategy to Reality* gives you a thorough introduction and practical steps to leverage the well-recognized methodology of business architecture to achieve your goals.

Lene Østerberg, COO, Linconomy

Despite decades of research and literature on the topic, strategy execution is no better today in most organizations than it was twenty years ago. Business architecture, if positioned correctly within an organization and staffed appropriately, can close the gap between business strategy formulation and strategy execution—a critical role that is missing or poorly functioning in many organizations today. This practical book focuses on many of the critical factors needed to do that.

Brian H. Cameron, PhD, Associate Dean for Professional Graduate Programs and Executive Education, Smeal College of Business, The Pennsylvania State University

Strategy to Reality gets everyone in your organization speaking the same language and builds a strong business foundation for your future. You will refer to it again and again. It truly takes a village to run a successful company, without Whynde and her book you are already at a disadvantage. The CIO understands that business architecture is the API—the ultimate connector—for strategy to execution. This book helps your organization on the journey towards realizing its full potential.

Robert Field, Vice President of Global Information Technology and Digital Solutions, Precipart

In *Strategy to Reality*, Whynde Kuehn explains in clear terms how to unleash the elegance and power of business architecture in a way that is equally compelling to those just starting out and to others who may be well down the path towards maturity. I recommend that you not only pick up this book, but keep it close at hand as your practice matures as it will continue to inform and inspire along the way.

William Ulrich, President, Tactical Strategy Group and President and Cofounder, Business Architecture Guild

Whynde is a true pioneer in business architecture and in a period of human history where change is on the doorstep of every leader. This body of work will be a true compass, making the impossible possible, enabling businesses to not only evolve but continue to stay relevant.

Michael Clark, Global Digital Innovation and Technology Leader

As one of the world's leading experts on the topic of business architecture, Whynde Kuehn needs no introduction nor accolades from me. However, I offer them anyway for her amazing work on the discipline of business architecture as well as the benefits an organization can hope to achieve by leveraging it. Too often, I have seen organizations fail to deliver digital transformation, agility, and value without business architects to connect the strategy to the execution for enterprise digital advantage. This book should be on every executive's desk and in the hands of every business architect and change maker.

Paul Preiss, CEO, Iasa Global

Whynde Kuehn is one of the most inspiring global leaders and true innovative pioneers for the business architecture community. Her modern, multi-dimensional approach, and holistic expert guidance has been the blueprint to support successful executive leaders, business transformation teams, and game changing innovation. *Strategy to Reality* will undoubtedly become the *go-to* guide for future leaders seeking to drive scalable business value in today's complex landscape.

Shaun Rolls, Managing Director, Closed Circle International and Global Head of EDM Council Innovation Lab

Strategy to Reality shares a vision of a business architecture practice that is fully embedded and influencing the business with universally valued strategy work. Enjoy exploring this vision to advance your agenda to create or turbo-charge the practice in your organization!

Grant Ecker, VP Global Enterprise Architecture at Walgreens Boots Alliance

Strategy
to
Reality

MAKING THE IMPOSSIBLE POSSIBLE
FOR BUSINESS ARCHITECTS, CHANGE MAKERS
and STRATEGY EXECUTION LEADERS

WHYNDE KUEHN

NEW YORK

LONDON • NASHVILLE • MELBOURNE • VANCOUVER

Strategy to Reality

Making the Impossible Possible for Business Architects, Change Makers and Strategy Execution Leaders

Published in New York, New York, by Morgan James Publishing. Morgan James is a trademark of Morgan James, LLC. www.MorganJamesPublishing.com

Proudly distributed by Ingram Publisher Services.

Morgan James BOGO™

A **FREE** ebook edition is available for you or a friend with the purchase of this print book.

CLEARLY SIGN YOUR NAME ABOVE

Instructions to claim your free ebook edition:
1. Visit MorganJamesBOGO.com
2. Sign your name CLEARLY in the space above
3. Complete the form and submit a photo of this entire page
4. You or your friend can download the ebook to your preferred device

ISBN 9781631958441 paperback
ISBN 9781631958458 ebook
Library of Congress Control Number: 2021951705

Cover Design & Branding by:
Stefanie Hartman & Whynde Kuehn
www.StefanieHartman.com
www.press-project.com
www.StrategyintoReality.com

Cover Graphics by:
Botond Kiss
www.kissbotond.info
Christopher Wray
www.communique-marketing.com

Figures by:
Christopher Wray
www.communique-marketing.com

Interior Design by:
Chris Treccani
www.3dogcreative.net

Morgan James is a proud partner of Habitat for Humanity Peninsula and Greater Williamsburg. Partners in building since 2006.

Get involved today! Visit MorganJamesPublishing.com/giving-back

DEDICATIONS

For my dad, William L. Kuehn.
I'll always have big shoes to fill.

CONTENTS

ACKNOWLEDGMENTS

This book is the culmination of a journey that began in 2003, so I can only be humbled and filled with gratitude for all the many people who have walked before me, taught me, influenced me, co-created with me, and believed in me. This book would not be if it were not for all of us.

To my parents—I am eternally grateful for how you shaped me, in head and heart. For my dad, William (Bill) Kuehn, who crossed over to the non-physical world during the writing of this book, often referenced by others as "the smartest guy I know," for his relentless commitment—and achievement—of true excellence in his professional life and everything he did. He built physical structures where I build conceptual ones, but I hope he will be proud. For my mom, Geri Kuehn, who taught me how to love the whole world and told me I could do anything. I believed her. LUMTA, Mama.

To my Inner Circle, students, mentees, and clients—thank you for the honor of walking alongside you on your journeys and for all that you have taught and given me. To Julie Decker and Steve McKenna and all the business and enterprise architecture practice leaders I have worked with—you will always have a special place in my heart. I recognize the special people you are—who day in and day out—catalyze change in your organizations with vision, courage, and conviction. And to Suleiman Barada—who is a catalyst for an entire region of the world. As I look back to the beginning—thank you to Marsha Barnett and Ray Carlson because it all started with you. And thank you to Greg Suddreth, my original collaborator and partner—your legacy lives on.

To all the architecture pioneers, leaders, and community builders (though I cannot possibly name all of you)—thank you for your tireless and brilliant contributions to formalize, scale, and bring business relevance to the business and enterprise architecture discipline. In particular, a huge shout out to my Business Architecture Guild® co-founders and collaborators William Ulrich, Mike Rosen, and Jim Rhyne, and to Jeff Scott for putting business architecture on the map in a new and practical way, to Dr. Brian Cameron for bringing business architecture as a facilitator of strategy execution into higher education, to Linda Finley for her leadership and community building, and to Paul Preiss for being an international voice and unifier for architects and the architecture profession.

To the strategy execution leaders, the global business architecture community, and all our advocates—here's to you. You are the real heroes. I laud you for your vision, courage, hard work, patience, persistence, and humility. For delivering real business results; for helping others to think differently; for relentlessly serving as advocates for your organizations and its customers. For lifting each other up. And for never giving up.

To all the readers and guest stars of the original StraightTalk blog series that paved the way for this book—thank you for being on this journey with me. And to Tamara Park—thank you for giving me the inspiration and courage to start the series in the first place and for cheering me on the whole way.

To Christopher Wray—where do I start? Thank you for bringing StraightTalk to life with the stunning and engaging visualizations that we all know and love. You have made an entire ecosystem of graphic resources a reality that serve the global business community. If I can dream it, you can design it—and better than I could ever imagine.

And speaking of bringing dreams to reality—a huge thank you to the whole team at Morgan James Publishing, especially David Hancock, Jim Howard, Gayle West, Heidi Nickerson and the design and support teams.

Thank you for believing in me and making my dream come true. I love what Morgan James stands for and I am beyond proud to be a part of this family.

To Stefanie Hartman—You have been a godsend. Thank you for coming alongside me and for your expert guidance and wisdom that has shaped me, my work, and the book. Simply said, without you, this book would not have been what it is or reached the hands it was meant to be in. I am so grateful for you. And we are only getting started.

To Charles Araujo—Thank you for the brilliant and inspiring Foreword that brings us back to the bigger context, relevance, and *why* for this book. And thank you for being a visionary, leader, and voice of clarity, to help us make the fundamental shift into the digital era, well-informed and with humanness.

To Ragny and Steinar, who generously gave me an island haven in the North Sea where I could write this book with solitude and the wonder of nature—tusen takk. I absolutely treasure you both.

To my dear friends Christine, Tracey, and Erik—thank you for your inspiration that has transformed my life. You showed me the difference that one person can make to change the world.

To Asbjørn, the epic love of my life—thank you for believing in me, for understanding me, and helping to make all my dreams come true, no matter how crazy they are. I love every moment of this incredible journey with you. You are my greatest gift.

And to *you* who are holding this book now—here's to you. We are bonded by our vision and commitment to something greater than ourselves. We need your talent, courage, and leadership. Remember that movements start small, and, as the late Nelson Mandela remarked, "it always seems impossible until it's done." This book—and all that I have ever done—has always been for you and because of you. Enjoy the journey.

You're Holding a Key
to the Future

By Charles Araujo

You hold in your hand something special. I know it feels like a book (or, if you're like me, a tablet), but it's something else altogether.

It's a key. It's a key that opens the door to the future. And not just your future, but the future of your organization. Cool, huh?

I know that sounds like hyperbole, but I promise you it's not. I've been studying, researching, and exploring the implications of digital transformation for over ten years and it has left me convinced of one thing: *we are entering a period of unrelenting change.*

"Tell me something I don't know," you're thinking to yourself. Fair enough. After all, we're already in the midst of this unrelenting period of change. But here's what you probably don't fully grasp—you ain't seen nothin' yet.

This period of continuous change is going to upend almost everything we know about how organizations function and run, and it will only be those leaders who can guide their organizations through this period of transformation that will come out on the other side. And you know this is true because you can already see it happening all around you.

If you want to be one of those leaders, you're going to need to collect a set of keys that are able to unlock the chains that bind your organization to the past and free it to adapt to the future. *Strategy to Reality*—and the methodologies within, based on the discipline of business architecture—is one of those keys.

The fuel that is powering this period of unrelenting change is what some are calling the experience economy. What it all comes down to is that whether we are wearing our customer, employee, or partner hat, we all want to engage with organizations who deliver a simple, intuitive, and delightful experience.

The problem is that most organizations were built for a different time—one in which the experience was an after-thought (if it was a thought at all).

This shift to the experience as the driver of value is happening everywhere. Long-standing companies and entire industries are being transformed by companies who are re-envisioning those customer, employee, and partner experiences.

In order to compete and thrive in this new era, you're going to have to adapt and change. You need a new strategy.

But even more importantly, you need to be able to execute against that strategy.

As Whynde so aptly puts it, "The challenge for organizations is less about having a poor strategy, than it is about having poor strategy execution." That's the real challenge, and why this book you're holding—the culmination of Whynde Kuehn's years of unique thought leadership and practices, experience and learned-the-hard-way expertise—is so critical to your future.

As a leader you undoubtedly understand this situation and what's at stake. You've probably had more meetings than you can count about your need to adapt and shift.

What you've lacked is a way to reliably and consistently execute—a way to change your organization from the inside out. That is, until now. In *Strategy to Reality*, Whynde makes the case that business architecture is one of the chief ways for you to do so—and I agree with her.

The reason is straight-forward. You have the opportunity (and mandate) to remodel your organization from one that was built for a different time into one that will be relevant and viable in a still-evolving future. And no different than remodeling a home, you need to start by understanding what you have to work with, and you need a clear vision of where you want to go so that your entire team can be working towards the same end-state. That's the essence of business architecture's value.

In this book, Whynde translates her passion for the value business architecture represents as an enabler of transformation into written words and makes a compelling case for why you should share in it. She explains that business architecture provides three overarching values: that it facilitates effective strategy execution, that it improves the design of organizations and their ecosystems, and that it informs decision-making.

Those value elements are foundational to any successful change or transformational effort.

She goes on to explain, however, that business architecture also helps organizations avoid the *transformation trap* (my words) of getting stuck on the idea of transformation, but failing to execute on it. In part, the discipline of business architecture does this by delivering tactical benefits that allow it to *pay its way*—things like reduced costs and risks, preventing compliance issues, facilitating M&A activity, breaking down organizational silos, and opening the door to future strategic options.

It does all of this by creating visibility and establishing a common perspective around which your organization can organize and rally. It's a powerful and enticing package that begs to be executed as fast as possible.

And that's exactly what this book aims to help you do.

If you're an executive, it will help you understand the importance of business architecture and why you must build this capability and fully embed it as a discipline in your organization. And it will serve as your guide as you do so.

If you're a business architect, it will help you find your true north and fight off the forces that will otherwise push you into myopic and small efforts that lead you astray. It will be your manual and an invaluable tool to help educate others and bring them into the fold.

In both cases, this book will help you see that adopting the discipline of business architecture—and Whynde's time-tested practical approach to it—may be one of the greatest, most sustainable tools you'll find to drive the cultural and organizational change that will enable you to pivot, react to, and take advantage of whatever shifts the market brings in the future.

See. I told you. Your key to the future.

But it's up to you to use it. So, congratulations on getting this far. Now turn the page and get started!

Charles Araujo
Publisher, The Digital Experience Report
Founder, The Institute for Digital Transformation
Author of The Quantum Age of IT, The Ecosystem Advantage,
and Performance-driven IT

INTRODUCTION

A coach once told me that my word was *big*. It's true. I love climbing mountains, physically and metaphorically. If there is one mountain I know well, it is *business architecture*. I've literally been one of the few who pioneered it, explored it, and lived it from every angle imaginable. Being a Sherpa for this mountain, and guiding business architecture leaders and practitioners around the world to the top, has been one of my greatest honors.

This book is based on years of those experiences as well as the trusted and popular StraightTalk blog series that was delivered twice monthly to subscribers on six continents. The series concluded a four-year journey with its 100th issue on 17 May 2021. *Strategy to Reality* is the culmination and celebration of that journey, which was dedicated to thoroughly explaining business architecture with the goal of advancing the discipline among global practitioners through shared and actionable knowledge.

Together we are about to explore business architecture from end-to-end, through the lens of questions. Yes, *your* questions. Why questions? Personally, I believe that questions are magical. They open a space for possibility and knowledge, and I insist that even the mysteries of the universe can be unlocked if we just ask the questions and let the answers unfold. The original StraightTalk series was oriented around questions, and that connected me deeply with the business architecture community. We co-created the journey together, through questions, and I always felt that we were in a continual conversation. Now I get to have that conversation with you.

My business architecture journey was inspired by observing how challenging it can be for organizations to move big ideas into action. I have found this to be true for all types of organizations, everywhere, from the largest to the smallest. There is a missing middle that is needed to translate and activate big ideas. Business architecture creates a holistic blueprint for an organization—or an entire business ecosystem—that is needed to create a clear, shared understanding and activate change. *Business architecture is the golden thread that connects strategy and execution.*

I believe wholeheartedly in the power of business architecture to support us in building better organizations and societies; to unlock new ways of executing strategy, collaborating, and creating value. For this to be possible though, we must share a common foundation of understanding and a vision bigger than ourselves, and we must deliver practical value.

Strategy to Reality explains the discipline from end-to-end, bringing together a vast number of perspectives and experiences all in one place. My goal is to give you the straight talk to clarify, simplify, and humanize business architecture, and make it practical and actionable. I wrote this book for *you*. I care deeply about your success and lifting *all* of us to a higher standard.

As we transform and reshape the world we live in, there has never been a greater need for a well-informed, holistic view to guide our future. If you are reading this book, you are likely a catalyst, a change agent, a champion for the bigger picture, relentlessly seeking ways to do things better, always asking *why*, and most importantly asking, *what if?* I will be your personal guide through all that is business architecture and its possibility. See you at the summit, my friend.

How to Read This Book

This book is for business architecture practitioners and leaders, current or aspiring, as well as their executive leaders. This book is also for business and technology executives who are seeking to improve the outcomes of their strategies and transformations, along with entrepreneurs, leaders of mission-driven organizations, and anyone interested in diving deeper into the discipline of business architecture. The concepts are applicable for organizations of all sizes, in all industries, and across all sectors, though many of the examples are oriented around a larger corporate environment. *Any* organization needs to be designed with intention to achieve its mission and deliver value to the people it serves as well as grow and continually adapt to change.

If you are a **business architecture practitioner or practice leader,** you may want to read the book from cover to cover, and then use it as a reference to come back to again and again as your business architecture journey unfolds.

If you are an **executive**, you may want to read Chapter 1, which provides a solid overview across all topics, and then turn to Chapter 3 to explore how business architecture can be leveraged for unique business value.

If you are **just looking to learn a little bit more about business architecture**, you may also want to read Chapter 1 for the overview and then skip to any additional chapters that pique your interest. If you work in a complementary role and partner with business architects in your organization—maybe you are a strategist, product manager, process professional, or IT architect—you can also check out Chapter 4. This will help you learn more about how business architecture interconnects with and brings value to your team.

Think of *Strategy to Reality* as your guru guide to business architecture. Hopefully soon it will be torn and worn, with multiple pages earmarked, and may you carry it with you always. Whether you need help preparing for that meeting with your executive leaders to explain the value of business architecture or creating a game plan to partner with another team, be confident that inside these pages is your 3 AM access to *What Would Whynde Do?*.

Note: You will also find an **online companion** to this book at **www.StrategyintoReality.com**, which includes downloadable diagrams and examples that correspond to the topics throughout to give you a more immersive understanding.

A Special Note

The *Guide to the Business Architecture Body of Knowledge®* (*BIZBOK®* *Guide*) published by the Business Architecture Guild® provides solid grounding for the book you are about to read. Having a shared base of knowledge allows practitioners to do much more together and with greater efficiency. However, an important distinction should be made between this book—*Strategy to Reality*—and the BIZBOK® Guide. *Strategy to Reality* does not represent that body of knowledge or the organization behind it. In fact, while this book draws upon key concepts found within the BIZBOK® Guide and helps to clarify some of its concepts, this book goes far beyond the BIZBOK® scope. *Strategy to Reality* offers careful curation of ideas and insights, perspectives on many new topics, specific approaches, expanded connections, contextualization, and practical usage throughout. It is important to note that the reader does not need to subscribe to any one specific method because this book is about embracing the straight talk, about building bridges, and about following the guiding light of business value and practicality.

1

Demystifying the What, Why, and How of Business Architecture

Picture this. You are building the home of your dreams. You can already see and feel yourself inside it, the years flashing through your mind filled with family gatherings, quiet moments, and just life. You send a one-line e-mail to your general contractor summarizing your vision. The following day, all the workers show up, ready to realize your magnificent concept into physical reality. What could go wrong?

Hold on. You would never build your dream home without creating a blueprint, and you would not just start knocking down walls to build an addition onto your home without consulting a blueprint or certified structural engineer, right? So why then do we embark upon major business transformations within our organizations without a cohesive understanding of where we are, where we are going, or how we will get there?

We all see entirely different and incomplete pictures in our minds about what we think our organization does, depending on our purview. Without a business architecture, no one sees or shares a common view of the organization in its entirety, yet we all expect to arrive in the same place and achieve our goals. (And yes, the one-line email is a real example, though it was created by an executive to articulate a two-million-dollar transformation effort to a technology team!)

The power of *clear intent translated into organized effort* not only builds dream homes, but gleaming cities, functional societies, effective organizations, robust business ecosystems, and every good and service we interact with in our daily lives. *Blueprints are a vehicle to create understanding and activate change. A business architecture is a blueprint of an organization that creates common understanding and aligns strategy and execution.*[1]

Business architecture tells us how an organization is structured to deliver value to its customers and support its operations. There are no other views or techniques like it. In our world of complexity and detail, what makes business architecture so unique is that we can see an entire organization and the business ecosystem in which it operates from a bird's eye view and through a refreshing new lens: the whole.

Every organization has a business architecture. This is true for companies of all sizes and across all sectors. An organization's business architecture may not be written down and some aspects may have been created unintentionally, but it does exist. The key is documenting it in a principled manner so that it can be used to support effective strategy execution, decision-making, and organization and ecosystem design. That is where the journey begins.

So, What Exactly is Business Architecture?

Let's start with the official definition. According to the Federation of Enterprise Architecture Professional Organizations (FEAPO), "Business Architecture represents holistic, multidimensional business views of: capabilities, end-to-end value delivery, information, and organizational structure; and the relationships among these business views and strategies, products, policies, initiatives, and stakeholders."[2] Just as a blueprint for a building has different views: structural, electrical, mechanical, plumbing, and so forth, a business architecture for an organization has views for ten different domains or perspectives.

Think about a business architecture as the one go-to place where you can see everything an organization does at a high-level. For example: *What customers does the organization serve and what products and services does it offer to them? How does it create value for its customers and stakeholders? What differentiates it from other organizations? How are people organized? What are the current strategic priorities and initiatives?* This shared business knowledgebase—from which countless views may be generated—serves as a *guidance system* that people can consult to understand what the organization does today, design what it needs to look like in the future to achieve its goals, and determine how best to get there.

The idea of creating a business architecture to holistically represent an organization might seem like an obvious idea, especially when we consider analogous situations such as blueprints for buildings or maps for geographies, but historically we haven't been too good at writing them down. However, the increased pace of change, the desire to deliver seamless experiences for customers, partners, and employees, and the need for external transparency and collaboration has moved business architecture from nice to have to *necessity* for organizations today.

What perspectives comprise an organization's business architecture?

Let's unpack the ten perspectives that are reflected in a business architecture. At the heart of any organization's business architecture are **value streams** and **capabilities**. Value streams represent how value is delivered from end-to-end, to a customer, partner, or employee. Capabilities define the *whats* of the business—the unique abilities that the organization performs across all business units and product lines. Capabilities are a crucial construct to organize and optimize the resources needed to deliver stakeholder value and evolve the organization through change initiatives.

Capabilities are the one domain that connects to all the others. They are like reusable building blocks that may be used many times within or across value streams.

Information forms the vocabulary of an organization through defined information concepts such as customer, product, partner, and asset. **Organization** represents business units, which may be internal business units or even external partners.

While value streams, capabilities, information, and organization are considered *core business architecture domains*, they may connect to the remaining six *extended business architecture domains*. **Strategies** capture various aspects of business direction, and **metrics** measure the performance of the organization. **Products** represent the goods and services that an organization offers to its customers. **Stakeholders** represent the external or internal players that participate in value streams to receive and/or contribute value. **Policies** guide the organization and may be externally-driven such as a regulation or internally-driven such as an internal human resources policy. Finally, **initiatives** represent any current or planned scope of work to implement change.

There are of course additional domains that represent other aspects of an organization, but they are outside the scope of business architecture. However, a capability and/or value stream, for example, can be connected to those other domains. A few notable connection points for business architecture include **journeys** (part of the customer experience design discipline), **business processes** (part of the business process management discipline), **applications** and **software services** (part of the IT architecture discipline), and **requirements** (part of the business analysis discipline).

Figure 1.1 illustrates the ten domains represented by business architecture along with a few key related domains. *Visit www.StrategyintoReality.com to download diagrams and other valuable resources.*

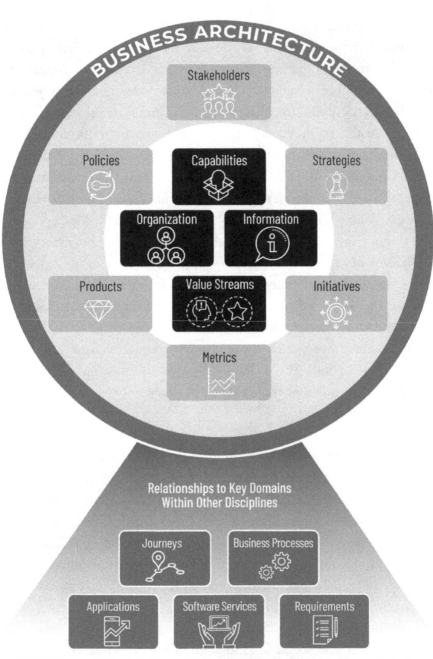

SOURCE: Content within circle diagram based on *A Guide to the Business Architecture Body of Knowledge*® (BIZBOK® Guide). "Relationships to Key Domains" copyright Whynde Kuehn.

Figure 1.1: Business Architecture Domains and Key Relationships

What differentiates business architecture?

What *exactly* is a business architecture then? It is essentially a componentized view of an organization, comprised of reusable, interconnecting pieces. For example, a capability named Customer Information Management defines the ability to collect, maintain, and track information about a specific customer, independent from any agreements, orders, or payments they have with the organization. Similarly, a capability named Payment Management defines the ability to determine, maintain, and track payments owed by or to an organization from its customers, partners, or employees. Many business units may have the same capability, and a capability can be used many times to enable different value streams.

Architectural thinking, and viewing an organization in a modular way, sets the foundation for facilitating reusable solutions, fresh innovation ideas, consistent and integrated experiences for people, and rapid business change.

We can think about a business architecture in three parts. We catalog the elements, we attribute the elements, and we create connections between the elements. That is essentially what forms a business architecture. *Our overall goal then is to build a repository, or knowledgebase, of reusable business components.*

Cataloging the elements. First, we capture the names of the individual values for each of the ten domains. This means listing the names of an organization's capabilities, products, business units, and so forth, each organized into a separate "bucket." In other words, all the capabilities are grouped together, all the products are grouped together, all the business units are grouped together, and so forth for each domain. Sorting different types of information into these different buckets (domains) is the architectural concept of *separation of concerns.*

Attributing the elements. Second, we define attributes for each of the values. For example, we would capture a description and outcome for each capability. We would capture a level, type, and description for each business unit.

Connecting the elements. Third, we create connections between the values. For example, we would create a connection between a capability and the business units that have that capability. We would create a connection between a product and the capabilities that enable it. These relationships form a rich tapestry of information that can be used to answer countless business questions and support a broad range of business usage scenarios.

Business Architecture Has Distinguishing Characteristics

There are a few key characteristics that distinguish business architecture from other documentation and approaches. These can and should guide its creation within any organization.

A business architecture represents the business. Business architecture is not an IT view or discipline. It is wholly business-focused, describing the scope of what the business does, in the language of the business. A business architecture can, however, be connected to an organization's IT architecture, which illuminates how the business is supported by applications and services, data and data deployments, and infrastructure.

A business architecture represents the entire scope of an organization and the ecosystem in which it operates. Business architecture is the big view. A business architecture does not exist in fragments across an organization. Each business unit does not have its own business architecture. There is one business architecture for an organization (unless it is a conglomerate or other structure which would dictate separation). A business architecture is one, top-down, cohesive view of everything an organization does.

A business architecture is described at a high level of detail. To make that scope of documentation attainable and usable, a business architecture is described from a higher elevation. In contrast to the detailed processes, rules, data, and systems we are immersed in daily, business architecture allows us to see the forest for the trees. This is by design for the value business architecture is intended to deliver.

A business architecture is reusable. Unlike the many documents, presentations, and deliverables that we create and archive, an organization's business architecture persists in a knowledgebase that is accessible to anyone. This translates into great time savings for onboarding and making changes to an organization because an understanding of the current state is always readily available.

Building Practical Business Architecture

Unlike the buildings in which we live or work that were a blueprint before they were built, our organizations rarely have a cohesive, documented business architecture. This means we must create one before we can start using it.

The entire reason a business architecture exists is to provide business value, so it is wise to take a practical approach to building it out over time. Many teams have been challenged by taking the *if we build it, they will come* approach, spending months or years building out content and then becoming disappointed when the businesspeople did not understand or want to use it—and furthermore questioned why the organization would invest in such an activity in the first place.

The best practice approach that has proven itself globally is to build a business architecture just enough, just in time, in direct support of the intended business value.

Here's how that breaks down. The first and most important step before building anything, is to gain an understanding of business architecture concepts and articulate the value proposition it will provide to an organization. Then, the next step is to build the business architecture baseline, which includes (1) capabilities based on clearly defined information concepts such as Customer and Product, (2) a few key value streams, and (3) a cross-mapping between capabilities and the stages within each value stream they enable. This baseline provides a solid foundation upon which to build and most importantly, start using.

The business architecture baseline should, of course, represent the entire scope of an organization and its ecosystem, and *it should be built in partnership with a cross-functional group of business experts working together.* This not only ensures ownership, but also that the business architecture is correct, complete, and represents a collective and rationalized view of the organization. A business architecture team may steward an organization's business architecture, but it is ultimately the businesspeople that own the business architecture.

With the baseline in place, the next step is to begin using it. Select an initial usage scenario(s) that is aligned with the defined business architecture value proposition for the organization. For example, create a view of the planned investment spend by capability or communicate a customer experience challenge framed by the value streams and capabilities which are particularly problematic. Depending upon the scenario selected, capture just enough additional business architecture content to support the current business needs. For example, if analyzing planned investment spend, capture the initiatives and strategies within the portfolios that are in scope. With the business architecture content now captured, blueprints or views can be produced to support the usage scenario.

It is safe to say that no business architecture has been perfect or complete on the first try. It only becomes refined with usage. As people start using the business architecture baseline, they will inevitably identify gaps and necessary adjustments—and this is a good thing.

From here on, rinse and repeat. Select the next usage scenario(s) and determine whether all the content exists to create the supporting blueprints and analysis. Perhaps the scenario may require defining another value stream, decomposing some capabilities into further detail, or capturing the list of products the organization offers.

Provided that a set of principles are followed to ensure consistency, this *just enough, just in time approach* allows an organization to build a robust business architecture over time while simultaneous delivering value. A business architecture is never complete, but rather will continue to refine and evolve as the organization expands and transforms. At some point—and ideally sooner rather than later—the business architecture should be captured in an automated knowledgebase tool. This will help to better manage the content and relationships and make it accessible to anyone throughout the organization in a variety of formats.

More on representing an organization through business architecture is discussed in Chapter 2.

Why haven't I heard of business architecture?

It's not you. Business architecture is a relatively "new" concept as compared to other functions and disciplines that have been around for decades. For example, we are all familiar with functions in an organization such as sales, marketing, finance, or human resources. In addition, many people have heard of disciplines such project management or business analysis, though early in the cycle of maturity, awareness of these disciplines would not have been as ubiquitous as it is today.

While the concept of business architecture has been part of the overall enterprise architecture discipline, in more recent years business architecture has become much more business-focused, more expansive, and more robust. This is due in a large part to the significant amount of work done by the Business Architecture Guild® and its members to mature and formalize the discipline. The Business Architecture Guild® is a not-for-profit association founded in 2010 to promote best practices and expand the knowledgebase of the business architecture discipline. It is the industry body responsible for the business architecture body of knowledge (the BIZBOK® Guide), certification, training accreditation, industry standardization, interdisciplinary alignment, and more.

As the business architecture discipline continues to be practiced around the world and as targeted efforts permeate executive suites, the academic community, and mainstream business literature, it will eventually reach the level of recognition and adoption that other disciplines like project management and business analysis have today. Business architecture will be embedded into the fabric of our organizations and become just how we work and think.

Is that really all there is to business architecture?

With much hope and anticipation for this new concept, some people find themselves feeling nonplussed and underwhelmed after they learn the definition of business architecture. It has a similar effect to asking, "what is a piano?" and hearing that it is a large musical instrument with a wooden case enclosing a soundboard and metal strings that creates sound when struck by keys on a keyboard. Well, that's disappointing. But just think about the role the piano has played throughout history. Think about the tremendous volume of music that has been composed for pianos, the cognitive and creative abilities that have been developed by an immeasurable number of musicians devoted to playing the piano, and the immense joy that music has brought to people of all walks of life around the world for centuries.

The key is to fall in love with *the why* of business architecture. For *the what* of business architecture to really make sense, we have to understand the opportunity or problem we are trying to address. The why of business architecture is where it really comes alive. This is the space where we can dream and reimagine how our organizations can be even better for the people we serve and all stakeholders involved.

Why Business Architecture: The Secret

Let me tell you a secret. Despite all this talk about business architecture, it's not really about the business architecture. The truth is that business architecture is a means to an end, and we must make sure that we don't make the means the end and forget what we were trying to achieve in the first place.

What this is all really about—what we architects, leaders, change makers, and catalysts are trying to achieve—is a new vision for strategy execution and new ways of working in our organizations and business ecosystems.

We are not drawn to business architecture because we like building blueprints, but rather we are compelled by a bigger purpose and ability to make a real difference. We share a vision and commitment to something greater than ourselves for the benefit of our organizations and societies. Building a business architecture is relatively easy. Change is hard.

Amidst the backdrop of a digital, globally connected, and ever-changing world, where customers are king and value is currency, we know that our organizations need to think and act differently to survive and thrive. We need an organizational *metanoia*, or a change in our thinking. Business architecture is still just a blueprint of an organization, but because of its holistic nature, it encourages a shift in peoples' mindsets and behaviors as they build and use it over time. They begin thinking in wholes, not parts.

- Business architecture facilitates *relentless customer value delivery*: shifting from an internal inside-out perspective to a customer-focused outside-in perspective.
- Business architecture facilitates *cross-organization collaboration*: shifting from silo orientation to enterprise optimization and cross-business unit partnership.
- Business architecture facilitates *big picture thinking*: shifting from narrowly focused investments and problem-solving to systemic thinking and approaches.
- Business architecture facilitates *end-to-end organizational agility*: shifting from a bias towards action and a focus on execution agility to focusing on doing the *right* things and agility from strategy through execution.
- Business architecture facilitates *intentional design*: shifting from solutions that meet the needs of today to an effectively architected and designed environment that will meet the needs of tomorrow.
- Finally, business architecture facilitates *business first thinking*: shifting from leading with technology and solutions to leading with business goals and outcomes first.

As these mindsets take hold within an organization, the outcomes, processes, and structures inevitably begin to transform.

What problem are we trying to solve with business architecture?

Consider the following:

> *"No organization can win if its parts are not all aligned to execute the same strategy and achieve the same goals. Even the "perfect" strategy within a competitively advantaged business model will ultimately fail if the organization is not fully aligned internally and does not understand how to execute the strategy, or if it works at cross-purposes."*
> – Rick Kash and David Calhoun[3]

The challenge for organizations is less about having a poor strategy, than it is about having poor strategy execution. Challenges in strategy execution manifest through a variety of different symptoms. For example, different business areas within an organization may create competing or misaligned strategies or may be carrying out strategic courses of action that are working at odds with each other.

As a strategy diffuses throughout the layers of an organization, it may become diluted and misunderstood. Strategy translation and planning in silos may lead to investment in conflicting or redundant solutions, which in turn creates fragmented and inconsistent customer experiences and increases cost. Investment decisions may be difficult because everything is a priority, which further stresses the already-overloaded resources. Funded initiatives may not always align with the organization's strategy and delivery on the intended business objectives may be jeopardized. Additionally, measurement may be difficult, particularly when trying to measure cross-initiative collective impact. In such cases, on-time and on-budget metrics become the primary gauge of success. But these metrics fall short of customer-centric analysis.

The statistics illuminating strategy execution challenges abound. Famous statistics such as "67% of HR and IT organizations develop strategic plans that are not linked to the enterprise strategy"[4] and "95% of employees in most organizations are unaware of or do not understand their organization's strategy,"[5] are alarming—even if dated—because we shrug and know that they are still true. However, strategy execution challenges in organizations have become like walking with a rock in one's shoe: we've become so accustomed to the annoyance, and so good at working around it, that we forgot that it's even there.

How Did We Get Here?

The well-established organizations and institutions that exist today are still here because they *succeeded*. Throughout their history, they have served customers or constituents, competed, adapted, expanded, and thrived. However, an established organization that has been around for some time, as it grew, became more complex and more interdependent. Silos likely formed, making collaboration more challenging across the organization. To meet the ever-increasing pace of the growth, solutions were built, quick fixes were employed, and perhaps some unintentional design happened along the way. For many organizations, this common condition plays out in today's complex business environment. As a result, there is limited cross-organizational visibility, fragmented customer experiences, redundant and inefficient operations, and difficulty or inability to react to the pace of change.

This complex state that many organizations find themselves in has now collided with high customer expectations and rapidly changing market forces. Due to digitalization, globalization, regulatory demands, stakeholder expectations, and other factors, constant change is the new normal. Whether the result of business strategy (defining where to play and how to win), operational strategy (designing the organization), or transformation strategy (changing how the organization works), organizations must do change well.

The ability to move business direction into action, and constantly innovate and adapt to change, has now become competitive advantage. The organizations that can execute in a coordinated way—and with agility—will win.

Business architecture gives organizations the ability to move business direction into action quickly and well. In for-profit organizations, having a business architecture can be a competitive advantage. For governmental, non-governmental, and non-profit organizations, business architecture enables more effective delivery on policy and mission.

What is the value of business architecture to an organization?

If business architecture had a six-word memoir, it might be something like: *Bridges strategy and execution; activates change.* Articulating the value and benefits of having a business architecture can be challenging because it can be used in many ways. For this reason, it is sometimes referred to as a Swiss army knife. In simple terms, we can think of business architecture as providing value in three categories. It helps to facilitate effective strategy execution, improve the design of organizations and business ecosystems, and inform decision-making.

Facilitating effective strategy execution. Business architecture, particularly through the lens of capabilities, ensures that there is alignment between an organization's strategy and how the people, processes, and technology are structured and working together to deliver it. When an organization adjusts a strategy or introduces a new one, business architecture plays a critical role to inform and translate that strategy into a shared vision for the future as well as a coordinated set of changes across the organization. Business architecture also provides the end-to-end traceability that aligns strategies, investments, initiatives, and results.

Leveraging business architecture throughout strategy execution helps to ensure a focus on the customer and their experiences. It also helps to optimize an organization's most precious resources—time, people, and funding—by focusing them in the most effective way: on logically scoped efforts of the highest priority to the enterprise. Business architecture's role in strategy execution also helps to increase organizational agility and decrease the time it takes to translate business direction into action.

Improving the design of organizations and business ecosystems. Business blueprints are ideal for analyzing an organization at a high level to identify opportunities for optimization and simplification in the business and technology environment. For example, through the lens of an organization's capability map (a blueprint representing all capabilities), we may discover there are redundant system applications automating the same capability and can drive action plans based on how important those capabilities are to the business. Or, by aligning businesses processes to a value stream, we may uncover opportunities to streamline how different business or product areas perform similar activities. Or, after two organizations have merged, their business architectures may be compared side-by-side to make decisions on how the people, data, and systems will be integrated.

While we can leverage business architecture to retroactively improve and simplify the current state, it should also be leveraged to architect the business and technology environment with intention going forward. Increasing efficiency and simplicity have benefits in their own right, such as to save time and cost, but helping an organization to be future ready and speeding up its pace of implementing change are invaluable.

Informing decision-making. The process of making decisions can be challenged by incomplete information, incorrect information, politics, emotions, pressure to move fast, and other factors. Business architecture's holistic blueprint provides more valuable information to the decision-making process than was previously available. It also facilitates greater objectivity and transparency. For example, a risk manager may quantify and represent different types of risks on an organization's capability map to help formulate and communicate mitigation strategies and priorities. Or, a product manager may perform *what if* analysis using the business architecture knowledgebase to understand whether the organization has the capabilities necessary to launch a new product along with the likely impact to business units, stakeholders, other products, processes, and technology.

Business architecture can contribute to countless decision-making scenarios within an organization. Depending on how it is used, it may help an organization to assess strategic options, reduce cost, reduce risk, prevent compliance issues, and achieve other business benefits.

So, to put it all together, business architecture is a blueprint of an organization, used to facilitate effective strategy execution, improve the design of organizations and business ecosystems, and inform decision-making. The benefits are many and depend upon how an organization chooses to leverage its business architecture. Chief among them are improved customer experience, increased organizational agility, simplified complexity, greater operational effectiveness, and reduced risk. Business architecture helps organizations execute strategy, operate effectively, and transform. Business architecture = competitive advantage.

How do organizations use business architecture?

Some of the top ways cited by leading organizations for how they use business architecture include aligning strategy and execution, connecting the dots, helping make the right decisions, managing complexity, prioritizing investments, reinforcing accountability, and solving strategic problems. The specific business usage scenarios for business architecture are only limited by the imagination. The more mature an organization's internal business architecture practice becomes, the greater the scope and complexity of usage scenarios it can undertake.

Organizations frequently use business architecture from end-to-end not only for translating strategy, but for business transformations of all types. This includes digital transformations and product-centric to customer-centric transformations. Other strategic usage scenarios include business model evolution, innovation, product management, and customer experience improvement. Business architecture is also frequently used to enable investment decision-making within and across portfolios as well as to inform initiative planning and prioritization.

A few common business usage scenarios that are more operational in nature include business simplification, cost transparency and reduction, risk management, policy making and compliance, and crisis management and preparedness. Leveraging business architecture for technology decision-making is common, particularly for business and technology alignment, application portfolio management, cloud strategy and migration decision-making, and leveraging emerging technologies.

Business architecture is increasingly used for cross-organization scenarios such as mergers, acquisitions, divestitures, and joint ventures. It has also been used to architect business ecosystems and cross-sector social initiatives. Finally, business architecture is ideal to help embed concepts such as sustainability and ethics throughout an organization because the blueprint helps to make changes actionable, measurable, and visible.

Business Architecture Bridges the Elusive Strategy Execution Gap

Why are strategy execution challenges so common in organizations? Afterall, organizations have been investing significantly for years to try to improve projects and delivery. The truth is that the *challenges begin upfront* in the strategy execution life cycle. The symptoms just manifest downstream.

One of the main root causes of strategy execution challenges is hiding in plain sight. *There is a gap between strategy and execution.* Organizations often jump from ideation to implementation, skipping the important activation stage in the middle. This is true for organizations of all types and sizes. We tend to go right from strategic thought to execution without any real, coordinated translation of what it means or in some cases without an understanding of the underlying problems. It does not matter how pretty the PowerPoint is describing the strategy—people throughout an organization need to understand how they fit into the strategy and what they need to do. Otherwise, that PowerPoint will just become a paperweight.

The big picture issues are often the true sources of the challenges—and if addressing them were easy, they would not exist in the first place. Translating strategy into execution can be overwhelming. There is often a giant leap between interpreting high-level business direction and converting it into all the changes necessary in the business and IT environment to make it real. In addition, organizations often translate, plan, and execute strategy in silos by business unit, product, or other organizational constructs. This can lead to redundant, conflicting, and fragmented business and IT solutions—which leads to poor customer experiences and inefficient, expensive operations.

Perhaps the greatest challenge of all is that organizations approach the process of strategy execution in a fragmented way. Multiple instances of the strategy execution process may occur in different silos. Teams working across the strategy execution life cycle are not always integrated well. Visibility and ownership for strategy execution from end-to-end rarely exists. Strategy execution is typically not even thought of as a cohesive process, let alone one that is important.

But, let's ask ourselves, *what if*? What if business direction was collectively translated, architected, prioritized, and planned from a business-driven and collaborative perspective—with the enterprise in mind—instead of performed disjointedly in silos? What if strategy execution were regarded as a critical capability of an organization, treated as a priority, and deliberately designed with transparency, ownership, and accountability from end-to-end? How much *more* successful could our organizations be?

Start with an intentional vision for strategy execution. If doing change well is at the heart of an organization surviving and thriving, then effective end-to-end strategy execution is not only essential but true competitive advantage. Business architecture can help.

What is the role of business architecture in strategy execution?

Business architecture is the often-missing bridge between strategy and execution. It plays a role to help execute strategy more effectively every step of the way and is the golden thread that connects all the pieces from end-to-end. There are two angles to this. First, we can leverage business architecture to translate business direction into a coordinated set of business-framed initiatives across the organization to execute that direction. Second, we can leverage business architecture to ensure alignment—from strategies and objectives to initiatives and investments, and from initiative results back to the original strategies and objectives. Even if business architecture was not leveraged upfront for the translation, which is often the case, it can always be used to help with alignment.

Figure 1.2 depicts a high-level strategy execution framework with an overlay highlighting the role of business architecture. This is a simplified framework representing the types of activities which occur and does not reflect nuances, feedback loops, or timing. For example, there is an overall iterative flow between strategy, architecture, and execution. Strategy drives change to the architecture and then architecture translates strategy for execution. Execution enables improvements to the architecture and architecture in turn informs and refines strategy.

The strategy execution framework is agnostic to the development methodology. It makes no difference whether the organization embraces waterfall or agile approaches. Alleviating the upfront strategy execution challenges is just as important in either case. Business architecture facilitates overall alignment and enables autonomy for all teams, including agile ones, by ensuring clear direction, providing common business components, and illuminating integration and coordination points.

The use of business architecture—and the unique role that business architects play—is heaviest upfront through the beginning of the Plan Initiatives stage. While the focus here is specifically on business architecture, it takes many roles and teams working together to successfully execute strategy. The traceability of business architecture along with the integrative role of business architects helps to knit these teams together from end-to-end.

How Business Architecture Facilitates Effective Strategy Execution

As shown in Figure 1.2, in the **Develop Strategy** stage, business architecture is leveraged to inform, assess, and rationalize business direction. Business leaders, strategists, and other decision-makers consult the business architecture to understand the current state and what the organization can do. Leveraging the business architecture knowledgebase, they can perform *what if* analyses to help assess the potential organizational impacts of different strategic options. Business architects help rationalize direction across business strategies, goals, objectives, and courses of action. Some experienced business architects may also serve as trusted advisors in the formulation of business direction. Business architects may also help to document business direction using various strategy mapping techniques, depending upon the need.

The second stage is the one that typically needs to be added into an organization's strategy execution framework and mindset. In the **Architect Changes** stage, business architecture is used to assess and collectively architect the changes needed to the business and technology environment across silos. While business architects participate in all other stages, this one is where most of their core responsibilities are performed, working hand-in-hand with business leaders, strategists, IT architects and other designers. First, business architects clarify and sometimes further articulate or decompose business direction and objectives. Using the business architecture knowledgebase, they inventory the aspects of the business and technology environment which need to change using value streams, capabilities, and other business and technology focal points.

At this point, there is an opportunity to step back and assess the best way to scope and architect the changes. For example, an organization may have multiple strategies and business changes that are targeting the same capabilities which could be addressed collectively instead of with siloed solutions. Business architecture provides a way to architect and plan initiatives across business and product areas because the blueprints are defined at a high enough level of detail and because the process naturally brings people together for this type of coordination. The outcome of this stage is a clear definition of the high-level changes needed to people, process, and technology, framed by value streams and capabilities, along with an actionable view(s) of the future (e.g., a target architecture) that can be communicated widely.

In the **Plan Initiatives** stage, business architecture is used to shape initiatives and support investment decision-making. Working together with business leaders and potentially planners and other designers, business and IT architects organize the defined changes into a logical set of initiatives, reflecting dependencies and integration points. For large efforts such as business transformations, these initiatives may be represented on a high-level strategic roadmap. The initiatives may be input to the portfolio management process. Separately, business architecture can also be used as a framework to support investment decision-making within and across portfolios, such as by using a capability map to show where plans may be redundant or misaligned.

In the **Execute Solutions** stage, business architecture is leveraged to provide high-level scope definition, accelerate requirements development, and ensure alignment of execution to direction. Business architects may provide counsel and oversight to initiative teams during execution, though this is not a full-time role. They may also help guide the translation of the architecture direction into requirements. Business architects report overall progress to leaders, often using target architectures and strategic roadmaps to communicate within a high-level business context.

In the **Measure Success** stage, business architecture provides end-to-end traceability to assess if initiative results satisfied the original objectives. Once an initiative is complete, business architects can help to report on the results achieved by comparing back to the business objectives that were defined in the first stage. The business architecture knowledgebase stores the full set of connections from strategies and objectives to value streams and capabilities to initiatives and requirements and more. This end-to-end traceability can also be used for a different purpose. If business direction changes, any initiatives that are connected to the impacted business objectives can be quickly identified and reconsidered or stopped.

Visit www.StrategyintoReality.com to download diagrams and other valuable resources.

Figure 1.2: The Role of Business Architecture Across Strategy Execution

How does business architecture help address silos?

Business architecture is an expert silo-buster. One of the key themes for business architecture's role in strategy execution, and most other usage scenarios for that matter, is its unique role in helping to break down and bridge organizational silos.

Silos are in many ways just inherently human, yet they can be detrimental to an organization's success. For example, internal silos can produce unhappy customers. If a customer contacts your company to change their address and unknowingly changes it with just one department of the organization that does not talk to others, the customer will continue to receive mail at their old address and wonder why their request was not honored. Silos can also decrease organizational performance by demotivating employees, slowing down processing times, increasing errors and rework, and even increasing risk due to a lack of transparency and coordination.

Business architecture alone cannot address the challenges that come with silos without a corresponding change in the organization and corporate culture, but it can help to break down silos and create bridges across disparate workplace divisions. Let's look at how business architecture can assist.

Business architecture helps everyone understand the whole. Everyone needs a holistic understanding of how the organization delivers value, to whom, and how things work at a high level. They also need to have a common language, because speaking different languages can further isolate people into silos. For example, the language used by the sales versus operations versus legal versus IT functions can all be very different. Business architecture provides a shared mental model and business vocabulary—at a level of abstraction that terms such as Customer, Partner, and Product can be shared across silos.

Business architecture creates a shared purpose. Without a common vision and objectives, employees and partners can be challenged to contribute effectively to the organization's goals. They can also feel disconnected from the bigger picture. Having more collaboration is not always the answer. Business architecture provides a clear and shared understanding of the ultimate business direction and helps each person see how they contribute to the bigger goals.

Business architecture identifies where to remove or bridge silos. While it is not always possible or logical to remove silos, sometimes it makes sense. On the other hand, identifying where and how to best bridge silos can be useful, such as where there are information, process, tooling, or cultural gaps. Value streams and capabilities provide an ideal enterprise business lens for identifying opportunities to remove or bridge silos. For example, value streams can provide an additional construct to help people work together across business units towards a greater goal of delivering value. Value streams and capabilities together can illuminate opportunities for sharing expertise, processes, or tools.

Business architecture facilitates a change in mindset. Potentially the most effective way to break down and bridge silos is to start with peoples' mindsets. This includes openness, sharing, collaboration, transparency, empowerment and truly caring about the customer and the entire organization and its mission. These changes are hard work. They need to start with leaders and be backed by the right incentives and motivational mechanisms. Business architecture does not change culture or mindset directly, but it provides the facts and transparency to illuminate where silos exist so they can be addressed appropriately. As a truly shared cross-organization framework, business architecture also provides a way for people to come together in support of something bigger than themselves to serve customers and the organization's mission.

More on leveraging business architecture for value is discussed in Chapter 3.

It Takes a Village: Business Architecture and Other Teams

Business architecture is not a silver bullet. It takes an entire ecosystem of teams working together for an organization to deliver on its promise to customers, support its operations, execute strategy, and transform when necessary.

One of the key indicators of business architecture maturity within an organization is how integrated it is with other functions, disciplines, and organizational processes for strategy, planning, transformation, innovation, solution development, risk management, procurement, compliance, mergers and acquisitions, and many others. Furthermore, strong partnerships with and buy-in from other teams is arguably one of the top factors that dictates whether a business architecture practice will be successful in an organization long-term.

When integrating business architecture into an organization, there are three areas of alignment to consider. Each of them helps to infuse architectural thinking and mindset shifts throughout an organization.

The first consideration is the business architecture itself. Business architecture blueprints can and should be used by anyone in an organization to help make better decisions and enhance their own role. The second consideration is the business architects. The role of a business architect is often new to organizations and needs to be formalized through the human resources department. Business architects help other people use the business architecture as well as leverage it to perform their own responsibilities which deliver new value to the organization than existed previously. Business architects also steward the business architecture knowledgebase to ensure it supports business needs. The third consideration is the business architecture practice, which provides the infrastructure and focal point to coordinate business architecture activity across the organization. This includes supporting the business architects and ensuring the discipline is delivering its intended value proposition. Regardless of where business architects report within an organization, these practice activities are typically managed by a central team, though in some cases it may be through purely virtual collaboration.

How does business architecture relate to enterprise architecture?

Business architecture is part of the overarching discipline of enterprise architecture. What is enterprise architecture? Simply put:

Enterprise Architecture =
Business Architecture + IT Architecture (Application Architecture + Data Architecture + Technical Architecture)

IT architecture as referenced here is comprised of application architecture for software applications and services, data architecture for data and data deployments, and technical architecture for infrastructure and network. Security architecture spans all of these.

Solution architecture, on the other hand, is another discipline. It focuses on a slice of business, application, data, and technical architecture for the scope of a specific solution or initiative. Solution architecture leverages the business and IT architecture to define the business needs and pinpoint the perspectives to be automated.

Scope is the primary differentiator between the enterprise architecture and solution architecture disciplines. While enterprise architecture focuses on the scope of the entire organization and its ecosystem, especially within the context of strategy execution, solution architecture focusses on the scope of solutions in support of addressing specific business needs or problems.

The importance of collaboration across all enterprise architecture domains cannot be overstated. Business architecture without IT architecture lacks the means to translate business needs into technology enablement—which in our increasingly digital world would be detrimental to any organization. IT architecture without business architecture lacks the direction and prioritization to guide the technology investments and solutions needed to support the business today and tomorrow.

Business architects tend to work closest with application architects and data architects, though all IT architects can benefit from consuming the language and direction business architecture provides. However, good working relationships should exist across the entire enterprise architecture team. Business architects also work with solution architects to advise on business direction and needs and provide ongoing consulting during solution development.

Creating Alignment Across the Enterprise Architecture Function

For an enterprise architecture function to be effective within an organization—regardless of where the business architects and IT architects report in the organizational structure—there must be alignment in three areas.

Business and IT architecture alignment. All business and IT architects should understand the domains for which they are responsible and how those domains are related to other ones. For example, business architects should have an in-depth understanding of the ten domains of business architecture and how capabilities, value streams, business units, and other business perspectives connect to domains within the IT architecture such as applications and software services. Business architecture and/or enterprise architecture knowledgebase tools should support the needs of both business and IT architects as well as any necessary integration.

Business and IT architect role alignment. The role of a business architect, application architect, data architect, and technical architect each must be clearly defined and differentiated. In addition, the interactions between roles, ideally within the context of specific scenarios, should also be clearly defined. For example, for a strategy translation scenario, architects should understand what roles are involved at what stage, what activities they perform together, and what deliverables they should consume and produce.

Enterprise architecture practice alignment. A shared understanding of the overall value proposition and positioning for the enterprise architecture discipline within an organization helps bring the team together. In addition, a shared methodology or playbook (and any training based upon it) creates consistency and guides architects on how to build and apply architecture and work together in different scenarios.

How have business architecture practices evolved related to enterprise architecture?

As the contemporary practice of business architecture has evolved, it has become the ultimate Venn diagram. On one side we have strategic management and on the other side we have the enterprise architecture discipline. As shown in Figure 1.3, business architecture plays a role right in the middle as a part of both. This evolution of business architecture helps to explain why people sometimes see business architecture in different ways. We simply look at the world through slightly different lenses depending on our experiences and education.

Visit www.StrategyintoReality.com to download diagrams and other valuable resources.

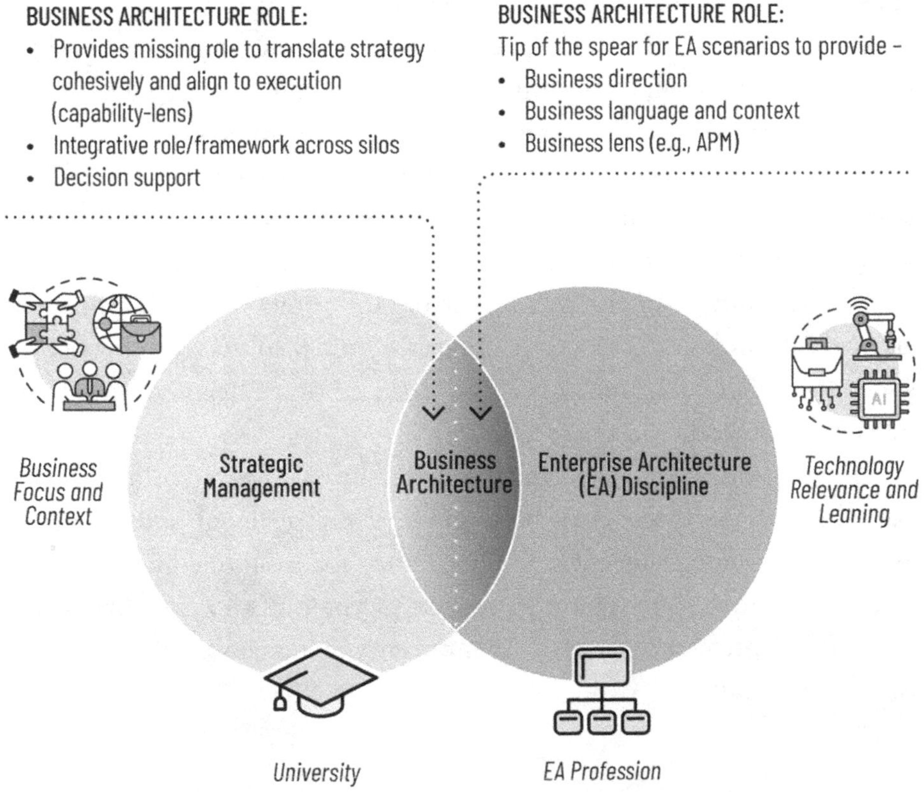

BUSINESS ARCHITECTURE ROLE:
- Provides missing role to translate strategy cohesively and align to execution (capability-lens)
- Integrative role/framework across silos
- Decision support

BUSINESS ARCHITECTURE ROLE:
Tip of the spear for EA scenarios to provide –
- Business direction
- Business language and context
- Business lens (e.g., APM)

Business Focus and Context — Strategic Management — Business Architecture — Enterprise Architecture (EA) Discipline — Technology Relevance and Leaning

University — EA Profession

Figure 1.3: Business Architecture Lives in Two Worlds

The role of business architecture and business architects in strategic management is as the missing framework and role needed to translate strategy cohesively and align it to execution, as an integrative framework and role across silos, and as additional support for more holistic decision-making. The usage scenarios are more strategic and business-focused such as those related to strategy, transformation, business model innovation, mergers and acquisitions, joint ventures, risk management, and financials.

On the other hand, the role of business architecture and business architects within the enterprise architecture discipline is as the *tip of the spear* for usage scenarios relevant within an enterprise architecture context, often more closely related to technology. For example, business architecture provides business direction, business language and context, and a business lens that can be leveraged for business and technology alignment, application portfolio management, and other scenarios.

As it pertains to education and approaches, the strategic management side draws more from higher education and specialized training while the enterprise architecture side draws more from the enterprise architecture profession. As business has evolved to require cross-organizational collaboration to provide integrated customer experiences, deliver on strategies, and effectively manage operations and risk, it is no surprise that we see a global uptick in the number of organizations now using business architecture and more practitioners entering the field. As a result, we may see more higher education curriculum focused on strategy execution and business architecture in the future.

Today's business architect must continually balance and bring together the goals and perspectives of both strategic management and enterprise architecture. Certain business architects may focus on one more than the other depending upon their organization's dynamics and their own experiences and preferences, but it is important to remember that both are equally necessary.

How does business architecture integrate with other teams?

When an organization begins leveraging business architecture, it can generate some initial confusion and concern about how it will be used, how business architecture is different than other disciplines or modeling techniques, and how the business architect role is different than other roles. However, when the lines are drawn right, business architecture does not overlap with any other disciplines or teams. For example, business architects *consume* strategic documentation from strategists and customer journeys from customer experience designers. Business architects *produce* initiative definitions as input to planners and business analysts and change impacts to organizational change managers—just to name a few.

Having conversations early on with the leaders of other disciplines and teams is a good way to establish long-term partnerships and diffuse any concerns about business architecture. Once people understand the value and intent of business architecture and how it can make their lives easier, they are often open to exploring it further.

A best practice is to communicate the engagement model for how business architecture relates to and interacts with other roles and teams. For example, it may reflect the value business architecture provides to each team or describe the inputs and outputs exchanged. It is also ideal to represent how business architecture interacts with other teams *within a relevant context* to the organization, such as its strategy execution framework, investment planning process, or agile methodology.

As business architecture gains traction and expands within an organization, the three areas of alignment mentioned previously guide the integration of business architecture with other teams and disciplines.

Domain alignment. Other teams should understand how their domains (if applicable) align with business architecture domains. A plan should be put into place to capture information within the knowledgebase just enough, just in time. For example, business processes for a designated scope of the organization may reflected in the business architecture knowledgebase and related to capabilities and value streams.

Role alignment. Since the business architect role typically addresses gaps and provides new value to other roles, existing roles and responsibilities typically do not change other than to reflect some additional partnership with business architects. (Changes are rarely made to the formal job descriptions.) For example, the roles and responsibilities of a strategist or organization designer might be adjusted to reflect key areas of partnership and exchange with business architects.

Practice alignment. Other disciplines should be aligned with the business architecture practice. This type of alignment is often reflected in the processes, procedures, methodologies, or playbooks maintained by other teams. For example, a set of procedures used by business analysts to perform their role may be updated to reflect the input of business architecture and guidance on how it should be translated into requirements.

An overview of how business architecture integrates with a common set of related teams is discussed further in Chapter 4.

The Unique Role and Talents of Business Architects

Business architecture can and should be used by anyone in an organization. It is not—and should not be treated as—an isolated discipline limited to a certain group of practitioners. In fact, widespread usage unlocks the value of business architecture and is another key indicator of business architecture maturity within an organization.

However, just as there has been a gap between strategy and execution, there has been a gap in the role to help activate, facilitate, and align the translation. A new role—and career path—has emerged for the business architect. Business architects play a critical and unique role in helping not just to build and steward an organization's business architecture, but most importantly to translate strategies into actionable initiatives, ensure end-to-end strategic alignment, facilitate effective organizational design, and support business decision-making.

Business architects are special people. They are recognizable. They have a distinguishing set of characteristics, competencies, and thought patterns. They are wired to see and care about the big picture.

People come to the business architect role from increasingly diverse backgrounds, often after having had a rich set of career experiences. It is not uncommon for someone to change careers and become a business architect—even towards the end of their career—because they finally feel they have found their calling. A common remark is *I didn't know there was a name for what I do.*

Depending on an individual's background and experiences, they will lean into the business architect role differently. This also fosters team diversity. For example, a business leader that moves into the role of a business architect will be a natural at connecting with the business and using business architecture in practical ways. They can learn the business architecture mindset and methods. On the other hand, the architectural thinking and methods will come easily to an individual who was working in an analyst or technology role, but they will need to develop their knowledge and empathy to connect with the business.

While people in certain roles are more naturally inclined towards the business architect role, there is no common path to business architecture or background required. To demand or assume it would only limit the possibilities.

The first recognizable trait of a business architect is in how they think. They tend to be structured thinkers with the ability to abstract and synthesize information, recognize patterns, and connect dots that others do not see. They can't *not* see the big picture. The second trait is in their disposition and how they act. They relentlessly ask *why*, they bring people together, they see what needs to be done and take ownership—because it is the right thing to do.

A career as a business architect is one of the most intellectually stimulating and meaningful roles. It lives at the heart of where organizational change happens. However, it also makes an excellent career steppingstone for those who have different intentions. It not only develops strong thinking skills but provides exposure to a wide variety of areas and initiatives within an organization. Business architects have gone on to become business leaders, product leaders, technology leaders, innovation and design thinking leaders, strategists, human-centered designers, entrepreneurs, consultants and more. They often claim that their business architecture experience and mindset made them better and more differentiated in their new roles.

They key then is for an organization to be intentional about how they leverage the unique talents of business architects and provide support for them to be successful.

What do business architects do?

The business architect role is a strategic one. Business architects produce outputs to support different business usage scenarios for their assigned scope of focus, but their overall aim is to *deliver the business value and outcomes for which they are accountable*, versus creating deliverables or repeating tasks. This mindset is what sets successful business architects apart.

Regardless of where a business architect reports within an organization, they serve as enterprise advocates. They think, speak, and act *enterprise*. Whether a business architect focuses on a set of cross-enterprise capabilities, one business unit, or some other scope of focus, they work together with other business architects, forming a mesh, to ensure the organization is architected and aligned.

There are a number of misconceptions about what business architects do, so let's start with what business architects do *not* do for contrast.

Not just modelers. Business architects do build and steward the business architecture knowledgebase for the organization, but the entire focus of the role is not just to model the business. The role is defined as business *architect*, not business modeler. This is a strategic role.

Not project resources. Business architects do not work as project resources. They work upfront in strategy execution and inform delivery, but their role is as a consultant and guide during delivery. Business architects guide, but do not typically write requirements or specifications.

Not business analysts. Business architects are not an extension of the business analyst role or any other roles. Business architecture and business analysis are two distinct, mutually beneficial disciplines and business architects and business analysts should partner closely. However, the roles focus on different scopes, outcomes, and deliverables.

Not IT resources. Business architects are not technology resources. Business architects should have a strong working knowledge of IT architecture and technology, particularly now that technology has new strategic importance and the lines between business and technology have blended. However, business architects are not responsible for designing or developing solutions, but rather they partner closely with IT architects and solution architects to inform and guide technology solutions to meet business needs.

Business Architect Responsibilities

We can think of business architect responsibilities in three categories. Business architects are professionals who facilitate the application of business architecture for business value, build and maintain the business architecture knowledgebase, and provide input and assistance with the internal business architecture practice.

Once an organization's business architecture baseline is established, most of a business architect's time should be focused on *applying* business architecture. However, some time and focus are always required to steward the business architecture knowledgebase and supporting practice infrastructure. The latter two ensure that an organization's business architecture practice is beneficial, consistent, and scalable.

Facilitating the application of business architecture for business value.
Delivering value is the entire reason why business architecture and business

architects exist within an organization. However, there is not a one-size-fits-all answer for what every business architect does in every organization. The business scenarios and scope upon which each business architect focuses depends on a variety of factors. This includes the organization's intended value proposition for business architecture, the individual's level of experience, and the organizational structure.

In one organization, a majority of business architects may be focused on informing, translating, supporting, and aligning major business transformations and strategies while a few others may be assigned to some additional usage scenarios. For example, a couple business architects may focus part-time to support portfolio investment decision-making during the planning cycle while others may support simplification and IT architecture transformation efforts. In larger teams, some business architects (or other support resources) may even be dedicated full-time to supporting the knowledgebase and/or practice. On the other hand, an organization that is doing a significant number of acquisitions may focus its business architects on supporting due diligence assessments and integration efforts.

Business architects bring their unique skills and mindset to whatever scenarios and scope they are assigned. They help others use the business architecture and often serve as trusted advisors to provide counsel and insights when needed.

Building and maintaining the business architecture knowledgebase. Business architects facilitate sessions with business representatives and capture the resulting content, mapped according to defined principles, in the knowledgebase. They work together with people from related disciplines and teams to reflect their domain content (e.g., processes or requirements) in the business architecture knowledgebase and cross-map it to business architecture perspectives such as capabilities and value streams. Business architects ensure the business architecture knowledgebase is created with integrity and kept up to date as the business evolves.

Assisting with the internal business architecture practice. In some organizations, the foundational practice responsibilities are the focus of a certain person(s) and in other organizations the responsibilities are spread across some or all of the business architects. For example, some team members may take ownership for onboarding new team members, some may help create and steward a how-to playbook, some may help with tool selection and usage, and some may get involved in socializing business architecture with other people. At a minimum, business architects typically provide input to practice activities, even if they are not responsible for them.

It is important to note that at the time of publication for this book, an industry standard business architect job description is still evolving. Whether one may be looking to hire a business architect or join an organization as a business architect, keep in mind that the understanding of the role can vary. No matter what side of the table you are on, asking the right questions and discussing expectations upfront will ensure the right match.

Where should business architects report within an organization?

The cross-cutting organizational role and strategic focus of business architects means they need to be positioned for success. The business architect role needs to be clearly communicated and visibly supported. Business architects need to report at a level and place within the organization that will provide them with credibility, access, and authority.

As the contemporary practice of business architecture has evolved, there has been an increasing trend of business architecture teams reporting to business leaders—and with good success. They have more access to decision-makers, more firsthand knowledge of business direction, and ultimately more buy-in for the discipline. *So, ideally the business architecture team should report within the business.*

Business architecture teams often report to business leaders responsible for strategy, transformation, innovation, or planning (or any combination of these), though there are many other examples, including teams who report to different C-Level executives. Business leaders who have responsibilities that cross business units and who care about business direction being executed well are ideal candidates for the business architecture executive leader role.

However, this certainly does not mean that a business architecture team reporting to a leader within the IT department will not be successful. In fact, many business architecture teams incubate in IT since there may be the initial buy-in and skills within that department to help get the practice off the ground. Some teams then shift to report to a business leader later on.

While having the business architecture team report to a leader in the business is ideal, we start where we can start, and ultimately the right answer is the one that works best for an organization. In addition, remember that business architects have one foot in two different worlds, one in the business and one as part of the enterprise architecture team. This means that no matter where the business architecture team reports, they will always need to maintain a close partnership with one side or the other.

What makes business architects unique?

Business architects are truly unique and consistently so worldwide. While there is of course great variation from any one individual to another, there are a few very special characteristics embodied especially by business architects.

Challenge status quo. Business architects relentlessly challenge the status quo for the sake of more effective strategy execution, organizations, and a better world. They relentlessly ask *why*. They are driven by value, outcomes, and results for the business and its customers. While there may be easier career choices, business architects choose the role because they want to make a difference and are often unsung heroes behind significant change.

Abstract and simplify. Business architects have great ability to rationalize, abstract, and synthesize information. They have a natural talent to see patterns. They create frameworks for looking at organizations and ecosystems in new ways and apply them to problems and opportunities to unlock new value and innovation. They simplify and visualize complex concepts and bring people together around a common understanding and direction.

Think big picture. Business architects always think big picture and long-term. They think holistically in terms of the overall system including their organization and the ecosystem in which it operates. Business architects are problem solvers and trusted advisors because of their structured thinking and rational approaches. Business architects see beyond the details and consider root causes and opportunities for solving a problem smarter.

Connect dots and build bridges. Business architects connect the dots between people and ideas. They build bridges across business units, between business and technology, between business and IT architecture domains, between teams to create seamless strategy execution, and even between the organization and its ecosystem partners. Business architects bring people together to facilitate collaboration and build consensus. They are *enterprise advocates*, always looking out for what is best for the customers and the organization overall.

Learn voraciously. Business architects are curious and inquisitive. They often come to the role after a significant amount of successful career experience because they are ready to learn and do more. Business architects appreciate intentional design and are continually gaining new knowledge and learning new techniques to improve and expand their abilities.

In fact, some initial research illuminates that business architects have some unique superpowers to be leveraged, particularly related to thinking. The first superpower is related to *connectedness*. Business architects are often non-linear thinkers and can see non-obvious connections between things and events that others might miss. The second superpower is related to *intellection*. Business architects bring wisdom and clarity to leaders and teams through their ability to think deeply into a challenge, idea, concept, or principle. Given the intellectually demanding and complex nature of the scenarios in which business architecture is leveraged, this helps to explain why business architects standout in their ability to solve problems and challenges.[6]

More on building a successful business architecture team is discussed in Chapter 5.

Starting and Succeeding with Business Architecture

How do we know that an organization has been successful with business architecture? A maturity model can be used to help an organization understand the level at which their business architecture practice is performing related to a standard set of categories. For example, maturity can be assessed as it pertains to the business architecture knowledgebase, management involvement, people, methods, tools, governance, and alignment with related disciplines.

The more mature a business architecture practice is, the more embedded it will become into the organization, and the more value it will deliver. *We are aspiring for business architecture to become fully embedded into the fabric of an organization, where it becomes just how the organization works—no longer a separate concept requiring special attention.* As part of this, business architecture should be fully integrated with related disciplines and teams, and key processes including the organization's strategy execution, investments, innovation, solution development, procurement, onboarding, finance, risk, compliance, audit, and any other organizing processes or frameworks.

We are also aspiring for business architects to become highly skilled and strategic resources. They should be at the table for strategic conversations and serve as trusted advisors for the organization. Finally, *we are aspiring for business architecture to deliver on the value proposition for which it was intended—whatever an organization defined it to be—and create advantage.*

We can observe some signs along the way that indicate an organization is on the right track with business architecture. **Commitment** is a good indicator of perceived value, which may be demonstrated through investment and visible executive support. **Acceptance** represents increasing buy-in and adoption by others. Most important of all is **usage**. Usage is the ultimate sign—when people ask for business architecture, speak its language, and use it as part of their daily work.

The real success is witnessed when we see a shift in the way people think and act. When people start thinking enterprise, when they make decisions based on what is best for the greater good and not just their area, when they start collaboratively setting and translating direction, making decisions, and investing together, then—and only then—have we arrived at a significant milestone, and the journey can continue to the next level.

How does an organization get started with business architecture?

The key to getting a successful start with business architecture is to quickly build a solid enough business architecture foundation and then start demonstrating value with it. However, before building models, *start with why*. Here is a five-step approach to starting a business architecture practice that is practical and proven. Be intentional and invest in these activities from the beginning because they form the foundation for long-term success and scale.

Step 1: Build the case for business architecture. First, gain a sound understanding of what business architecture is. Then, build a case for the discipline that is relevant to the organization and start socializing it. Clearly articulate the value proposition of business architecture, even if just an initial working idea. This is also the time to secure executive business sponsorship. However, while executive sponsorship is undoubtedly a critical success factor, if it is not possible at this point, it can be obtained in the future by demonstrating results and building partnerships and buy-in.

Step 2: Select an initial usage scenario(s). Next, select an initial usage scenario(s). This is important because it will help to provide context in conversations, guide practical usage, and potentially inform priorities for building out the business architecture baseline.

The initial usage scenario(s) should be related to the defined value proposition. The scenario does not need to be large, but it does need to highlight the strengths of business architecture. For example, a usage scenario that highlights how business architecture can provide an aggregated view across business units is better than a detailed usage scenario for a very small scope. Most people do not fully grasp the concept of business architecture until they can see it. In addition, what people *see* has more bearing on their understanding of business architecture than what they *hear*, so choose the initial usage scenario wisely. Having the right sponsor for the effort (if different than the overall business architecture executive leader) is also important. Find someone who is open to trying and advocating for new ideas, potentially someone you already know and can trust.

Step 3: Build the baseline. Build the business architecture baseline for the scope of the organization and its ecosystem, working in close partnership with a cross-functional group of business experts. The baseline should include capabilities based upon defined information concepts, a set of key value streams, and a cross-mapping between the capabilities and the value stream stages they enable. The creation of a business architecture baseline can be accelerated by prioritizing certain areas of focus and leveraging business architecture industry reference models.

When the baseline is complete and approved by the business representatives, publish it, and make it available to others. Some organizations publish their initial baseline widely, while other organizations share it among a smaller group of people until business architecture gains traction. Introduce a light process to manage changes to the baseline on an ongoing basis.

Step 4: Leverage business architecture. With clear direction, commitment, a team, and a baseline in place, now you can leverage business architecture on your first usage scenario. Deliver it well and tell the story (hopefully a successful one) to communicate the value and learning with others. Rinse and repeat.

Step 5: Create a roadmap for the practice. Finally, as momentum starts to pick up, start getting deliberate about the practice of business architecture. A good place to begin is to create a roadmap for establishing and maturing the business architecture practice within the organization over the next 6 to 12 months. There are always three aspects upon which to focus: applying business architecture for value, building and maintaining the knowledgebase, and establishing, maturing, and socializing the practice. These aspects must always be in balance, guided by the mantra *lead with value, build as you go.*

More on the approach to building an internal business architecture practice is discussed in Chapter 6.

How long does it take to establish business architecture within an organization?

Establishing a successful, sustainable business architecture practice is a journey that takes time, especially within large organizations. With the right conditions in place, much can be achieved within a one-year time frame and again by the three-year mark. The better the starting conditions are, the quicker a business architecture practice can be established. However, there is some limit on growth because business architecture changes the way an organization works, and change takes time.

The most ideal starting conditions would include a **C-Level executive sponsor and mandate** along with a **mission critical initiative** that requires new ways of thinking and working. For example, customer experience transformations and legally mandated initiatives have a way of accelerating business architecture adoption because people must rally around something bigger than themselves and their silos. The ideal conditions would also include a **core team of people who are highly experienced** in building and applying business architecture and establishing a practice. In addition, there would be **visible leadership commitment** and **ample**

investment for the resources and tools necessary to grow and support the team. This entire set of conditions is not typically the norm, but small and mighty business architecture teams with the right advocates have made astounding progress.

Within the first year, a business architecture team can be selected, trained, and mobilized, a value proposition defined, a business architecture baseline built and captured within a tool, the initial business usage scenario(s) delivered upon successfully, a maturity assessment complete, and a practice advancement roadmap in place for the next year. At the three-year mark, business architecture teams can really hit their stride with a competent team in place delivering on some significant initiatives for the organization, integration with key strategic and solution delivery processes, and key components of the practice maturing such as governance and shared methods.

It can take a business architecture team many years to reach the highest maturity at levels 4 and 5, especially when we consider that business architecture is meant to be practiced as an enterprise discipline. It simply takes time for it to roll out and mature across an organization. As an organization's practice matures, business architecture can be leveraged for increasingly large and complex opportunities and challenges. However, business architecture will bring value from day one.

Startups and smaller organizations should create their business architecture baseline right from the start. It can be used for immediate value but furthermore, it embeds architectural thinking into the DNA. As the organization scales up, the business architecture will grow with it, providing a valuable foundation necessary for growth. It may also serve useful in heading off some of the common challenges we see arising in larger organizations, such as the complex, inflexible business and technology environments that can slow down agility and innovation.

How does an organization succeed with business architecture?

Successful business architecture teams create a cohesive business architecture practice. Business architecture makes the greatest difference when it is practiced as an enterprise discipline, not as a toolbox of available techniques. One shared business architecture helps bring together an entire organization. Treating business architecture as a set of tools and templates that are available for each business unit to use as they wish, will only reinforce the silos that exist. In the worst-case scenario, an organization creates multiple mini-practices within each business unit or initiative, each with their own business architectures, tools, role definitions, methods, and relationships. We have plenty of fragmented views and techniques in our organizations today. Business architecture is an opportunity to do things differently.

The foundation for business architecture as an enterprise discipline is ensured by two immutable principles. The first is *there is one shared business architecture for an organization* (unless it is a conglomerate or other structure that warrants multiple). The second is *business architecture practitioners share one methodology.* The first principle ensures the same architecture is used and the second ensures that the architects use it consistently and have a shared education and frame of reference. These principles apply regardless of how an organization's business architecture team is organized. For example, a business architecture team with a purely virtual center of excellence can still adhere to these principles through intentional collaboration among practitioners.

Successful business architecture teams are business oriented and value-focused in everything they do. They have in common a few tried and true approaches that can by now be interpreted as critical success factors. These include:

Executive sponsorship. Obtain visible, committed executive level sponsorship as high in the organization as possible, as soon as possible.

Repeatable value delivery. Define a clear value proposition for business architecture in the organization, deliver it through repeatable services, and build the knowledgebase and practice just enough, just in time. Business architecture services provide the mechanism for applying business architecture to common usage scenarios in way that delivers consistent outcomes.

Strong partnerships. Build strong partnerships with other roles and teams. Successful business architecture teams see themselves as an internal service provider to their organization. They focus relentlessly on helping people and building bridges.

Ubiquitous business architecture. Make business architecture for everybody. Having this aim from the start instills the right mindset and accelerates the adoption and usage of business architecture.

The business architecture journey requires patience, persistence, and passion. There is only one way to get to the top of a mountain and that is one step at a time. Getting to the business architecture summit is no different. Nonetheless, every step adds up to a journey worth taking and the opportunity to make a meaningful difference to your organization.

2

Representing an Organization Through Business Architecture

You know what business architecture is. You know your why. There are people in the organization who can't wait to start using business architecture. This all sounds like a good idea. Now what? The process of building out a business architecture can seem daunting, especially as one begins to uncover the breadth of mapping principles, guidelines, and options. However, trust the process laid out here, because it will give you a mental framework to think about the work that lies ahead.

It is important to get the business architecture baseline as "right" as possible up front. This means it represents the organization correctly and completely in the language of the business, is aligned with industry principles, and is stable. The rest of the business architecture will be built upon this foundation, so while the baseline will naturally evolve and expand, it should not be at risk of a total remodel.

However, once the baseline is in place, keep going. Keep capturing content for all the other domains just enough, just in time. Each domain is like a side of a prism reflecting a view of the business from different angles. In fact, the best way to understand the utility of additional domains such as strategies, initiatives, products, and policies is just to start capturing and using them. Learn by doing and evolve along the way.

Sources for detailed mapping principles and methods are contained in the additional resources provided. Please see Call to Action for more information.

Business Architecture Represents the Business Ecosystem

Two of the most crucial guiding principles for building a business architecture are related to its scope and its orientation. There are places to bend the rules, but these are not them. Business architecture gives us a golden opportunity to see things differently, and it starts right here.

The first overall guiding principle is that a business architecture represents the scope of an organization and the ecosystem in which it operates. For example, if an organization outsources a capability to a partner, that capability is represented in the organization's business architecture. If an organization resells a product for a partner, that product is represented in the organization's business architecture. If an organization is comprised of multiple different legal entities, the collection of what those entities do should be represented in the organization's business architecture.

The second overall guiding principle is that in a business architecture, customers and products always reflect the external perspective. Customers are the entities (individuals or organizations) with whom an organization has an agreement or who otherwise receive or benefit from an organization's products and services. For example, for an insurance company a customer could be a policyholder or their beneficiary. For a shipping company, a customer could be the person who pays to ship a package as well as the recipient.

Products are the goods and services that an organization offers in the market for customers. A good test if something is a product or not is if it is listed in the organization's product catalog viewed by customers. For example, a product could be an insurance policy, a piece of apparel, or an electronic device, appliance, or vehicle with a warranty.

The terminology for customers and products may need to be adapted to an organization's business model and sector. For example, a governmental organization might have constituents and government services instead of customers and products. Depending upon the organization, they may refer to their customers as clients, members, patients, or other alternatives.

There Are No Internal Customers or Products in a Business Architecture

In a business architecture, "internal customers" with whom value is exchanged are not categorized as customers. For example, a businessperson who sponsors a technology initiative is not a customer. In the business architecture they would be considered a human resource. In addition, key partners with whom the organization works are not customers. For example, for an insurance company, an independent insurance agent would be considered a partner.

In a business architecture, "internal products" are not categorized as products. For example, a portal is not a product. A customer would not see Customer Service Portal in the product catalog as something they can purchase. In the business architecture, this would be considered a technology asset represented in the IT architecture, which delivers the capabilities that ultimately enable a customer-facing product or service.

The customer-facing orientation of a business architecture is so important because it creates a crystal-clear understanding of the big picture, and it always brings us back to who we are ultimately serving: *the customer*. We can maintain the spirit of treating each other as "customers"—and even keep it in the daily vernacular—but when it comes to representing an organization's business architecture, it is customer with a big "C" and product with a big "P."

How does an organization scope its business architecture?

First, it may be helpful to reflect upon the entire scope of what the organization does, even beyond the entities or functions that are typically considered to be the core. Consider depicting the scope of the ecosystem using a value network or other technique to represent the various legal entities that make up and interact with the organization along with the value exchanged between them.

With the full scope of the business ecosystem in mind, now a decision can be made whether an organization has one business architecture or multiple. Keep in mind that just because an organization is large and business units do different things does not mean that the organization should have more than one business architecture. Lean towards having only one unless there is a solid case for having multiple (though there are many justifiable cases).

Consider creating one business architecture if business units share customers, partners, assets, or investments, or if an IT architecture automates shared capabilities across business units. In addition, if the business units on their own—or the organization on its own without other legal entities—are not enough to represent a complete business model that delivers customer value, then consider creating one business architecture.

Does the scope change if business architecture is starting in just one business unit?

As some organizations start their journey, they may only have buy-in for business architecture within one business unit or perhaps on a large change initiative. We always start where we can start, but this does not change or reduce the scope of the business architecture.

In these cases, it is just as essential to represent the entire scope of the organization in the baseline for two reasons. First, with the full scope represented, that business unit or change initiative can now assess and communicate their full breadth of impacts, coordination points, and reuse opportunities. Second, it subtly conveys the intent of business architecture, which sets the stage for expanding business architecture to the enterprise level in the future.

When creating the baseline in these instances, the key is to *build with the enterprise in mind but focus on the details that the business unit or change initiative needs*. For example, the top level of the capability map can be mapped out for the entire organization and then only capabilities within the area of focus can be decomposed into more detail. Industry reference models can be leveraged to fill in gaps.

Does a business architecture represent the current state or future state?

Generally, the business architecture knowledgebase represents the current state of an organization. However, future state ideas can be mixed in. For example, while most capabilities will represent the current state, there may be some new capabilities planned because of a business model change, strategy, or acquisition and they may be included, ideally with an indication that they represent the future state. In addition, planned or potential products, policies, initiatives, and other domains can include future representations as well. This concept applies to any cross-mappings as well such as a planned process or system application.

There is a school of thought suggesting that when documenting a business architecture, one should skip the current state and go right to the future state. However, this is based on several misconceptions, most of all the level of detail represented in a business architecture.

Business architecture is created at a level of abstraction where there is not a significant difference between the current state and the future state. The operating model details however, inclusive of people, process, and technology, are much more voluminous and detailed, and making deliberate decisions about current state versus future state modeling here *is* highly important.

Does IT have its own business architecture?

An organization's IT department does have a business architecture: the same one as the rest of the organization. Within this context, the IT department is considered a business unit just like any other. Every business unit plays an important role to deliver value to an organization's customers and support its operations. IT is no different and no more or less special. Every business unit sees themselves as important and worthy of having their own view but splitting out or elevating any one over the other is detrimental to our ability to see the whole.

For example, IT manages strategies, plans, initiatives, policies, assets (both software and physical assets), partners, agreements, finances, and human resources as other business units do. IT's capabilities, value streams, and other business architecture focal points are woven into the overall business architecture.

There are numerous frameworks for representing IT as a business and there is good intent behind them to deliver great service for an organization with efficiency and agility. They may certainly exist as separate frameworks for specific purposes, but they are not part of an organization's business architecture, which is business-focused, leveled consistently, principle-based, and cohesive.

There is no us and them—there is only us and us. An organization is united by one business architecture and that includes everyone. Views, however, can help each business unit to see its own unique scope and how they fit into the bigger picture.

Value Streams and Capabilities: The Heart of a Business Architecture

Ideally both value streams and capabilities will be created as part of an organization's baseline, not just one or the other. Value streams help us see the business in motion, but it is capabilities (and the people, process, and technology they employ) that enable them. Capabilities help us to see the business at rest, but without value streams they lack context for how they are used to create value.

Value streams and capabilities together are the heart of a business architecture. Both have significant value on their own, but when cross-mapped together they form what is arguably the most important blueprint of business architecture. They provide the lens into the rest of the business architecture, IT architecture, and the operating model.

Creation of a business architecture baseline is an entirely introspective and enlightening experience for all those who are involved. It is the start of the mindset shift in an organization.

What is the minimum business architecture baseline needed to get started?

The minimum business architecture baseline includes three components: (1) capabilities, (2) value streams, and the (3) cross-mapping between them. All three components should be in place for the greatest benefit, but there are ways to scale back the scope of each when availability of subject matter experts is limited or the need to release the baseline is urgent. As long as each component is in place to a minimum level, the *just enough, just in time* approach to evolving the knowledgebase will address any gaps over time.

Minimum Level of Content for Capabilities

For capabilities, the minimum level of content is to include all level 1 capabilities, which reflect the highest level of detail. For example, this would include capabilities such as Customer Management, Product Management, Asset Management, or Human Resource Management. It is essential to include all level 1 capabilities because it frames the entire capability map and ensures the correct leveling before it is decomposed into more detail. It also communicates that the capability map is an enterprise-wide view. Depending on where business architecture gets initial traction within an organization, for example if it is in just one business unit, there can be some consternation about representing capabilities outside of one's scope. However, the appropriate disclaimers can be added, and reference models can greatly speed up the task.

Ideally though, the baseline capability map would include capabilities down to a level 3 or potentially level 2. The level indicator implies a degree of detail, so level 1 capabilities are the highest level of detail and become progressively more detailed at levels 2, 3, and beyond. A capability map that is decomposed down to level 2 or 3 is still a bird's eye view but provides enough granularity that is useful for making decisions and framing challenges, opportunities, and initiatives. Depending upon the constraints, just a subset of capabilities can be decomposed from the level 1s, potentially with a focus on all customer-facing capabilities or those which are relevant for the business unit or change initiative where there is currently traction.

Finally, the capabilities need to be based on defined information concepts. This helps people interpret capabilities consistently and it also creates the high-level vocabulary of the business. This essentially means that creating a portion of the information map (with the information concept names and definitions) is part of the baseline as well.

Minimum Level of Content for Value Streams

For value streams, the minimum level of content is one fully articulated value stream. Ideally though, the baseline would include 3-5 value streams, typically those which are customer-facing, a key organizational priority, and/or relevant to the initial business architecture usage scenario(s). Starting with just a few value streams is a practical approach regardless because actual usage will inform the next round of mapping efforts.

Minimum Level of Content for Value Stream/Capability Cross-Mapping

For the value stream/capability cross-mapping, a relationship should be created between the stages within each value stream and the capabilities that enable them. One way to scale back this activity is to only cross-map level 1 capabilities to stages or to only cross-map the most important capabilities (across varying levels) to stages.

How are capabilities represented in a business architecture?

Capabilities are the centerpiece of a business architecture. A capability map creates a powerful mental model, underpinned by a common business vocabulary, so that every person in the organization shares the same picture in their minds to see and communicate about what the organization does.

Capabilities define *what* an organization does, not how it does things. Capabilities are the unique abilities that an organization performs across all business units and product lines to deliver value to its customers and support its operations.

Capabilities Are Organized into Tiers

We often speak of capabilities within the context of the blueprint that represents them: the *capability map*. Organizations also refer to it as a capability model or business capability model (BCM). A capability map organizes each level 1 capability and its "child" capabilities into three tiers which convey the overall context for each.

The **Strategic tier** contains capabilities which have more bearing on the direction of an organization, such as Business Entity Management, Market Management, or Policy Management. The **Customer-Facing/Core tier** contains capabilities which are customer-facing or foundational to what the organization does, such as Customer Management, Channel Management, and industry-specific capabilities such as Shipment Management for a transportation company or Financial Instrument Management for a financial services company. The **Supporting tier** contains capabilities which are necessary to operate such as Human Resource Management or Finance Management. A little-known fact is that these three tiers were originally inspired by the Porter Value Chain.

The capabilities in the Strategic and Supporting tiers are common and can be found in most organizations. The capabilities in the Customer-Facing/Core tier reflect differentiation by industry and business model. However, since capabilities are highly abstracted, many of them will look the same for organizations in the same industry. On the other hand, how each organization puts together the people, process, and technology behind those capabilities (the operating model) to deliver exceptional customer experiences and operate with advantage is what truly differentiates them competitively.

Key Characteristics of a Capability Map

Below are a few characteristics to keep in mind when creating or interpreting a capability map.

Non-redundant. A capability map is a non-redundant view of an organization. Capabilities are defined once for an organization, regardless of who performs them or where they are used. For example, many business units may have a capability for Customer Information Management if they interact with customers or use the information. A capability for Payment Management may be used within the context of receiving a payment from a customer, providing a refund to a customer, making a payment to a partner, or paying employees through payroll.

Not process or organization. A capability map is not a process view or organizational view. It does not mirror product or service offerings, business units, or processes. A capability map represents categories of abilities—not a cohesive flow.

Comprehensive. A capability map represents an organization comprehensively. It encompasses everything an organization does, from top to bottom, levelled consistently. Everyone should be able to find pieces of what they do, even if at a high level.

Stable. A capability map is relatively stable. Since a capability map is the centerpiece of the business architecture with all other domains connected to it, it needs to remain relatively stable. The high level of abstraction achieves this. When an organization's business model changes or strategy requires, capabilities may be created or evolved, but this is more the exception than the rule.

Decomposition not encapsulation. A capability only decomposes into other capabilities. Capabilities do not break down into, become, or encapsulate anything other than more detailed capabilities. For example, they do not become processes or requirements or anything else, but rather they cross-map to these perspectives. Capabilities decomposed to level 3 provide just enough detail to support many strategic scenarios. However, decomposing them further clarifies what the organization does in more detail and may also be useful for initiative framing and detailed scenarios. Capability decomposition is not limited, but typically does not go beyond level 6 otherwise it tends to start reflecting operating model details.

The BIZBOK® Guide achieves these characteristics in a capability map through a set of rigorous principles, the core of which is that it bases capabilities upon *business objects* (a.k.a. information concepts for purposes of simplicity). It guides that each capability is based on one and only one object and produces a concrete outcome. The syntax of a capability then becomes *object action*. Business objects not only form the business vocabulary but ensure stability and tangible outcomes.

However, regardless of how an organization chooses to achieve these characteristics, most importantly, a capability map should be mutually exclusive and collectively exhaustive (MECE).

Each capability should have a **definition**, and its **outcome** may be defined as well. Capturing these additional attributes is essential to create common understanding.

If some of these concepts seem unfamiliar, remember that the capability map is *fit for purpose*. It gives us a new lens to uncover where people do things the same versus focusing on where they are different. A capability map's form follows its function and when created according to these guidelines, can illuminate powerful new insights.

How are value streams represented in a business architecture?

Value streams are high-level frameworks that describe how value is delivered from end-to-end to a customer, partner, or employee. The value stream construct truly guides a new mindset. Value streams help us focus on the things that create value, and they allow us to look at what an organization does from the perspective of its stakeholders.

An organization typically has approximately 25 value streams. However, there can certainly be more, especially if an organization has a complex business model and does many diverse things that deliver distinct value.

Anatomy of a Value Stream

A value stream is triggered by a **triggering stakeholder** who may be external such a customer, partner, or regulator, or internal such as a hiring manager, a product manager, or a finance officer. A value stream produces a **value proposition** at the end, such as a product being built to requirements on time for a Manufacture Product value stream.

A series of stages define the steps of a value stream. Each stage includes a **description**, a list of **participating stakeholders**, **entrance criteria** and **exit criteria**, and a **value item(s)** that provides value to the triggering stakeholder.

Value streams and the stages within them are named with a *verb noun* syntax, where the nouns are based upon the organization's defined set of information concepts. In fact, what creates the "flow" in a value stream is an information concept such as a customer, product, shipment, or claim changing state and moving in and out of stages as it meets the entrance and exit criteria.

Key Characteristics of a Value Stream

Here are a few characteristics to keep in mind when creating or interpreting a value stream.

Business unit and product agnostic. Value streams are business unit and product agnostic. Because of their level of abstraction, they almost always involve more than one business unit. For example, a value stream for Acquire Product would be used when a customer purchases any of an organization's products, and a value stream for Establish Product would be used when any product areas create or update a marketable product or service. Analysis at this elevation provides opportunities for streamlining, consistency, and reuse. For example, Acquire Product can highlight opportunities for making the customer experience more integrated and consistent across products. Establish Product can help different product areas share best practices and streamline how they create products using shared solutions.

Encompass all scenarios. Value streams represent the superset of any number of possible scenarios for which it could be used. For example, a value stream for Settle Financial Accounts is a bi-directional value stream which could encompass any inbound or outbound payments to or from an organization and its customers and partners. In fact, a good way to test the completeness of a value stream is by walking through scenarios and ensuring that it can handle each.

Focused on value delivery. Value streams must deliver value in the eye of the triggering stakeholder. This means that the way an organization scopes its value streams is highly important. Value streams represent logical groupings of value delivery. Value streams are not life cycles, especially considering that the aim of a value stream is to reach the end. For example, if a value stream was defined to include the entire employee life cycle from hire-to-retire, this would imply that the purpose of hiring people would be to retire them. Instead, there would be one value stream for Onboard Human Resource and a separate one for Develop Human Resource Career which includes developing people and supporting their retirement.

Not processes or workflows. Value streams do not represent process or workflow details, though they may be cross-mapped to processes or event models to make the connection to the operating model.

Named based on outcome. Value streams and the stages within them are named for what they ultimately produce. For example, a value stream for Onboard Human Resource covers the scope from a position being requested to an employee or contractor being fully onboarded. It goes beyond just the onboarding process and is named after the desired outcome: a human resource hired, onboarded, and ready to contribute.

How are value streams and capabilities cross-mapped in a business architecture?

Cross-mapping can begin when both the capability map and value streams are finalized, or at least stable enough where they are not likely to change significantly. Capabilities are cross-mapped to each stage within a value stream that they enable. *The relationship is made from a value stream stage to the highest level of capability where all the lower-level capabilities apply.* For example, if the level 2 Customer Information Management capability is cross-mapped to a value stream stage for Initiate Product Interest, then all of its the level 3 capabilities and beyond must be applicable to the stage. *A value stream/capability cross-mapping should represent the superset of all potential capabilities needed for any scenario through a value stream.*

Following a checklist or sequence can help make the activity of cross-mapping easier and more repeatable. For example, for each stage, first identify the applicable information concepts and then follow them through to the applicable capabilities. Next identify overall capabilities to handle communications, information, work, and other concepts. Standard patterns can even be created to define the capabilities that enable certain types of stages.

Tooling is of great help in creating and maintaining these cross-mappings and others. Once cross-mapping begins, it often becomes the tipping point for seeking tool support beyond Visio, Excel, and PowerPoint.

How do the information and stakeholder domains relate to the baseline?

While value streams and capabilities are the focal point of the business architecture baseline, information and stakeholders play an important supporting role. Most organizations do not map out the information or stakeholders in detail at the same time they are building their baseline. This is simply because they want to publish and start using the baseline quickly as possible. However, more rigorous information and stakeholder mapping upfront can make the value streams and capabilities even more solid. Otherwise, these activities can easily be revisited after the baseline is published, ideally within 3-6 months, and any resulting updates made to the value streams and capabilities accordingly.

These four domains also have something else in common: their source. While not readily obvious on surface, the content for each of the ten domains of business architecture is sourced differently. Value streams, capabilities, information, and stakeholders are abstracted. They should be defined by the same group of business representatives and are essentially made up, though of course mapped according to principles. For example, the business team will decide whether a capability is called Payment Amount Determination or Payment Calculation or whether a value stream is called Establish Product or Launch Product.

On the other hand, content for the remaining domains is sourced from information that already exists in the business. For example, if a regulation (policy) is named GDPR, that is the name we use. Or, if a business unit is named Business Transformation and Innovation, that is the name we use. We do not abstract or alter the naming of these values.

How is business information represented in a business architecture?

The information map provides a pure business perspective on how the business defines its information concepts and their relationships. An information map (blueprint) provides a focused view of business information, helpful for facilitating conversations related to decision-making, reporting, solution design, and much more. It also informs an organization's data architecture.

Information concepts are ubiquitous throughout an organization's business architecture and are worth the time and effort to define well. For example, information concepts are the basis for capabilities. The states of information concepts create the flow in value streams. Information concepts can be used to categorize stakeholders. Information concepts are critical for data and solution design as well.

While a portion of the information map is captured as part of the business architecture baseline, specifically the **information concept names and definitions**, the remaining portions to be captured include the types, states, and relationships for each.

Information types. are especially useful because they describe additional business granularity, which is intentionally not represented in the capability map. For example, the capability map would contain many capabilities within Asset Management, but they are generalized for Asset Information Management, Asset Performance Management or Asset Inventory Management. However, the information map articulates that the types of assets can be, for example, Tangible and Intangible.

Information states. list the superset of potential states an information concept may be in. For example, an asset may have a state of Requested, In Preparation, In Use, Retired, or Disposed. Information states also allow for a simpler capability map to be created. For example, instead of having multiple capabilities to manage leads, prospects, and customers, one set of capabilities can be created for customers where a customer can be in a state of Prospect, Active, or Inactive.

Information relationships. are made between information concepts. For example, a customer *has* an agreement, or an agreement *contains* products. The relationships are captured within the knowledgebase and may be represented through a variety of rich visual views.

How are stakeholders represented in a business architecture?

Stakeholders provide a people lens into the business architecture. For example, a customer experience issue may be explored by assessing the value streams that customers trigger or participate in. Stakeholders can also provide a focal point for assessing the collective set of changes planned for a certain group of people across initiatives.

Stakeholders refer to individuals, not entities. For example, Auditor would be a stakeholder, not Internal Audit department, which would be considered a business unit. Stakeholders are also abstracted and do not refer to job titles such as Senior Internal Auditor.

In business architecture, stakeholders are the players in the value streams. They are not a generic list of the organization's stakeholders or a list of stakeholders participating in initiatives. This means that the inventory of stakeholders that exists in a business architecture knowledgebase is essentially a rationalized list of people who trigger or participate in a value stream.

While the **names of stakeholders** who trigger or participate in value streams are captured as part of value stream mapping, additional attributes can be captured for each stakeholder. This includes its **category**, **type**, and a **short description**.

The deliberate rationalization and attribution of stakeholders performed during stakeholder mapping is a valuable and introspective exercise, which often illuminates opportunities to refine the stakeholders captured during value stream mapping.

How should the creation of a business architecture baseline be facilitated?

Having the right people involved with creating a business architecture baseline is a critical success factor. First, ensure there is an active sponsor from the business. If the business architecture executive leader does not report within the business, it may be helpful to engage an additional business leader to serve as a sponsor for the baseline building effort.

Second, co-create the business architecture baseline with a group of cross-functional business representatives. They should ideally be at a leadership level where they are still close enough to the business details but can think *enterprise*, make decisions, and influence others. The business team should play an ongoing role to develop future content, review proposed changes to content, and serve as an advocate for business architecture. They are also essential to capturing the right content and helping to facilitate adoption.

If it is not feasible to bring together a group of businesspeople, then the baseline may be defined by proxies for the business, potentially the business architecture team. However, as business architecture gains traction, the baseline should be reviewed retroactively with a business team and adjusted accordingly.

The Business Architecture Baseline Jumpstart Approach

A business architecture baseline jumpstart approach is effective for quickly creating a solid starting point and momentum. A three-day facilitated workshop with the business team provides a good balance of achieving significant results without overburdening their schedules. This approach may be extended to five days or broken into a series of shorter work sessions, but the concepts are the same.

With the three-day approach, capabilities are the focus in the morning and value streams are the focus in the afternoon. This is a good rhythm because capabilities tend to be more taxing and can be covered while workshop participants are fresh.

Day 1. On the first day, the business sponsor will typically kick off the sessions, reaffirming what the goals are for the session and how the organization plans to use the resulting business architecture. A very light business architecture primer can be presented, keeping the mapping details to a minimum. Keep in mind that the businesspeople do not need to become mapping experts, but rather they need to understand just enough of the principles and guidance to appreciate and effectively participate in the mapping activity.

The first topic of discussion is to confirm the scope of the business architecture. This is followed by the first capability-related activity in the morning, which is an information concept brainstorm. The business team shouts out the important *nouns* of the business, which are listed on a large whiteboard or digital equivalent. This activity gets the group working together, keeps the conversation high level, and lays the foundation for capabilities. The information concept brainstorm is what shifts capability map creation from daunting to doable. Next, through facilitation, the information concepts are rationalized and defined. For example, if the brainstorm uncovered Strategic Alliance, Supplier, and Distributor, these might be rationalized to an information concept for Partner.

The first value stream-related activity in the afternoon is to create a value stream inventory. Reference models are a key input to the list as well as expertise from the business team. Next, the business team prioritizes 3-5 value streams (or whatever number desired) to flow out as part of the baseline. If time, the first value stream is mapped out. Each value stream starts with a working name and the two bookends: the triggering stakeholder and value proposition. From there the stages and their detail are defined.

Day 2. On the morning of the second day, rationalization of the information concepts continues. When it is complete, the team renames each information concept in capability syntax (e.g., an information concept for Partner becomes Partner Management) and organizes the concepts into the three capability tiers. The level 1 capability map is now complete.

In the afternoon, the next value stream(s) is mapped out.

Day 3. On the morning of the third day, the business team will start decomposing the capabilities. They may focus on a certain set of priority capabilities or perform a rough brainstorm of the things they do for each level 1 which can later be considered during capability decomposition activities. With the three-day approach, it is common for small group conversations to continue after the sessions with individual business representatives and/or their teams in order to complete the capability decomposition.

In the afternoon, the final value stream(s) is mapped out.

At the end of the day, the next steps are confirmed, especially related to any responsibilities of the business team. The ongoing role of the business team may also be discussed as it pertains to developing future baseline content, reviewing changes to it, and advocating for or using it.

After the Jumpstart Sessions. The business architecture team leverages the content from the sessions along with the reference models to complete and refine the value stream and capability content, with assistance from business representatives as needed. Once the capability map and value streams are final, they are formally reviewed with the business team and then published.

At this point, the value stream/capability cross-mapping can be created. The business architecture team may co-create the cross-mapping with the business team or create a draft which may be reviewed with the team. Once the cross-mapping is complete and reviewed, it may be published as well.

How should business architecture reference models be leveraged?

Leveraging business architecture reference models means that you can spend less time building your business architecture and more time using it. Industry reference models, particularly those offered in the BIZBOK® Guide, are tremendous accelerators for the mapping of an organization's business architecture baseline and additional domains as well. The reference models are based on BIZBOK® Guide principles and the content are coherent across models. This makes it easy to leverage multiple models to represent an organization, or even architect across organizations. Even if there is not a reference model available for a particular industry, the models are abstracted to a level where a significant portion of any related models can still be leveraged, including a common reference model.

Any reference model will need to be adapted to the vocabulary and business model of a particular organization. Immerse in learning the reference models *prior* to facilitating any mapping sessions. This way the sessions can be facilitated in a way that feels organic, yet is based upon standard information concepts, capabilities, and value streams. It also ensures that the tough questions are asked, and the group can be guided towards creating a principle-based baseline. After the initial mapping sessions, the reference models are instrumental to inform detailed decomposition and definition.

There are a wide range of reference models available in the market. When using a non-BIZBOK® Guide reference model, keep in mind that it will not likely be based on the same set of principles or even a set of principles at all. However, additional reference models may be useful to provide additional starter ideas for content to include.

How long does it take to create a business architecture baseline?

With the right conditions, a business architecture baseline can be created for an organization in a duration of approximately three months. Building a baseline is typically not full-time work, but a three-month period allows for the right conversations, reviews, and iteration to occur. However, a larger and more complex organization, such as one operating globally with a sweeping scope of markets, products, and value propositions, may require more than the three-month period.

Conditions which accelerate business architecture baseline creation include **active business sponsorship**, **the availability of business representatives**, and **a compelling reason(s) that motivates people to buy into mapping efforts**. From a mapping perspective, **dedicated business architects**, **mapping know-how** on the business architecture team and/or support from an external expert as well as the **use of industry reference models** are key accelerators. Following the business architecture baseline jumpstart approach described earlier can also help to boost the initial efforts.

How can capabilities and value streams be made more relatable to other people?

Capability maps and value streams can seem foreign to people, especially because they are intentionally abstract. Most people are used to looking at the world through their specific context and often at a deeper level of detail.

To address this very important challenge, first *make sure the purpose for business architecture within the organization is clear.* If people understand that the business architecture is represented in a way that is fit for purpose, it can help make its reason for existence more logical. For example, if people understand that the capability map will be used to help inform investment decision-making—and that it does not replace other views such as the organization chart or processes—they may be more open to adopt it. Or, if they understand that the business language created by the information concepts does not replace their daily dialect but rather gives them the ability to speak *enterprise* in cross-business unit forums, they will better understand the intention.

In addition, *a variety of presentation layers or views may be created to put a more familiar and contextual lens over the capabilities.* In conversation, it is most important to translate and speak in the business dialect of whomever one is speaking with. Educational sessions or interactive tools can also be used to help others learn value stream and capability content in simple ways.

Another approach is to simply *not show the capability map or value streams beyond a limited group of people until the concept starts gaining traction.* Furthermore, when they are shown, they should always highlight insights such as a heatmapped view to represent organizational costs or application health—not just simply the maps on their own.

What if an organization's baseline is not aligned with industry principles?

Some organizations have been on the business architecture journey for some time and have capability maps and value streams that were created using an approach other than the BIZBOK® Guide principles. There are two options to realign an existing capability map and/or value streams: fix them or rebuild them. Fixing them often takes more time and effort than rebuilding from scratch, because the paradigms are often entirely different.

Some organizations prefer to phase in changes to their business architecture over time, while others choose to republish a new capability map and/or value streams at a specific point in time. The best approach depends on an organization's dynamics, such as the level of usage and adoption of the business architecture. Socialization and messaging are highly important so that people understand why the changes are being made and for what benefit.

Organizations with longstanding capability maps may have system applications or other types of content cross-mapped to their capabilities. To address this, the cross-mappings from applications or other content can be changed from the legacy capability map to the new one. Alternatively, a translation can be created from the legacy capability map to the new one so that existing relationships can stay in place and be phased out at the right time.

Does the mapping approach to value streams and capabilities really matter?

Following an industry standard mapping approach is beneficial for a few compelling reasons. First, the principle-based approach creates a consistent and defensible architecture with the rigor necessary to achieve the intended outcomes. For example, a capability map that does not create the intended non-redundant view of an organization will not be able to effectively highlight duplicative spend or opportunities for reuse.

Second, a standard approach creates acceleration. This comes from leveraging reference models as well as creating a common frame of reference among the team. If all team members, including new hires, share a common set of principles, it can greatly reduce the time it takes to create and interpret a business architecture.

Finally, if organizations create their business architectures in consistent ways, it enables architecting across organizational boundaries. This is becoming increasingly important in the connected, digital world. Architecting across organizations is particularly relevant for situations such as mergers, acquisitions, joint ventures, whole of government architecture efforts, or business ecosystem design. At a broader level, following industry accepted mapping standards serves to codify business architecture, helps to legitimize the discipline, and strengthens its merit universally.

The Non-Negotiables, With Practicality as the Guiding Light

However, it is worth remembering that we are not performing surgery or sending humans to the moon. We are modeling a business and the methods we use can evolve. In fact, let's be honest: the methods *have* evolved over the years and different people have different experiences and perspectives.

If we take a step back, there may be times when we need to flex to make sure business architecture is consumable and continues to advance for the greatest good. However, ensuring overall cohesiveness in the discipline is critical and we need to hold precious a few core beliefs.

Boundaries of the business architecture discipline. The scope of business architecture is defined as the domains in the BIZBOK® Guide. Top level agreement on what makes up business architecture is the starting point for consistency and provides sharp clarity on how business architecture relates to other disciplines.

Positioning of business architecture. The positioning of business architecture is between strategy and execution. Business architecture is a strategic discipline, most effective when leveraged upfront in strategy execution. It is used to inform and translate strategy into a coordinated set of actions across an organization.

Scope of a business architecture. The scope of an organization's business architecture should represent the entire organization and the ecosystem in which it operates. We have plenty of fragmented views of our organizations and the intent of business architecture is to help us see the whole.

Capabilities are the core. Capabilities are a necessary construct to help organizations organize and optimize the resources needed to deliver stakeholder value and execute change initiatives. Capabilities should provide a non-redundant view of an entire organization at a high level.

Capabilities require context. Capabilities alone are not enough and need a flow- or value-based construct to provide context for their usage. The BIZBOK® Guide defines these as value streams. Capabilities and value streams are particularly powerful when related to and used in conjunction with each other.

Regardless of the mapping method your organization chooses, the value streams and information concepts as defined in the BIZBOK® Guide are two of the most powerful connectors within and across organizations. Overlaying them onto any of your existing models can help to highlight new connections and opportunities for reuse that may not otherwise be identified.

Beyond the Baseline: Other Domains of Business Architecture

Once the business architecture baseline is in place, the rest of the domains can be captured opportunistically to support business needs. From this point forward, we are building the knowledgebase one piece at a time, maintaining any new information we capture along the way.

When capturing information for any domains beyond the core, determine the scope and level of detail necessary based on the business usage scenario(s) at hand. For example, when helping a product leader with a new strategy, capture just the products that are in their scope along with any other products necessary for impact analysis. When supporting a compliance review, capture only the policies which are in scope and cross-map them to the capabilities they guide. Or, when just looking to get some high-level connection points in place to support enterprise-wide impact analysis, do not capture details such as the individual product or policy names, but just rather make the linkages at the product or policy category level.

Capturing and maintaining content for additional domains typically requires collaboration with new partners in the organization. For example, a human resources expert may provide information about the organization's business units, or a legal expert may provide information on policies.

How is organizational structure represented in a business architecture?

Looking at a business architecture through an organizational lens can be invaluable for bringing transparency to how an organization really works without the politics. It also helps to inform organization design, outsourcing decision-making, and impact analysis, especially during restructuring.

Business architecture provides a unique and politically agnostic take on organizational structure. It does not replicate the organization chart or include people, titles, or hierarchical management structure. Organization mapping is simply a representation of an organization's business units (including how they decompose into sub-business units) and their relationships to other domains such as capabilities.

There are three types of business units that can be used to represent a full business ecosystem, even beyond the legal boundaries of an organization. **Internal business units** are the organization's internal structures, which may be referred to as business units, divisions, departments, or other terms which may vary across sectors and organizations. **External business units** are partners of any type such strategic alliances, vendors, or even regulatory bodies. **Collaborative teams** are informal structures such as steering committees, governance bodies, councils, or teams (including agile teams).

Business units reflect an organization's actual business units or partners—they are not abstractions. In fact, if organization mapping reveals sub-optimal structures (e.g., multiple business units that are redundantly performing the same capability), the current state should be represented exactly as it is. This technique can provide transparency and clarity to help people understand an organization's structure today and identify opportunities to improve or transform.

Business units can be decomposed into lower-level business units. As with any domain of business architecture, organization information can be represented textually or visually to show business units and their relationships.

Stakeholders belong to business units, and this relationship can be made in the business architecture knowledgebase. For example, an internal stakeholder of Claims Adjuster would belong to the P&C Claims business unit. An external stakeholder of Auditor would belong to a certain external audit firm. However, the most important relationship to make is the cross-mapping from business units to the capabilities they have.

How are products and services represented in a business architecture?

Products represent both the tangible goods and intangible services that an organization offers to its customers. As mentioned, in a business architecture, the definition of products must always be customer-facing, never an internal definition of product.

Product mapping can help to build a common understanding of an organization's product offerings. Products are based on the actual names of an organization's products or services, not abstractions, and may be sourced from product managers, product catalogs, or other lists. Products can be organized into families, lines, or other categories. The exercise of product mapping often becomes more introspective than expected. On the surface people tend to believe that everyone knows the products that an organization offers, but the conversations can reveal differences in understanding as well as nuances such as what is a product versus a package.

One of the most important relationships to make is the cross-mapping from products to the capabilities which enable them. When a new product is being considered, an assessment can be performed to determine if any existing capabilities can be leveraged or if they need to be uplifted in some way. On the other hand, if new capabilities are needed, the business architecture helps inform the decision on whether it is best to build them internally or outsource them to a partner. Products can also be cross-mapped to the value stream stages to which they directly contribute value.

How does business architecture fit with a product mindset?

Many organizations are going through a shift from a *project mindset* to a *product mindset*. Product-based delivery helps to organize resources around "products" instead of IT systems or functions. This is a step in the right direction and organizations are receiving benefits from a product-based approach. However, there are a couple important considerations which underscore the importance of leveraging the business architecture for additional perspective.

The first consideration is that the definition of "product" in this context is an internally defined product which can also be for internal customers. As a result, the business ecosystem view that business architecture provides is a critical counterbalance to help everyone keep the bigger picture in mind to serve the *actual* end customers.

The second consideration is that internal "products" tend to be defined as capability or system groupings, but do not always identify all the areas of integration, coordination, or potential reuse of common business components. One of the most practical ways to uncover these types of opportunities is by overlaying the business architecture value streams and information concepts on top of the product groupings. For example, this may illuminate that customer communication-related capabilities or the Settle Financial Accounts value stream may be reused across product groupings.

How are regulations and policies represented in a business architecture?

Policies represent external directives, such as regulations, industry agreements, or treaties, or internal directives such as internal policies and rules. Policies can be organized into categories and may be defined at different levels of detail depending on the business need (e.g., a policy name or a specific section within a policy).

Policy mapping can help to centralize policy definition and tracking for an organization. However, the policies captured within the business architecture knowledgebase are not meant to replace any existing repositories where policies are managed, but rather to create a connection between policies and the rest of the organization. For example, a policy can be cross-mapped to another policy to indicate how an internal policy supports an external regulation. In addition, policies can be cross-mapped to the capabilities they guide.

Policies are based on the actual names of an organization's policies and can be sourced from different people and documentation related to human resources, compliance, audit, corporate law, finance, product development, sales, information management—potentially anywhere throughout the organization.

Policy mapping enables bi-directional impact analysis. For example, if a new policy is introduced or an existing one is changed, the impact can be readily assessed by following the relevant capabilities through to the business units involved, and the value streams, products, processes, and system applications impacted. On the other hand, if a capability is being targeted to change because of an initiative, any potential policy impacts can be identified upfront as well.

How is business direction represented in a business architecture?

Strategies represent different aspects of business direction, often with a focus on **goals**, **objectives**, and **courses of action**. Objectives are the key focal point and can be cross-mapped to the value streams and capabilities they impact, as well as the business units that have them and the initiatives which will deliver them. Courses of action can also be a useful bridge between strategy, architecture, and execution because they create focus. For example, if an organization has an objective to increase revenue, this could be achieved in any number of ways from entering a new market to offering a new product to acquiring another company, so the course of action would specify the chosen direction.

Metrics are represented as a separate domain in the BIZBOK® Guide and help to drive business performance. Metrics can be used to make objectives measurable. For example, a metric of Customer Satisfaction Score may be used to measure the achievement of an objective related to increasing customer satisfaction.

In addition, business metrics can be captured for value stream stages or capabilities to help measure value and performance. For example, Application Processing Time may be one metric used to measure a value stream stage for Approve Application within an Acquire Product value stream.

Furthermore, a special set of metrics typically associated with the concept of capability assessments may be captured for capabilities and even value stream stages to help to assess business performance and target improvements within an architecture context. *More on capability assessments is discussed in Chapter 3.*

Business architects may work with business leaders, strategists, or other business representatives to capture these aspects of business direction. The information is maintained in the business architecture knowledgebase to create end-to-end traceability. It can also be used to facilitate alignment across strategies and from strategies to architecture to initiatives.

Beyond maintaining this traceability and facilitating alignment, business architects may also help executives and strategists to represent strategy as needed using a variety of techniques, such as SWOT analysis (strengths, weaknesses, opportunities, and threats), Porter's five forces, Kaplan Norton strategy maps, Hoshin Kanri, and a variety of others.

How are initiatives represented in a business architecture?

Initiatives represent any defined scope of work to implement change. An initiative may be in-flight or planned, and of any size or type, from a large effort such as a program to a sprint.

Initiatives may be captured in the business architecture knowledgebase at any stage and may be used at any altitude. For example, a set of *in-flight* initiatives may be captured for retroactive analysis and alignment back to strategy. A *proposed* set of initiatives may be captured to support portfolio leaders in making investment decisions. A set of *planned* initiatives may be defined as part of translating strategy with business architecture.

Initiatives may be sourced from a wide variety of existing lists, repositories, and people including any number of business leaders or representatives, strategists, product managers, portfolio leaders, business planners, Project Management Office (PMO) team members, program and project managers, or others.

Initiatives are often cross-mapped to the objectives to which they are contributing, the business units that are sponsoring them, and the value streams and capabilities they are impacting.

More on leveraging strategies and initiatives for strategy and transformation is discussed in Chapter 3.

Putting It All Together

With a solid understanding of the pieces, the next question is how to put them together and where to store all this information. VEP (Visio, Excel, and PowerPoint) will only get you so far and it is best not to try to stretch these tools beyond their abilities. An automated business architecture tool should ideally be deployed within the first year of establishing a practice. Even better is to have the tool in place at the time of baseline creation or at least ready for value stream/capability cross-mapping.

First, gain some understanding of business architecture and how it will be used within the organization. Then, acquire a business architecture tool as quickly as possible. Good tools that are industry aligned can actually *help* people to learn business architecture by using them.

However, purchasing a tool is not always feasible for organizations that are just beginning their journey and may not yet have the buy-in or budget. The good news is that some excellent business architecture tools are available which are lighter weight and industry aligned. Some even cover just a slice across strategy, business architecture, and initiatives which can be used to gain traction and help make the case for a full business architecture tool.

These business architecture tools can typically integrate with other enterprise architecture tools. However, some organizations prefer to leverage a robust enterprise architecture management suite as a repository for both the business and IT architecture together.

How do all the pieces fit together?

There is a formal concept called a *metamodel* which officially defines (and visualizes) the domains that make up business architecture as well as all the relationships between each of them and the domains in other disciplines.

The BIZBOK® Guide contains a rigorous metamodel. At the time of publication for this book, the Business Architecture Guild® is taking that metamodel through the process to become a formal, adopted standard. This will help to further expand the market of available tools and service providers who are aligned to a common understanding.

Adopting the BIZBOK® Guide metamodel is the most expeditious and sound approach to put a business architecture practice on a solid foundation. The metamodel is based on a neutral, widely accepted perspective (most likely to become a standard) and it can be adapted as needed.

From a practical perspective though, learn the relationships between the business architecture domains and other domains. Then, when building out the business architecture knowledgebase just enough, just in time, be deliberate about not just the scope of domain content captured, but also the *relationships* created. For example, when capturing business units in the knowledgebase, it is probably more important to first create the cross-mapping to capabilities, but the cross-mapping between business units and stakeholders can be made later when business need dictates.

What should we look for in a business architecture tool?

An automated tool for the business architecture knowledgebase should first support the content. Reflecting on what essentially forms a business architecture, this means any tool should support defining the elements, attributing the elements, and creating connections between the elements—with the ability to customize where needed. It should also support related discipline domains and the ability to connect the business architecture domains to them. Some of the most common related domains include customer journeys, processes, requirements, events, and of course the IT architecture.

Fully supporting business architecture content is the essential foundation of a business architecture tool. One of the most common errors made by business architecture teams is selecting a tool that does not ultimately meet the needs of business architecture—even if it is an excellent tool that supports the IT architecture well. It is not unheard of for business architecture teams to revert to VEP, even after significant time and money has been invested, because an enterprise architecture tool still does not meet their needs. In these cases, it is a better choice to select a robust, aligned business architecture tool that fully supports the discipline and then integrate with the enterprise architecture tool.

Select a tool that is aligned with the BIZBOK® Guide metamodel. Even if a business architecture team does not follow all the BIZBOK® Guide methods or use all the domains it defines, this still provides a solid foundation for long-term success, flexibility, and expansion. BIZBOK® Guide-aligned tools often support other methods and approaches as well.

In addition to the core ability to support content in an industry-aligned way, *a business architecture tool should support visualization and reporting.* Keeping in mind the usage scenarios for business architecture, explore the blueprints, heatmaps, roadmaps, reports, and other views that a tool offers. Visualization and reporting are tremendously important for business architecture to be consumable and engaging by leaders and people throughout an organization. Some organizations leverage an additional tool(s) for powerful analytics and visualizations on top of their business architecture knowledgebase tool.

Beyond these major categories of requirements, assess the factors which one would consider for any vendor or tool, among them the intuitiveness and ease of the user interface and the ability to integrate with other tools. When conducting business architecture tool assessments, ask the hard questions and ask vendors to show you how their tool supports these requirements. *Do not assume that you are speaking the same language.* In fact, many tools today are based on a slightly different paradigm of business architecture and do not support all ten domains.

The potential for business architecture in an organization is significant and the return on investment for tools will far outweigh the costs. Excellent tooling options exist today, and more are likely to emerge.

3

Leveraging the Unique Value of Business Architecture

Equipped with clear intent and a solid baseline, it is now time to start putting business architecture into action as envisioned in the beginning of this journey. Now you get to start seeing the ah-ha moments, new groups of people collaborating, different questions being asked, different decisions being made, and new initiatives getting started with a better foundation. There will be all these wonderful experiences and much more. There may also be some unexpected ones.

It is normal for some people not to share the same excitement about or willingness to use business architecture, especially in the beginning. There may even be situations where the business architecture helped to objectively uncover new truths or highlighted a new path forward that would be best for the entire enterprise. But the decision-makers that be didn't choose that new path forward. They said, "thank you" and made the same decisions as they do today.

Remember that business architecture introduces change, and it is underpinned by a mindset shift. Keep moving forward because you will also meet the people who are challenging the status quo, who want more for the organization and its customers, and who have the courage to make new decisions even when they are hard and push against the current of the organization's culture and structure. Together, you are catalysts to transform the organization, one step at a time to the top of the mountain.

Using Business Architecture: Start Small, Dream Big

We all start small when we introduce business architecture to an organization. Movements start small. The catalyst is often a passionate practitioner or leader within an organization, or a small group of them. Even if a business architecture team had a mandate from the CEO to use business architecture on the organization's largest transformation starting tomorrow, they would still need to build the capacity to deliver on that and build buy-in throughout the organization.

What makes all the difference though is having a strategic vision of business architecture for an organization, backed by the determination and continual steps to achieve it.

Business architecture can indeed be leveraged for large and complex efforts. However, contributing value with business architecture does not always need to be epic. Small wins matter too. They build understanding, momentum, and capacity. What is most important is just to begin. Try using business architecture in different ways and find what really resonates and makes the greatest difference to the organization.

Success can be measured in small ways too. Did someone gain insights they never had? Did someone make a different decision than they normally would have? Is someone walking around with a business architecture view and showing it to others? Did someone better realize how they fit into the bigger picture? Did someone request business architecture involvement within a key conversation or effort?

How specifically do we use business architecture?

Business architecture can essentially be used in two ways: as a framework to represent information and as a translator from strategy to execution (i.e., supporting a sequence of steps).

Business architecture can be used as a **framework to organize, analyze, and communicate insights.** Just as we can use a map of the world to represent data, the blueprints of business architecture work in a similar way. For example, we can overlay data for population or average temperature onto a map of the world and color code the countries accordingly. Similarly, we can overlay risks or costs onto an organization's capability map or value streams and create heatmaps to color code where they are highest.

Business architecture blueprints make such ideal frameworks for overlaying information because they are high-level, comprehensive, business-focused, and shared by the entire organization—just as we all have a shared understanding of the country boundaries as they appear on the world map.

Business architecture blueprints are commonly used to show **impact footprints**. For example, the impact of a potential new regulation may be shown by highlighting the capabilities, value streams, customer journeys, business units, stakeholders, products, processes, and system applications that will be impacted in some way.

Blueprints are also commonly used to show **heatmaps**, which take impact footprints a step further by representing the degree of impact. For example, potential risks may be overlayed onto the applicable capabilities and value streams, and color-coded red, yellow, or green depending on the cumulative amount of risk. This not only provides a birds-eye view of the situation but can guide prioritization based on the business criticality of the capabilities and value streams impacted.

Business architecture blueprints can also be used for **framing and providing context for business opportunities and challenges**. For example, a customer experience issue could be pinpointed as having a root cause related to a certain capability within a few specific value stream stages. This helps to communicate the issue with clarity and focus solutions on addressing the true root cause.

On the other hand, business architecture can be used **in a flow as a translator from strategy to execution**, using the sequence of steps described in Figure 1.2. This applies to a variety of usage scenarios including translating a strategy, business model change, or business transformation. It also applies when implementing major change initiatives such as a regulatory response, an internal reorganization, or an organization-wide simplification effort. Furthermore, business architecture is used as a translator for crafting and implementing the action plans from a merger, acquisition, divestiture, or joint venture.

Leveraging business architecture does not always require elaborate deliverable creation. Sometimes business architecture can simply be used to frame a challenge or provide some contextual background for a conversation. When we are initially trying to build buy-in, it can be tempting to try to overuse it or overly draw attention to it. However, it is often best *not* to overemphasize the use of business architecture to others. When we go to a doctor, we expect them to use their expertise to diagnose why we are not feeling well without explaining the tools and technical methods they used to get to that diagnosis. It is the same with business architecture and it should be leveraged naturally within the course of daily work.

What are some good ways to start using business architecture?

There are initial business usage scenarios and quick wins. **Initial business usage scenarios** are good places to start at the beginning of a business architecture journey because they require minimal content and clearly demonstrate the potential of discipline. **Quick wins** are ways to leverage business architecture in hours, days, weeks, or up to three months and these are always relevant. Here are a few short-term but impactful usage scenarios which primarily leverage capabilities as the main framework for analysis, though other domains such as value streams may be used as well.

Usage Scenarios That Take Hours or Days

Perform a business impact analysis to assess the impact of a potential business model change, strategy, innovation idea, product, policy change, anything. For example, help a business or technology leader make a decision or understand the scope and impact of an idea. Or, help an agile team identify shared solution opportunities, collaboration points, and stakeholders to involve. *Performing business impact assessments is a common initial usage scenario for business architecture teams.*

Frame a challenge or opportunity to scope, analyze, and solve a problem or opportunity within the fullest, relevant business context. For example, this scenario can help to uncover a problematic capability that should be fixed within the context of many value streams, even if the original problem was identified within just one.

Usage Scenarios That Take Weeks

Support analysis and decision-making for investments, risks, cost allocations, business unit responsibilities, partner outsourcing and performance, business and technology simplification, and any other aspects of the business. *This is a common initial usage scenario for business architecture teams.* One of the top scenarios is to analyze the strategic alignment and planned spend for proposed initiatives by capability, at an aggregate level, within or across portfolios. Another top scenario is to aggregate the system applications supporting each capability and analyze them for redundancy, health, and risk within a capability context.

Visualize the focal points of strategic direction to reflect the most important capabilities and value streams required to enable the organization's strategies. This provides a visual comparison point against which anyone can evaluate planned or in-flight work.

Reflect a Capability-On-A-Page to illustrate an aggregate dashboard of key information such as a capability's current state and future state effectiveness ratings, impacted value streams and stakeholders, and active strategies and initiatives. This can be used to build a common understanding for decision-making and coordination.

Usage Scenarios That Take Months

Translate one strategy to identify business and technology impacts, design a target state architecture, and create a strategic roadmap for execution. While this is more involved, it demonstrates value and business architecture's true role in translating strategy into initiatives. *Translating a strategy is also a common initial usage scenario for business architecture teams, especially as they become comfortable with the business architecture.*

Driving Business Change with Capability Assessments

The capability assessment is one of the most well-known business architecture techniques which gives a pulse on business performance, identifies improvement opportunities, and guides investment decisions. Essentially the idea is to capture unique metrics by capability to measure its strategic importance and effectiveness. While capabilities are typically the focal point, value stream stages may be assessed as well.

Capability assessments are commonly used because the results can be leveraged in so many ways and they offer a data-based view of business performance, at an aggregate level, that no other discipline provides. They can be conducted as standalone efforts or as part of other usage scenarios. Performing a capability assessment, even if only for a limited scope, is also an excellent initial usage scenario for new business architecture teams.

As with anything beyond the business architecture baseline, capability assessments can be performed just enough, just in time. Some or all capabilities can be assessed either upfront or on an ongoing basis. For example, when translating a strategy, the capabilities and value streams impacted by the scope of that strategy can be assessed to identify any changes or improvements that need to be made.

Regardless of the timing though, any assessment information captured becomes a part of the reusable business architecture knowledgebase. This information must be kept up to date over time as initiatives make changes and improvements to the capabilities.

What does a capability assessment include?

There are two categories of assessment to consider: *how well things work* and *why we care*. While each aspect reveals valuable information on its own, they are often used in conjunction with each other to provide the full context for a situation. For example, a certain capability may be highly ineffective, but if it is rarely used and only by a small group of people internally, then it may not be a high priority for investment.

Strategic Importance Metrics: Why We Care

The *why we care* metrics establish the importance of each capability to the business. This goes beyond the tier to which a capability is assigned on the map, which only provides overall context. For example, while Information Management capabilities may be categorized within the Supporting tier, an organization may consider them to be of strategic importance for its digital business model.

In this category, the BIZBOK® Guide offers two metrics, Business Impact and Business Breadth. **Business Impact** reflects the frequency of use, external visibility, and relative impact. **Business Breadth** reflects how ubiquitous a capability is across an organization, depending upon its occurrences in value streams, business units, and other places.

In addition, organizations may use a **Strategic Importance** metric as a binary indicator of whether a capability is currently a strategic differentiator or strategic priority. Alternatively, the Strategic Importance metric may characterize a capability's contribution to customer and financial value by assigning it to one of four quadrants: Advantage, Strategic Support, Essential, or Business Necessity. Capabilities characterized as Advantage (top right quadrant) create distinctive value for customers and drive financial results. Capabilities characterized as Strategic Support (top left quadrant) create high value for customers but contribute less to financial results. Capabilities characterized as Essential (bottom right quadrant) drive financial results, but not customer value. Finally, capabilities characterized as Business Necessity (bottom left quadrant) do not drive either customer value or financial results. Business Necessity capabilities may be good candidates for outsourcing, while Advantage capabilities are not likely to be outsourced.

Effectiveness Metrics: How Well Things Work

The *how well things work* metrics assess the quality and extent of enablement for each capability. This ultimately comes down to the people, process, and technology behind each capability and how effectively and completely they support the organization's strategic and operational needs. Capabilities help to frame where enhancements or uplifts to people, process, and technology are necessary along with the actions needed to achieve them. This provides a critical foundation for strategy translation and initiative planning.

The resulting scores for this category of metrics are often referred to as capability maturity. While this is a simple way to refer to the concept, it can lead to some misunderstandings because the focus of assessment is more nuanced than it appears to be on the surface. A generic Capability Maturity Model (CMM) and its five levels tend to be a better measure for processes and do not provide value in this context. We are essentially focused on two assessments for a capability: the quality of its enablement and the completeness of its enablement.

Assessing the quality of a capability focuses on its health or how well it is enabled by people, process, and technology. For example, do the people performing this capability have the right competencies? Is there enough capacity to deliver the capability within the expected timeframe? Is the capability automated to a level that is acceptable to the business? Does the availability of enabling systems meet the expectations of the business? The resulting score, often a rating from 1 to 5, defines the current state health of a capability. A desired future state score may be established as well towards which the organization can work. Scores are often heatmapped, with more positive ratings color-coded as green, average ratings as yellow, and less favorable ratings as red.

From a capability quality perspective, the BIZBOK® Guide offers two metrics, including Business Effectiveness and Automation Level. **Business Effectiveness** reflects an aggregate assessment of the quality of a capability. **Automation Level** reflects the extent to which a capability is automated.

An overall Business Effectiveness score for a capability can be approximated or derived from individual scores for the effectiveness of people, process, technology, and any other dimensions as desired (e.g., experience, information, assets).

Assessing the completeness of a capability's enablement focuses on whether its enabling aspects of people, process, and technology do everything necessary to support what the business needs. This is especially relevant within the context of business change. For example, if a new strategy targets a capability for Customer Preference Management, is the organization able to capture or derive all the necessary types of customer preferences? Do customer-facing roles know how and when to use those preferences? The result of this assessment, if scored, is a rating typically from 1 to 5, that defines the **Progress Towards Target State** for the capability. The rating scale used can be generic or customized to each capability and its target state. Of course, the definition of target state will continue to evolve as the organization does.

Both the quality and extent of enablement for each capability are important to delineate and consider with intention, even if their results are rolled together in one score called **Capability Maturity**.

Where does the information for capability assessments come from?

Capability assessment rating information can be sourced both subjectively and objectively. Effectiveness assessment information is often provided by business subject matter experts, who rate the capabilities based on their knowledge. Multiple business representatives may even have collaborative conversations to rate capabilities together based on their collective understanding or provide scores for their specific capability instances.

Clear rating criteria is of utmost importance to ensure as much objectivity and consistency in the rating as possible. It is also important to capture not just the scores, but the reasoning behind each rating to make them defensible and useful to others who were not involved in the conversation.

Beyond being logical, involving business representatives in the assessment process helps to build partnership and long-term ownership for the information. Business engagement is also essential to explain the ratings (especially any unfavorable ones) to leaders and to guide the next steps for improvement.

On the other hand, some metrics can be assessed more objectively using business architecture focal points. For example, the Business Breadth metric can be assessed by counting the number of value stream stages that a capability enables. Automation Level still requires subjective input, but the conversation can be framed objectively by reflecting the applications that automate a given capability, derived from the business and IT architecture together.

How is a capability assessment performed?

The first and most important step is to determine the purpose and scope of the assessment. A clear purpose guides decisions such as which metrics to collect and the level of capability detail to assess. Then, collect and analyze the assessment information from business representatives and other sources. Create heatmaps or other views as applicable and present them to stakeholders along with supporting insights. Here are a few additional tips for success:

Keep it simple. Keep the capability assessment process as simple as possible to support the business purpose. It can take time to conduct the assessment as well as keep the information up to date, so be intentional about what is captured. For example, if only a directional notion of performance is needed, use fewer metrics, and assess the capabilities only at a level 2.

Go granular when needed. Instead of assessing a capability at the aggregate level, it may also be assessed at the *capability instance* level. An instance could exist for a capability within the context of a given business unit, value stream stage, or other aspect. For example, a capability may be working effectively within one business unit but highly ineffective within another.

Define the assessment methods. Document the assessment methods and apply them consistently, especially if multiple people are performing assessments at different points in time. For example, clearly define each metric along with detailed criteria for each of its values in a way that can be consistently interpreted. Pay special attention to any nuances in weighting or aggregating capability scores. For example, a capability such as Customer Information Management could work effectively from each individual business unit's perspective (i.e., at the capability instance level), but if the information is replicated across each business unit, this may lead to a fragmented view of a customer and suboptimal customer experiences.

How are the results of capability assessments used?

Capabilities assessments may be leveraged as part of translating business direction. Any necessary capability enhancements related to quality and/ or completeness can be addressed through targeted initiatives, and value delivered over time in increments. A capability's importance to the business can further inform prioritization of initiatives.

Standalone capability assessments can be performed with the intent of identifying improvement opportunities or to inform other decisions, such as which capabilities to outsource. Any potential improvements can be achieved by scoping new initiatives or potentially inserting them into planned or in-flight initiatives. If all initiatives are framed by the capabilities they target, this information can be readily determined. Improvements should be prioritized in alignment with business priorities, as defined by the business objectives associated with a capability as well as its strategic importance metric ratings.

Capability assessments help inform investments. At a macro level, investment pools can be created to help prioritize funding. For example, a larger percentage of the investment portfolio may be allocated to Advantage and Strategic Support capabilities with less allocated to Essential and Business Necessity. At a more detailed level, assessments can be performed at the initiative level. For example, scores may be calculated for a large list of proposed initiatives to help filter out those which are clearly not a priority, so that further analysis can be performed on those that require further analysis.

Leveraging Business Architecture for End-to-End Strategy and Transformation

Translating strategic business direction into cohesive execution is an incredibly challenging activity, especially considering the scope of impact and massive details to sort through, accompanied by time pressures. The ability to translate strategy requires quite a unique set of competencies and knowledge. One needs to understand the organization and its external context. One also needs to understand the organization's business architecture and how to traverse it. Both are critical to bridging the large and nebulous gap between the desire to achieve something and the concrete and coordinated steps required to do so. It is a true exercise in making black and white out of gray to create the path to action. Business architects are naturally adept at helping to bridge this gap space.

Business architecture shifts an organization from strategizing and planning with an initiative mindset to a capability and end-to-end value delivery mindset. This alone is a game changer. The orientation around capabilities opens new conversations about collaboration and ownership across organizational silos and initiatives. For example, should the organization have executive ownership to set and govern direction for a capability or set of capabilities? Should we also have executive ownership to ensure end-to-end value delivery? Regardless of how we have drawn the lines up to this point, what should the scope of each product delivery team really be? Regardless of how we would typically scope initiatives, how might we better utilize our precious resources if we organized around capabilities and value streams?

Business architecture also provides new and expanded visibility so people can ask different questions. It provides objective data that transcends silos and politics so people can make the hard decisions that are best for the *enterprise*. For example, if an initiative is not aligned to our strategic priorities, should we continue investing in it? If two strategies conflict, should we pause and reconcile our direction first regardless of the timelines we set for ourselves? How will we handle accountability for an initiative that does not deliver the expected results?

Leveraging business architecture as the translator for strategy does not necessarily make this challenging activity easier. However, it does produce powerful results and naturally instills an important new mindset through the process.

What role do business architects play in strategy formulation?

While business architects can and often do inform strategy formulation, they are not ultimately responsible or accountable for it. When business architects are heavily involved in strategy formulation, this is often a function of their personal competencies, experiences, and preferences versus the intent of the role. However, business architects can provide invaluable support to business leaders and strategists throughout the process of formulating strategy.

Business architects are well-versed in how the organization works as well as its external landscape including the market, competitors, and trends in business models and technology. This makes them **excellent thinking partners** for generating ideas and facilitating innovation. For example, business architects can help leaders identify creative ways to leverage the organization's existing capabilities to deliver new customer value and products.

Business architects can also **support strategic decision-making**. They can help leaders and strategists understand the organization's strengths and ability to support the proposed strategy as well as narrow down and focus strategic options. For example, the business architecture knowledge-base can be used to quickly determine the organization-wide impact of a potential strategy.

Finally, business architects can help to **ensure that the final strategy documentation is articulated** in the clearest way. While they may or may not be engaged to map strategy using formal techniques, they will certainly capture the goals, objectives, metrics, and courses of action in the business architecture knowledgebase and tie them to impacted business architecture focal points. The very act of capturing this information often leads to conversations that uncover gaps, overlaps, or areas for additional clarification or decomposition.

The critical supporting role business architects play during strategy formulation underscores the importance of positioning them in the right place within the organization. The reporting structure and dynamics should allow for their engagement in strategy formulation to occur naturally, informally, and early on.

How are value streams and capabilities used for strategy translation?

Value streams and capabilities are intended to be stable frameworks for an organization. This means that they simply offer a frame, structure, or the *scaffolding* to which other things can attach. *As a result, value streams and capabilities typically do not "change."* More often the changes occur to people, process, and/or technology (the operating model) within the context of a capability and the value stream(s) and stages that it enables.

Value streams or capabilities *can* indeed be changed, for example by modifying a value stream to include an additional stage. New value streams and capabilities can also be created, but this is typically the result of a business model shift, transformational initiative, or other major change of this magnitude.

For example, an established automotive company that has been operating for decades would still have many of the same capabilities as it did the day it opened its doors. From the very beginning, it sold vehicles, manufactured vehicles, transported vehicles, built relationships with customers and partners, managed its finances, managed its employees, and so forth. The difference is in *how* it did those things, which evolved over the years. Just consider the simple example of creating an agreement with a customer buying a new vehicle. This agreement would have originally been created on paper and stored in a filing cabinet, where today there would be a robust IT architecture and systems to automate it. In this example, the capability of Agreement Management did not change, but rather the implementation of it changed. Of course, new capabilities *have* been created by automotive companies as they shift their business models and transform (e.g., to capture information from connected vehicles), but many of the value streams and capabilities do remain the same.

Value streams provide context for capabilities, and capabilities help to align and optimize the components of people, process, and technology to deliver value. This means that the role of value streams and capabilities in strategy translation is to provide context for, frame, and align the changes necessary to achieve a desired state.

How can business architecture help translate strategy into actionable initiatives?

Meet the golden thread. Translating strategy into initiatives may still be challenging, but this approach will guide you toward new ways of conceiving initiatives, facilitating cross-functional coordination, and creating alignment.

The golden thread shown in Figure 3.1 works from left to right to help translate strategies into initiatives and measure the results delivered by those initiatives. While ideal, working from left to right is not always feasible for organizations that are new to these concepts. However, the golden thread works equally well from middle out or right to left, to help ensure alignment within and across strategies, architectures, and initiatives.

Though the golden thread certainly does not represent the only traceability that can or should be captured in the business architecture knowledgebase, it does highlight the simplest end-to-end traceability from strategy to architecture to initiatives which can be used for some of the most common translation and alignment scenarios.

Visit www.StrategyintoReality.com to download diagrams and other valuable resources.

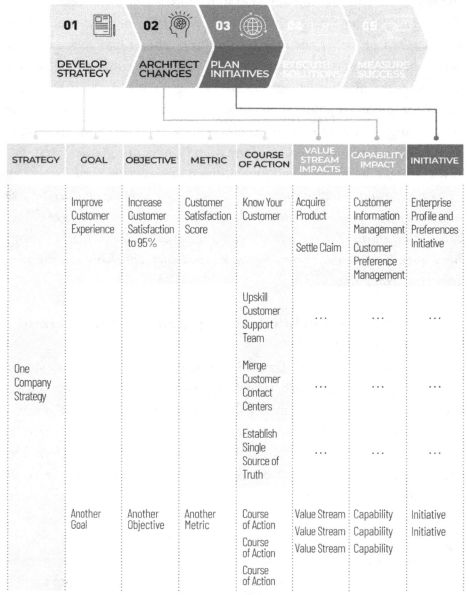

Figure 3.1: The Golden Thread: Translating Strategy into Initiatives

Here's how the process of translating strategy works, underpinned by the information captured across the golden thread. This information should of course be managed in an automated business architecture knowledgebase to enable analysis and reporting.

Step 1: Clarify and Articulate Strategy

Once a strategy has been formulated or is stable enough to start analyzing, the business architect(s) will categorize information into the discrete focal points of **strategies, goals, objectives, metrics,** and **courses of action.** (Shown in the columns for Stage 1 within Figure 3.1.) This activity and the conversations it facilitates can help to clarify the strategy further for all consumers. *Clear intent must be the starting point.*

As shown in Figure 3.1, the One Company Strategy has a goal to Improve Customer Experience, which is supported by an objective to Increase Customer Satisfaction to 95%. The results will be measured using the Customer Satisfaction Score metric. This objective will be carried out by four broad courses of action for Know Your Customer, Upskill Customer Support Team, Merge Customer Contact Centers, and Establish Single Source of Truth. This example represents a small subset of the direction that could be articulated. There could be multiple goals for the strategy, each with multiple objectives and metrics. The objectives may decompose into more detailed objectives. A course of action may apply to multiple objectives.

In this example, the goals are articulated to be aspirational, the objectives are measurable and have a corresponding metric, and the courses of action are broad themes or categories that narrow down how the objective will be achieved. However, organizations can and do model these domains differently. Some organizations may use only goals or objectives. Some may not create standalone SMART (specific, measurable, achievable, realistic, and time-bound) objectives, but rather create them through the combination of objectives and metrics together.

What is most important is that these strategy focal points are clearly defined and consistently used across an organization. This is often an area that requires discussion and standardization as business direction can be documented in vastly different ways across an organization, which only contributes to the challenges of strategic alignment.

There are two ways to approach this standardization. The first and most ideal approach is to organize any directional content into the clearly defined focal points. For example, one business unit may create OKRs (objectives and key results), but according to the standard definition of an organization's focal points, their objectives may get categorized as goals while their key results get categorized as objectives and metrics. The other approach is to allow for some flexibility in how business direction is articulated across the focal points and start bringing it together through the cross-mapping to value stream and capability impacts.

Step 2: Assess Impact

Once the strategy focal points have been captured, the impacted value streams and capabilities can be identified for each objective and course of action. (Shown in the columns for Stage 2 within Figure 3.1.) Value streams are the first lens for assessment because they not only provide the value context, but also help to narrow down the potential set of capabilities that could apply. Ideally the assessment will identify the impacted stages within a value stream and the impacted capabilities *within* those stages. This part of the process can be very iterative if the business direction is still evolving and refining. In addition, the process of identifying value stream and capability impacts can uncover new questions or gaps that may need to be resolved before proceeding further.

There is an important distinction of what *impacted* means in this context. *Since value streams and capabilities typically do not "change," an impact signifies that a capability within the context of one or more value streams will need to be enhanced in some way from a people, process, or technology perspective (or additionally, information, assets, or other dimensions).* The value streams and capabilities just frame and organize where the changes need to occur. For example, in Figure 3.1 for the Increase Customer Satisfaction to 95% objective and Know Your Customer course of action, some changes will be required to the *enablement* of the Customer Information Management and Customer Preference Management capabilities within the context of the Acquire Product and Settle Claim value streams.

When the business direction and impacted value streams and capabilities are final enough, additional impacts may be assessed. At this point, business architects begin working hand-in-hand with IT architects, especially strategic application architects and data architects. The business architecture knowledgebase is instrumental to identify other impacted focal points such as impacted business units, stakeholders, products, policies, processes, system applications, and so forth. The result is an inventory of the pieces that will be involved in the change, framed by formal architecture focal points from the knowledgebase. This inventory can be visualized as an **architecture impact footprint**, valuable for leaders and stakeholders to see the scope of change planned for the business and technology environment. It also provides business and IT architects with the concrete focal points they will need to examine further to define the enhancements to be delivered through initiatives.

Initiatives are only captured at this point if they were already outlined by business leaders or the strategy team. (Shown in the column for Stage 3 within Figure 3.1.) However, even if they were, they should be revisited and potentially reshaped based on the business architecture perspective.

Step 3: Architect the Change and Identify the Gaps

With an understanding of *what* needs to change, business and IT architects can now help to define *how* it needs to change. This collaborative step is a major divergence from how organizations typically proceed, where each business unit, initiative team, or other silo translates the direction into their own set of initiatives. Instead, the architects bring many people together across the organization and across disciplines to help define the changes that will become initiatives.

This step is where new innovative and reusable solutions that would not have otherwise been envisioned can be realized. This is how initiatives become scoped in the most effective and non-overlapping way. This is where leaders step up to collaborate on initiatives, even if it pushes on business unit, product, or portfolio boundaries—because it is the *right* thing to do for the enterprise. This is what accelerates the downstream delivery because the right stakeholders are already identified up front as are the dependencies and integration points.

The defined set of changes are assessed and framed within the context of a capability, within the impacted value stream(s). At a minimum, the people, process, and technology for each capability are interrogated to determine what enhancements (or new aspects) are necessary to support the strategy effectively and completely. Capability assessment results are very helpful input to this analysis, including an understanding of strategic importance to help inform decisions. Other focal points may be used as well. For example, a new product or policy may need to be created.

The result is a **high-level definition of the enhancements for each capability**. For example, a strategy targeting the Customer Preference Management capability both within an Acquire Product and Settle Claim context, may specifically require a change to allow for customers to indicate their language and communication preferences (e.g., contact via phone, e-mail, or SMS). From an information and technology perspective, this would require modifications to all relevant systems to allow for the capture and sharing of these new preferences. From a process perspective, this would require modifications to all relevant processes to reflect the capture, usage, and sharing of customer preferences. From a people perspective, this would require training for customer-facing representatives on how to locate, capture, and use customer preferences per the modified processes and systems.

While the business architects (and IT architects) are helping to drive conversations and pull the pieces together within a value stream and capability context, this aspect of translation requires partnership and collaboration with many other people. This may include business leaders and representatives, strategists, technology leaders, human-centered designers, business process practitioners, organization designers, and many others. The actual work is not done at this point—that happens during execution. Only *just enough* should be done to define a solid overall target state and define the work that needs to be done. However, this collaboration is invaluable to diagnose any problems and define the enhancements needed. For example, a new process may need to be created or an existing one reengineered, but the business process team will complete this work as part of a planned initiative.

For larger scopes of business direction, as typically warranted by a new strategy or transformation, a **target state architecture** (and **current state architecture** for comparison) may be created to represent a collective picture of the future state. These diagrams can be invaluable to help people see what the organization is working towards, especially if it will be delivered via many initiatives. The essence of the future state is often reflected in the operating model details, but it is *framed* by the business architecture with overlays for the IT architecture. For example, the current state architecture for a large simplification initiative may depict many business units and system applications enabling a set of capabilities. The target state architecture may show a streamlined set of business units and shared applications enabling that same set of capabilities.

Step 4: Plan Initiatives

With a clear understanding of the *actions* that need to be taken for each capability, now the work can begin to bundle them into the most logically scoped set of initiatives. Business architects and IT architects may again work with many partners to complete this activity, including planners, product managers, or program managers.

Initiatives are scoped around capabilities in value stream context. For example, if a few capabilities need to be enhanced, which span across the stages in a value stream, initiatives may either be scoped by stage, where enhancements for all capabilities are delivered for each stage, or initiatives may be scoped by capability and enhancements delivered applicable to all stages. Furthermore, initiatives may be anchored back to the capability assessment ratings. For example, an initiative or set of initiatives may help a capability move from a less favorable Business Effectiveness or Progress Towards Target State score to a more favorable one.

Keep in mind that the initiatives being scoped at this point are typically big chunks of work that establish a coordinated path of action. They will be further decomposed into or consumed by programs, projects, products, operational teams, or other delineations.

Each initiative should define the actions to be taken, framed by value streams, capabilities, and other focal points. Not only does this ensure clarity, but if every initiative can be tied back to the capabilities it is enhancing, then capabilities become the Rosetta stone to create connections across strategies, transformations, product teams, and operational efforts that may be targeting the same capabilities. Provided that the information has been captured, the business architecture knowledgebase can highlight any planned or in-flight initiatives that may be targeting the same capabilities and require coordination.

At this point the planned initiative names can be captured in the knowledgebase (as shown in the column for Stage 3 within Figure 3.1) and cross-mapped to the applicable business objectives, value streams, and capabilities. A **strategic roadmap** may also be created to represent a collective view of the initiatives planned for a strategy or transformation along with their sequence and a general notion of timing.

The Results

In summary, because of the approach outlined, the business direction has been harmonized and refined to a greater degree due to the conversations and interactions that occurred during the translation. A target state architecture and strategic roadmap have been created, which helped to drive business and technology leaders to consensus on direction and can now be used to help others in the organization understand where the organization is going and how it will get there. A set of strategy-aligned capability enhancements have shaped the portfolio of work that can now be approved for investment. Delivery teams have clearly defined initiatives and can hit the ground running with the upfront coordination already completed. And the traceability from the strategy to the architecture to the initiatives is in the knowledgebase to be used for ongoing alignment with other strategies and initiatives, and to dynamically replan, if needed. *This is how clear intent is translated into organized effort through business architecture.*

How can strategy be translated if it is not clear or detailed?

Translating strategic direction that is articulated at a high level (read: vague) is a common challenge in many large organizations. There is often a wide gap between the brilliant big ideas and a cohesive plan for what needs to change in the business and technology environment to make them real.

When business direction is high level or unclear, the best approach is to just work through the process of translating strategy. This will drive the conversations that will make ambiguous business direction increasingly clear. Trust the golden thread. What *doesn't* work is asking leaders to explain all the answers and details. It is more effective to take ownership for closing the gap, working in partnership.

To help close the gap, walk through the strategic direction with the leaders and strategy team to gain a better understanding. Next, take a first pass at organizing the information into goals, objectives, metrics, courses of action, and impacted business architecture value streams and capabilities. Make assumptions and fill in gaps. Then, review the interpretation with the leaders and strategy team, identify changes needed, and iterate.

When business architects take ownership for the gap, it minimizes the time required from busy leaders and strategists. In addition, leveraging business architecture for the translation, along with the consultative role of business architects, can uncover new insights that enable leaders to think differently about how to achieve their goals. The process also ensures that business direction is clearly articulated for others who will eventually consume it. Furthermore, these interactions can even illuminate gaps and opportunities to enhance the strategy formulation and communication approach going forward.

Sometimes organizations lack business direction entirely—or some people perceive that this is the case anyway. It is difficult to translate business direction where it does not exist, but business architecture may be used to *reverse engineer* it in a way. For example, an organization's planned and in-flight initiatives may be assessed and played back to describe the "strategy" they are leading the organization towards. Value streams and capabilities help to aggregate and frame the results for leaders who can either stay the course or adjust direction to course correct.

How can business architecture facilitate strategic alignment?

The golden thread in Figure 3.1 is a visual representation of the key domains involved in strategic alignment and how they form an end-to-end traceability. As mentioned, this information can be used in a variety of different ways, including from middle out or right to left, particularly when supported with an automated business architecture knowledgebase.

Leveraging business architecture to assess and ensure strategic alignment is relevant to different audiences at different points across strategy execution. For example, leaders and strategists can assess **alignment across strategies** to ensure that objectives and courses of action are not conflicting. Business and IT architects can assess **alignment of enhancements** being made to the same value streams, capabilities, and other architecture focal points across strategies and transformations. Portfolio leaders can assess **alignment from proposed initiatives back to strategies** as well as **alignment across proposed initiatives**. Initiative stakeholders, including sponsors and product, program, or project managers, can assess **alignment of initiative results** back to the original strategies and objectives. In-flight initiatives can even be assessed for alignment back to the business objectives they are supporting and the value streams and capabilities they are uplifting, and any necessary course corrections made. Additionally, business analysts can assess **alignment of initiative requirements** back to the value streams, capabilities, and business objectives they are enhancing.

Beyond leveraging the knowledgebase for these unique views, the integrative role of business architects can also help to facilitate alignment. Their roles often provide broad visibility across an organization and their competencies are naturally suited for dot connecting.

How can business architecture inform portfolio management and initiative investment decisions?

Business architecture does not just shape individual initiatives but also informs initiative investments within and across portfolios, with an eye to what is best for the enterprise. This is one of the most common and valuable ways to leverage business architecture and is suitable as an initial usage scenario. *Business architecture supplements portfolio investment decision-making with a framework that can be used to analyze potential initiatives against strategic direction and against each other.* Here is an overview of how to capture, represent, and leverage this valuable information to inform investment decisions.

Representing Initiative Strategic Alignment and Planned Spend
Capture Basic Initiative Information. Obtain a list of initiatives within the scope of the analysis, either within one portfolio or across multiple portfolios. Capture basic information for each such as a name, description, owner, and planned spend.

Relate Initiatives to Key Focal Points. Then, for each initiative, indicate the objective(s) that it supports as well as the capabilities it will be enhancing. Additional information may be captured for each initiative such as value stream context for the targeted capabilities or the sponsoring or participating business units. These connections are ideally captured within the business architecture knowledgebase, which allows the content to be reused and more in-depth analyses and visualizations generated.

Consider that an initiative may target the enhancement of *more than one* capability and this should be captured in order to find initiative gaps and overlaps. For example, an initiative focused on making improvements to a claim system would certainly target capabilities related to Claim Management. However, it may also be targeting Customer Management and Payment Management, which other initiatives are likely targeting as well.

Assess Alignment. With the information now collected, each individual initiative can be assessed for (1) alignment back to strategic direction and (2) alignment against each other. Strategic alignment may be assessed both against the business objectives as well as capability assessment results. For example, if a proposed initiative is not supporting one of the organization's objectives and if the capabilities it is targeting are all functioning effectively, the necessity and priority of the initiative may be questioned. Initiative alignment may be assessed by performing a series of checks across initiatives for overlaps, gaps, conflicts, dependencies, and sequence considerations.

Visualize the results through heatmaps. Heatmaps that aggregate information across capabilities can be highly enlightening. For example, an **aggregate view of planned spend by capability** is often eye-opening, showing where the top areas of spend are within and across portfolios. It can illuminate where redundant or conflicting initiatives are planned as well as highlight additional considerations for sequencing and integration.

The planned spend for heatmap analysis is valuable in its own right, but when compared side-by-side with an **aggregate view of strategic enablement by capability** (i.e., representing those capabilities most important to the organization achieving its strategy), the comparison can quickly highlight where there may be misalignment. For example, if a given capability is reflected as a low strategic priority but that same capability is in the top-third of the planned spend, then it may be worth exploring further. The difference may be due to a critical investment for purposes of compliance or business reliability. On the other hand, the difference may reveal a true misalignment in where the organization plans to invest compared to what the strategy truly requires.

Institutionalizing the approach

This concept can be institutionalized, and the data made readily available for future analysis simply by adjusting the requirements for submitting investment requests. For example, the request template could be updated to require supporting objectives and capabilities targeted for enhancement to be listed. Business architects can support investment request submitters in their selection of targeted capabilities until the thought process becomes familiar. Furthermore, embedding business architecture in a process as critical as an organization's investment process helps to give it some teeth and facilitates a mindset shift.

How can business architecture be leveraged for business and digital transformation?

Leveraging business architecture for business transformation, and even specifically digital transformation, is entirely based on the process and techniques related to how business architecture enables strategy execution. A business transformation is just a very large, potentially enterprise-wide, instance of business direction flowing through the strategy execution framework. *Leveraging business architecture and business architects not only leads to more successful transformations but also builds an organization's capacity for continuous change.*

Business architecture **provides the fundamental structure for transformation**, allowing people to readily view what the organization does (without spending time rediscovering it) and then methodically assess and redesign how it will change, no matter if that entails digitalizing existing capabilities and offering them in different channels or completely reinventing an organization's business model.

Business architecture is tremendously useful for **scoping transformations**. It helps organizations decide how to *eat the elephant*, because defining and implementing change across regions, business units, and products for potentially the largest scope encountered to date can be incredibly intimidating. Value streams and capabilities help scope the work in a logical and interlocking way. Different leaders and teams may be responsible for delivering shared capabilities or cohesive value streams. For example, one set of teams may be responsible for delivering ready-to-use capabilities organized around customer information and preferences, customer communications, or money movement. Another set of teams may be responsible to ensure that different value streams such as Acquire Product or Settle Financial Account are streamlined, unified, and integrated across business units and products, and ready to leverage the capabilities.

Business architecture also **helps people to envision the future**. A target architecture and strategic roadmap can be created for each major set of capability or value stream work to help people visualize what the organization wants to achieve, how it will get there, and how it integrates with each other major set of work. These views **provide a mental image and framework for grasping the complexity of change**, which can be consumed by everyone in the organization as well as external partners involved in the transformation.

Business architecture **creates a composable organization**. This concept and the mindset that goes along with it has become increasingly important for continuously delivering innovation, adapting to change, and creating integrated experiences and solutions within and across organizational boundaries.

> *"As business needs change, organizations must be able to deliver innovation quickly and adapt applications dynamically—reassembling capabilities from inside and outside the enterprise. To do this, organizations must understand and implement the "composable enterprise."[7]*
> – Gartner

Of course, an entire business architecture is essentially a componentized view of an organization, comprised of reusable, interconnecting pieces, but capabilities are the Rosetta stone that knit them all together. Capabilities set the stage for composable technology such as reusable software services that can be exchanged within an organization as well as outside of it with partners. In addition, capabilities facilitate a composable thinking mindset in business leaders and people throughout an organization, to inspire new ideas for innovation and agility with interchangeable building blocks.

Finally, a business architecture-scoped transformation **creates the foundation for long-term business ownership**. A business executive or steering committee can be established to set the direction for a set of capabilities or value stream(s) and govern the evolution to them. Target architectures and strategic roadmaps provide ideal structures for business leaders to make decisions and govern because they are high-level and entirely business oriented.

While it requires a solid level of business architecture maturity, leveraging the discipline for transformation can help an organization through one of the most important things it will do. It can also be the tipping point for full business architecture adoption.

How does an organization start practicing this approach to strategy execution?

There is often no quick or easy answer here. It is a journey, and it requires the hard work of formulating and sharing a vision for more effective strategy execution, partnering with other like-minded people, and working the change from within the organization day after day. Business architects often see and care about the bigger picture challenges and opportunities for strategy execution. While they cannot solve it on their own, they can help to catalyze and influence others towards new ways of working. Below are a few practical steps to shift an organization's approach to strategy execution.

Assess the current approach. The first step is to assess the organization's current strategy execution approach and results. For example, are there multiple "instances" of the strategy execution process occurring for different portfolios, business units, products, or other silos? How well are the teams integrated across strategy execution? Does enterprise coordination and decision-making happen when it needs to? Is business architecture leveraged as an enabler?

Present a case for change. If there is opportunity for improvement and a sufficient level of organizational readiness to get started, make the case. Present to your leaders (or peers depending on your role in the organization) or other relevant leaders who would be ideal sponsors for this change. The case will likely be better received by leaders who have cross-organizational responsibilities as well as by those who are heavily invested in the successful execution of business direction. In addition to C-Level executives, this may include leaders such as those responsible for transformation, innovation, strategy, customer experience, portfolio management, or planning. Discuss relevant challenges and opportunities along with quantifiable impacts where possible, a compelling vision for strategy execution, and quantifiable benefits.

Start making progress. The outcomes of presenting the case could vary widely but start where you can start and keep moving forward. For example, if there *is* buy-in to move forward with a cohesive enterprise strategy execution vision, then consider adapting a strategy execution framework such as the one shared in Figure 1.2. Leverage it to communicate the vision and start aligning and streamlining the various instances of strategy execution using it.

On the other hand, if there is buy-in to apply a cohesive strategy execution approach for a limited scope, such as for a specific portfolio or business unit, start there. The key is to still act with an enterprise mindset, otherwise it simply reinforces a siloed approach. Again, start by adapting a common strategy execution framework, create alignment, and find opportunities to apply it within the chosen scope.

Of course, it is possible that there is not any initial buy-in to approach strategy execution differently. However, keeping the vision in mind, share the insights, ask the tough questions, and continue to take steps wherever possible. Even if the steps are small, they will demonstrate value and help to inspire the vision, which will lead to bigger and more deliberate steps in the future.

> *"...a great strategy is valuable only if a company is capable of executing that strategy. And whether or not a company can execute its strategy depends largely on whether it is designed to do so. In other words, it depends on business architecture— the way a company's people, processes, systems, and data interact to deliver goods and services to customers."*[8]
> – Jeanne Ross

Business Architecture in Action: Other Business Usage Scenarios

Business architecture can bring new value to just about any business scenario, whether through the expanded views it offers, the shared language it creates, or the traceability it provides. What follows is a brief overview of how business architecture can provide unique value for a few common usage scenarios to improve the outcomes beyond what would normally be achieved. These do not represent a complete set of scenarios, but rather a starting point for inspiration. On the contrary, the uses of business architecture within and across organizations are only limited by the imagination.

Customer Experience Improvement

When business architecture combines with customer experience design (and the broader umbrella of Human-Centered Design) it creates a powerhouse for marrying the outside-in with the inside-out to help organizations maximize their customer value delivery and results.

Business architecture pinpoints the root causes of customer-related issues. A customer experience issue that is occurring at a certain stage(s) within a customer journey can be traced through to the value stream stages that are enabling that portion of the journey, and then further traced to the potentially problematic capabilities within those value stream stages. From there the people, process, technology, or other focal points can be explored to uncover the root cause. For example, the customer issue may be occurring because a team is understaffed, or an internal policy is misaligned with customer needs.

Business architecture safeguards the customer experience. Business architecture supports a range of customer experience impact analyses. For example, if a significant change is planned to a process or solution, it can be traced to the impacted capabilities, then to the impacted value stream stages, and ultimately to the specific customer journey stages that could be affected. Or, a business architecture-based checkpoint could be inserted in the initiative decision-making process to assess the potential customer experience impact of any proposed initiatives before they are prioritized and approved.

Business architecture helps create consistent, streamlined customer experiences. Capabilities that leverage reusable solutions help create consistent experiences for customers across business units and products. Value streams help streamline the delivery of customer journeys from end-to-end across an organization's entire ecosystem, including its partners. Value streams also help to orchestrate the capabilities, information, stakeholders, products, and technology across the customer journey at the right place and time.

Finance and Cost Management

Business architecture enables objective, holistic, and capability-based cost transparency across an entire organization, including its partners. Business architecture provides a business framework for assessing how costs are allocated to help identify opportunities for strategic alignment and cost efficiency.

Business architecture provides a methodical and repeatable business framework to assess costs across an organization. Business architecture provides the comprehensive skeleton structure to which costs may be assigned. Costs may be aggregated by capabilities for concrete focal points in the business architecture knowledgebase minimally to include business units and system applications. For example, the people costs can be aggregated by business units, including partner outsourcing costs, and technology and other asset costs can be aggregated at the business unit level or distributed accordingly. Costs can be aggregated around other focal points such as products as well.

Cost information can be stored in the knowledgebase, making it reusable, repeatable, and defensible—in contrast to a one-time framework and spreadsheet used for a cost study. The availability of an existing agreed upon business framework also allows costing efforts to hit the ground running.

Business architecture provides a strategic view on costs. Business architecture brings the analysis up to a higher level, related to capabilities or other viewpoints. It also helps to depoliticize the cost allocations and put them into a broader business context for decision-making. Business architecture can help connect cost results to other key information in the organization. For example, how does the spend by capability align with the capabilities necessary to support the organization's strategic objectives? If a capability has a high spend, what is its role in value delivery and its strategic importance? Is the organization spending on the right priorities? How does the organization's spend compare with industry benchmarks for the same capabilities?

Business architecture makes cost assessment results actionable. Once cost reduction goals are set, business architecture can help pinpoint the most logical actions to achieve them by following targeted capabilities through to their enablement. In contrast to the approach of asking different leaders to find a certain amount of cost savings, this methodical approach considers what cost reduction measures will be most effective for the organization overall.

Policy Making and Compliance

Business architecture supports internal and external policy making and embeds compliance and ethical thinking into the structure of an organization.

Business architecture helps identify where policies are needed. Consulting the business architecture knowledgebase is a methodical way to identify where policies are needed and ensure there are no gaps. For example, an organization's capabilities can serve as a focal point for identifying policies such as information privacy or anti-spam policies for the Customer Information Management and Partner Information Management capabilities, or identifying policies related to the security of credit and debit card transactions for the Financial Transaction Management capability.

Business architecture supports policy development. Business architecture can be used to assess the impact of a proposed or finalized policy, quickly and comprehensively. This can be especially useful to assess the impact of a new law or regulation proposed by a governmental body to provide feedback that will inform the final direction. Business architecture can also be used to assess the impact of a newly published regulation with which an organization needs to comply or to assess the impact of an internal policy or rule before it is created.

Business architecture helps translate and document policies. Policies can be cataloged at a high level in plain language in the business architecture knowledgebase and then connected to any other aspect of the business and technology environment. This makes the bigger picture information accessible to everyone, and within a shared, relevant business context. In addition, as policies are translated, policy impact assessments may be performed as well as risk assessments.

Business architecture helps to implement and communicate policies. As policies are implemented, business architecture can track the interrelationships among policies. For example, within the business architecture knowledgebase, a regulation can be related to the internal policies that implement it. Related policies across business units and regions can be connected to ensure consistency in implementation and stakeholder communication as well as coordination on any changes later. Furthermore, business architecture excels in translating policy-related changes into action in a coordinated way across an entire organization.

Business architecture helps to facilitate and demonstrate compliance. Business architecture may be used to demonstrate end-to-end traceability from policies to capabilities, business units, and value streams—with the ability to drill down to the relevant processes and systems that implement them. This is invaluable for internal and external audits and to demonstrate compliance with policies. Not only is the information available for the entire enterprise-wide scope, but it has business context and exists at a high level so that the big picture can be assessed first and details like processes or system applications can be targeted when needed.

Business architecture ensures that policy consideration and compliance is always brought to the forefront in the right conversations—and without someone from the compliance team having to be involved to personally remind everyone. For example, a capability targeted for enhancement may be quickly checked to identify what policies need to be considered prior to starting an initiative.

Crisis Management and Preparedness
Business architecture helps organizations prepare for and respond to the unexpected. The unexpected may include incidents caused *by* an orga-

nization, such as a data breach or the release of a defective product. It may also include incidents that happen *to* an organization, such as a natural disaster, pandemic, political situation, or other man-made disaster.

Having a business architecture in place is one of the best ways to be prepared to respond to an incident so that people do not need to spend time inventorying and agreeing upon what they do during a time of crisis. This includes the identification of critical business capabilities for which continuity is necessary, such as those that are customer-facing or necessary for operations. However, during the crucial time of responding to an incident, business architecture enables an organization to make more informed decisions, more holistic decisions, and quicker decisions.

Business architecture helps assess the impact of an incident. Business architecture helps to clarify and isolate the scope of the incident. It also helps to quickly identify who is impacted (e.g., stakeholders, business units, and partners), where (locations), and for what (value streams, capabilities, information, and products).

Business architecture helps prioritize essential versus non-essential activities to help control, contain, and resolve an incident. The critical business capabilities, as determined prior to the incident, can now help to guide the priority and sequence of actions. In addition, the knowledgebase can be used to perform *what if* impact analysis for different response scenarios.

Business architecture helps maximize capacity to deliver essential activities. Business architecture can be used to guide decisions on how to reallocate or reprioritize people or technology resources. For example, people working on non-critical business capabilities may be freed up to focus where the effort is truly needed.

In addition, business architecture can highlight options to increase capacity. For example, it may illuminate a partner who can take on extra workload for a certain capability. Or, it can even be used to identify ways to repurpose the organization's products, capabilities, and value streams in new creative ways during a time of need. For incidents with longer lasting impact, business architecture can also help identify strategies and initiatives that can be put on hold.

Business architecture supports stakeholder communication. Business architecture can be used to quickly identify the people impacted by an incident and the right response team members. Business architecture also helps to identify any stakeholders who need communication, both internal and external to the organization.

Application Portfolio Management

Business architecture supports rationalization, analysis, and decision-making for the system application portfolio from a business perspective.

Business architecture frames technology decisions with a business lens. Business architecture elevates the conversation from focusing on specific system applications to focusing on business capabilities, which may be automated by *many* applications. This puts the application landscape into a business context, which inevitably leads to different decisions. For example, measurements of the level of automation, application redundancy, application risk, or technical debt can be aggregated and assessed at the capability level. When combined with the business priority and strategic importance of those capabilities, it leads to prioritization and decision-making that is best for the business overall. Business decisions can be made with eyes wide open, including areas where risk is acceptable, or technical debt is tolerable because it provides efficiency gains or competitive advantage.

Business architecture builds business and IT partnership. Having technology conversations in a simple, shared business language and context can improve partnership between business and IT. It allows people to communicate regardless of their business or technology backgrounds. This not only results in better decision-making, but also better understanding, engagement, and ownership by the business for issues such as technical debt and modernization. It also facilitates important conversations about building a scalable, adaptable, and future-ready technology foundation to support the business as it evolves.

Business architecture drives technology investments from a business perspective. Through its connection with the IT architecture, business architecture helps to guide the modernization or technical debt remediation approach. Business-driven roadmaps can be created to implement the planned courses of action, in harmony with other initiatives targeting the same capabilities and impacted stakeholders. Business architecture can also be leveraged to prevent future application redundancy or technical debt by inserting a business architecture-based checkpoint or metric within business and initiative decision-making processes.

Cloud Strategy and Migration Decision-Making

Business architecture provides critical business context to inform decision-making for cloud strategy and migration.

Business architecture articulates business direction. An understanding of how an organization is planning to compete, transform, and improve is essential input to cloud decision-making. Business architecture reflects an organization's business model and strategy along with any planned internal structural changes to departments or external ones related to mergers, acquisitions, divestitures, and joint ventures. Business architecture also reflects how this direction will impact various aspects of the business and technology environment as well, including value streams, capabilities, business units, and system applications.

Business architecture informs cloud strategy and migration decision-making. Business architecture provides the business context and priority for defining what an organization should put in the cloud and when.

Together the business architecture and IT architecture can guide decisions on a whole array of questions. For example, which capabilities (i.e., their enablement) should be moved to the cloud? Which outsourced cloud services could be leveraged, especially factoring in the strategic importance of certain capabilities? How ready are candidate capabilities to move to the cloud depending upon their level of redundancy, interconnectedness, and effectiveness? In which order should capabilities be moved to the cloud? What business information is critical and is the business comfortable keeping it in the cloud? What is the impact to the business and technology environment for each potential cloud strategy we are considering? What is the impact to the business and technology environment if we move certain capabilities to the cloud?

Business architecture facilitates readiness for cloud migration. Business architecture can help to prepare data so that it is rationalized and consistent across silos. It can help to drive IT architecture transformation from a business perspective, for example by providing a business framework for reusable software services, so the organization can take full advantage of cloud benefits. Business architecture can also drive and frame cloud migration roadmaps and plans from a business perspective and harmonize them with other work across the organization.

Mergers, Acquisitions, Divestitures, and Joint Ventures

Business architecture is invaluable for assessing and implementing structural changes, including mergers, acquisitions, divestitures, and joint ventures. This is an example of how business architecture can be leveraged across organizational boundaries. Business architecture is also useful for internal structural changes, including the creation, splitting, or merging of internal departments. The blueprints of business architecture provide expanded decision-making support, and business architects are vital thinking partners to bring to the table.

Business architecture supports pre-deal due diligence and decision-making. Business architecture provides a framework to assess the fit, synergies, and alignment between organizations. For example, for a potential merger or acquisition, a side-by-side comparison of two organizations' business architectures can reveal alignment related to strategic direction, business models, customers, products, and value delivery, capabilities, business information and vocabulary, and operating models. Business architecture can also help to assess the potential impact of a merger, acquisition, divestiture, or joint venture on an organization's business and technology environment. It can also highlight stakeholder impacts and identify those who need to be involved.

Business architecture creates a shared view of the future. Business architecture helps people envision a common view of the organization in the future because of a potential or planned structural change. For example, an acquisition or joint venture might lead to a new or expanded value stream. Or, a planned divestiture might mean that a set of capabilities are no longer performed by an organization. From an internal perspective, an organization map could reflect the merging of two departments into one and the combined set of capabilities that will result.

In the case of a joint venture, not only will the business architectures for both organizations reflect changes, but a shared business architecture for the venture may be created as well. For example, a combined business model or a shared end-to-end value stream resulting from the collaboration of both organizations may be created to help people picture the new vision they are working towards.

Business architecture creates readiness for structural changes. For example, in the case of a planned divestiture, the capabilities to be divested may be highlighted and communicated. This can inform decisions and actions to ensure that the enablement of those capabilities can be cleanly and quickly separated from the rest of the organization. For instance, a business architecture-based checkpoint or metric could be inserted within the organization's investment process to ensure that technology investments are made in a way that capability enablement is standalone versus intertwined with shared system applications and infrastructure.

Business architecture facilitates post-deal integration. Business architecture is an essential part of post-deal integration through its role in translating business direction into actionable initiatives that provide the most efficient path forward. This includes harmonizing the actions taken for a merger, acquisition, or joint venture within existing initiatives or helping to reprioritize them. Business architecture is even more critical for an organization performing many acquisitions so the process can be streamlined and made consistent.

Architecting Business Ecosystems

Business ecosystem design takes cross-organization architecting to another level. The concept of a business ecosystem is multiple organizations working together towards a shared purpose, to create greater value for customers, society, and themselves beyond what they can do individually. An ecosystem may be comprised of many organizations, of all sizes large and small, and of all types including for-profit, non-profit, and governmental organizations.

The global movement towards business ecosystems provides unparalleled opportunities to solve some of the greatest challenges of our time while also fostering business growth and prosperity. It represents an important shift in how we think about the role of a firm and how value is defined by society. Business architecture is an essential guide to help organizations move into this new paradigm well-informed, with a strong foundation upon which to scale, and with a smooth and accelerated journey to success.

Business architecture helps to drive a new ecosystem mindset. Business architecture inherently pushes a new mindset because it encourages big picture thinking, working across silos, and applying a value lens to decisions and design. The structure of business architecture also lends itself well to working across organizational boundaries. After all, an organization's business architecture (1) represents the scope of its entire business ecosystem, (2) creates rationalized, high-level views of information concepts and capabilities, (3) is focused on end-to-end value delivery which transcends any one organization, and (4) includes external perspectives such as customer, partners, regulators.

There is a spectrum of business ecosystem scenarios that result as organizations progress from an internal orientation to a broader ecosystem orientation focused on value delivery in partnership with other organizations. Three examples are explored here. Any type of cross-organization architecting will be greatly accelerated if all business architectures adhere to the same set of principles and leverage a common, integrated set of reference models. This creates a shared mindset and vocabulary as well as a common set of business components that can be leveraged *across* organizations.

Business architecture facilitates cross-entity coordination within an organization's scope. This scenario includes situations such as a government that wants to define and deliver reusable government services across agencies, leading to a more integrated citizen experience as well as operational efficiencies. It also includes scenarios such as a company that wants to facilitate opportunities for sharing innovations and resources across its operating companies, brands, or other entities. Having a shared business architecture in place across entities is essential to provide a common framework for identifying these types of opportunities and pinpointing areas for coordination. It creates a common language and framework to streamline communication across entities and identify areas of commonality that may become opportunities for sharing resources and knowledge, as well as a shared IT architecture and solutions.

Business architecture facilitates collaborative cross-organizational ventures. This scenario involves two or more organizations that intend to deliver an expanded value proposition together. For example, a realty company, a financial institution, and a retail store may come together in partnership to define a collective Acquire Home value stream. Each organization contributes capabilities so that a customer can seamlessly move from selecting a home, to obtaining a loan for the home, to furnishing the home. By delivering greater value to the customer, each organization benefits such as by gaining new customers and revenue sources. This scenario also includes cross-sector collaborations such as government agencies, non-profit organizations, and for-profit organizations that partner to address a key area of need like education or health for an emerging nation or targeted population.

Business architecture creates a common language to facilitate communication across organizations and can be used to create a collective view of the venture including business direction, a shared business model, the end-to-end value stream(s) and enabling capabilities. It also helps to highlight key integration points and areas for data sharing, agreements, or policies between organizations.

Business architecture facilitates ecosystem architecting and collaboration. This scenario includes situations such as open banking and others where organizations in disrupted industries need to shift their strategies away from being a full-service provider to a more focused role delivering products and services, managing customer relationships and distribution, or providing shared services to others. It also includes ecosystems with many players that form around integrated solutions such as smart homes, smart cities, or the connected vehicle.

In addition to creating a shared language, business architecture defines the collective purpose, goals, and business model(s) of the ecosystem. It can also be used to design the overall ecosystem as well, including its value exchanges between organizations, value streams, capabilities, information, products offered, and applicable policies. Business architecture also helps to highlight key integration points and areas for data sharing, agreements, or policies. It also drives the IT architecture for the platform or solutions that will support the ecosystem.

4

Integrating with Other Teams and Disciplines

An organization is far more than the sum of its parts. Every individual, role, and team play a unique part in collectively helping an organization deliver on its promise to the customer, support its operations, execute strategy, and transform when necessary. Together, different functions and teams create an organization that is a living organism, fluid and ever evolving to deliver on its purpose and improve and reimagine itself. To do this well though, teams need to be integrated and aligned.

While business architecture and business architects may have a distinct part to play of their own, the blueprints and role are also invaluable to help align other teams. Business architecture connects people to the purpose and strategy of an organization and helps them see how they contribute to the bigger picture. Business architecture also provides the scaffolding to connect teams together. It offers end-to-end traceability through the business architecture knowledgebase and the dot connecting activities that business architects contribute as a part of their role.

By helping other teams to be even *more* successful, business architecture can help to enrich an entire organization. Whether helping to run the operations smoothly or implement change, business architecture is a powerful tool to help teams make better decisions, design the organization holistically, and of course successfully translate strategy into reality.

Business Architecture Is a Bridge Between the Business and Operating Model

Business architecture plays the role of an important middleman. It's not just a bridge between strategy and execution, but also a bridge between an organization's business model and its operating model. While an organization's operating model should be in alignment with its business model, that alignment should happen *through* the business architecture. This is not always evident because both business models and operating models have been in widespread usage well before business architecture started gaining traction.

For instance, if an organization shifts its business model, those changes should be translated through the business architecture, targeting the value streams and capabilities that need to be enhanced or created, along with any of the other business architecture domains. If that organization is now offering a new value proposition as part of its business model, in the business architecture this could require a new value stream, new capabilities or changes to existing ones, a new product, new partners (represented as external business units), and adherence to new policies. These macro level changes, framed by the business architecture, ripple through to target concrete focal points in the operating model that need to change including the people, processes, or technology.

Business architecture helps inform business model design with a holistic understanding of the business ecosystem—including how that ecosystem could be impacted by any potential changes. Business architecture helps inform operating model design with a holistic understanding of how value is created, for whom, and how it is planned to progress over time. Business architects are valuable thinking partners, interpreters, and guides for the design and evolution of an organization's business model and operating model.

How does business architecture align with business models?

"A business model describes the rationale by which an organization creates, delivers and captures value."[9] The *business model canvas* has become the de facto standard for representing an organization's business model on one page with nine standard building blocks. An organization's value proposition is shown in the middle of the canvas. The right side of the canvas focuses on value and includes building blocks for customer segments, customer relationships, customer channels, and revenue streams. The left side of the canvas focuses on enablement and includes building blocks for partners, key activities, key resources, and cost structures. The concept of a business model applies equally to for-profit, non-profit, and governmental organizations, though some terminology can be adapted.

Business models create a shared understanding and mental model about what an organization does and why, and the customers it serves. It provides a framework for reimagining an organization's value proposition and how it is delivered. It facilitates innovation and new ideas for product design and revenue streams. It provides a comparison point for competitive analysis and uncovers opportunities for business model improvement, such as where there are conflicts or weaknesses. A business model can be used to design and communicate a new legal entity or cross-organizational venture.

The business model is not a defined domain of business architecture (and is more of an artifact), but there is a critical relationship between the two. An organization's business model drives what its business architecture needs to be as well as any changes needed to the architecture over time.

Cross-mapping relationships are not typically made in the business architecture knowledgebase between an organization's business model canvas and its business architecture content, though there should be *conceptual* alignment. For example, in concept, the value propositions delivered by an organization's value streams should collectively enable the organization's value proposition as defined within the business model canvas. Or, the organization's stakeholders as defined within the business architecture should collectively encompass the customer segments and partners defined within the business model canvas, and so forth.

At what level should a business model be created for an organization?

Looking through a business architecture lens, there should be one business model (and thus one business model canvas) for an organization—unless of course an organization truly has different, unique business models, which is indeed applicable in many cases. An organization with one business model may, however, have multiple different value proposition canvases for different customer segments.

There can be a desire to create separate business model canvases for individual business units, products, regions, teams, or even initiatives. Many people appreciate the simple, visual nature of the canvas and they want to have a view where they can "see themselves," and understandably so. However, organizations already have plenty of siloed views and creating business models along the same lines will only serve to reinforce those silos—and perpetuate the blurred and competing definitions of customers, products, and value. Remember that the opportunity with business architecture is to *unite* an organization, to *transcend* business units and products, and to look at the organization and the ecosystem in which it operates *holistically*.

Stay true to the business architecture intention and mindset and create the business model at the overall organization level. If separate business models for business units, product areas, or other delineations are desired or needed, create the overall business models(s) *first* and then decompose it into separate views, like layers of an onion. The business model decompositions should align with and inherit from the top-level business model. Stay true to the enterprise vocabulary, reserving terms such as customers and partners for external concepts (e.g., use a name such as *business leaders* versus referring to them as *internal customers*).

For any other special representations such as a high-level, visual summary of an initiative-on-a-page, create a custom canvas. This will allow the business model canvas format to be distinguished for the enterprise context only.

How are business architects involved with business model creation and evolution?

The business model is equal parts business direction and business structure—it is a perfect Venn diagram. A business model is entirely strategic and directional, yet it also represents an organization's structure.

This means that an organization's business model is ideally created, evolved, innovated, and communicated through partnership between business leaders, strategists, and business architects. For a variety of reasons, business architects often take the role of **stewarding an organization's business model documentation**. However, *everyone* should be able to understand an organization's business model and use it.

Once a business model is created, business architects can be valuable thinking partners and trusted advisors to help **assess and reimagine business models**. They can facilitate objective analysis using techniques such as business model canvas-based SWOT analysis and business model type, pattern, and archetype analysis. These techniques can uncover business model opportunities, conflicts, or unfavorable tradeoffs being made.

Business architects can help **facilitate efforts to evolve and innovate business models**, not just from a creative perspective but also from a structured thinking perspective, using different focal points of the business model and business architecture. For example, an existing set of business capabilities can be assessed to identify how they may be reconfigured to deliver new value propositions and products to the customer. These techniques can identify opportunities to expand, evolve, or transform a business model for greater value.

Business architects are also invaluable to **help communicate business model changes**. They translate business model changes into specific business context and tangible actions through the business architecture, making it easier for individuals to understand where they fit in, what impacts to expect, and what they are responsible for.

How does business architecture align with operating models?

There is not a consistent definition of operating models or the elements they contain, but they frequently include people, processes, technology, assets, and locations. The focus on people, process, and technology specifically is common across organizations. *However, an operating model is more than a sum of its parts—it is about how the elements successfully combine to deliver an organization's purpose and value.*

The MIT CISR matrix[10] is a common operating model structure which focuses on an organization's degree of business process integration versus degree of business process standardization. Another common structure is the Operating Model Canvas[11] which positions itself as covering the left side of the business model canvas, specifically the building blocks of key activities, key resources, and key partners. Other operating model structures that are frequently referenced include those from Deloitte, Bain, and Strategy &.

An organization's operating model is not the same as an organization's business architecture. The clearest and most effective way to delineate them is by recognizing their different domains, levels of abstraction, and overall intentions, as have been described previously. *This also means that a target architecture, used for defining the future state of a large and complex change, is different than a target operating model.* The two artifacts are often confused though both may be relevant and used for strategy translation and transformation.

An organization's operating model should be framed by the scope of its business architecture and any changes to the operating model resulting from organizational strategies or business model changes should be translated through the business architecture.

If the leaders within an organization ask for an operating model to be created, first define the intended goals and outcomes. In many cases, the goals may be achieved not by creating an operating model view, but rather by capturing content for the relevant set of operating model focal points (e.g., roles, processes, or system applications) in the knowledgebase and cross-mapping them to capabilities and value streams. Since business architecture is a relatively newer concept, leaders may be requesting the operating model artifact simply because they are unaware of the views and insights that can be produced with the business architecture knowledgebase. When operating model views are created, the documentation should reflect the exact names of any concrete focal points contained in the knowledgebase where applicable.

Partners In Change: Business Architecture and Other Disciplines

Every discipline has its own unique purpose, methods, roles, domains, and artifacts. The interaction of business architecture with related discipline teams is multi-faceted because most teams play different roles at different times to help run or change an organization. For example, business architecture and business process roles may work together to help diagnose the broader root causes of an operational issue or to reengineer processes with an end-to-end enterprise lens. Or, within a strategy execution context, those same roles may work together to identify new processes necessary to realize the defined business direction.

Generally speaking, though, there are similarities in how business architecture interacts with certain teams that share a common context or purpose. For example, strategy and innovation are directional and upstream from business architecture. Organization design, business process management, and the IT architecture form key people, process, and technology integration points for business architecture from an operating model perspective, whether in an operational or strategy execution context. Customer experience design and business architecture are the starting point for the outside-in and inside-out views of an organization and are also relevant in both an operational and strategy execution context. Program and project management, business analysis, and organizational change management are typically most relevant within an initiative planning and execution context to introduce change to an organization.

What follows is a summary of how business architecture relates to a subset of important teams and disciplines. This includes key domain relationships to be defined and unique benefits that can be achieved by leveraging business architecture blueprints and engaging business architects with the corresponding roles.

How do we create cohesive alignment between business architecture and other teams?

To integrate business architecture with other teams, focus on the three areas of alignment: the domains, the roles and interactions, and the overall practices. This is achieved through intentional collaboration and relationship-building over time.

An *engagement model* represents how business architects work together with other roles and where business architecture is consumed. Most important though is to put this information within a relevant context for an organization. An end-to-end strategy execution context, such as the one shown in Figure 4.1, is relevant for all organizations at the highest level and is a good starting point. The interaction of business architecture and business architects may be overlaid onto other macro level processes or frameworks relevant to an organization as well. For example, this could include an organization's processes for innovation, investment decision-making, initiative delivery, procurement, mergers and acquisitions, and many others.

Figure 4.1 shows an overlay of business architecture and other teams across strategy execution, including their level of involvement in each stage.

Views such as these drive conversations and understanding between teams to a deeper level. For example, this strategy execution perspective may reveal that multiple teams believe they are defining business direction, but they are actually defining it at different levels of detail and in different stages. Where a business leader may be defining the overall strategies for the organization in Stage 1, a product manager may be defining product strategy at a lower level in Stage 3.

Visit www.StrategyintoReality.com to download diagrams and other valuable resources.

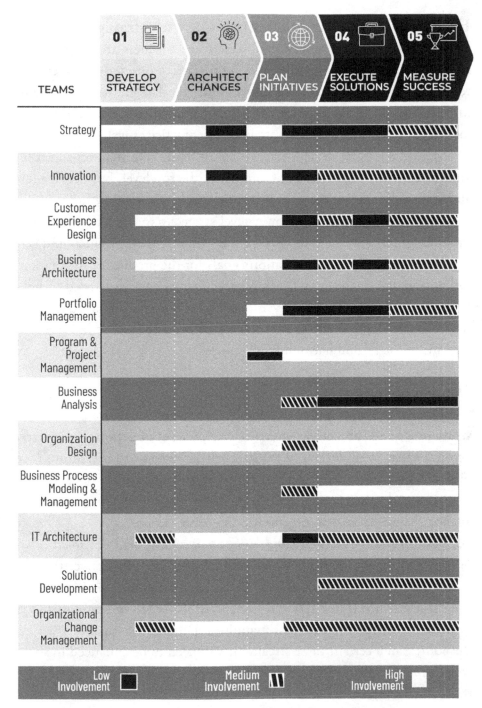

Figure 4.1: Team Involvement Across Strategy Execution

How does business architecture align with strategy?

The alignment and collaboration between business architecture and strategy is arguably one of the most important. Considering the critical role of business architecture to inform and translate strategy, this alignment is not only important for the benefit of an organization but for the long-term success of a business architecture practice as well.

Strategies may be developed at different levels within an organization and for different purposes. For example, at the top level, business leaders and strategists may define an overarching corporate strategy for an organization, which cascades into lower-level strategies for each business unit. Product leaders may develop strategies to innovate their products and services and deliver on an organization's goals for the product in the market. Other business leaders may develop specialty strategies as needed to help transform the organization in various ways, such as a digital strategy or workplace strategy. Business architecture can and should be leveraged to inform, translate, and harmonize all strategies.

Domain Alignment

Some of the most important domains in the realm of strategy include **strategies**, **goals**, **objectives**, **metrics**, and **courses of action**, particularly because these are all leveraged for strategy definition and execution. (See Figure 3.1 for traceability and context.) Other domains may be used such as **vision** and **mission**, which do not change frequently, but can help to anchor change back to an organization's greater purpose.

Business strategies leverage and build upon existing organizational capabilities. Consequently, from a business architecture perspective, the key relationships to make include the cross-mapping from an **objective to the value streams it impacts** and from an **objective to the capabilities it impacts**. Specifically, these cross-mappings signify that a capability within the context of a certain value stream(s), will need to be enhanced in some way from a people, process, or technology perspective in order to achieve the business objective.

Other beneficial relationships may be created as well. For example, a **course of action may be cross-mapped to the value streams and capabilities it impacts** to facilitate strategy translation and alignment. **Metrics may be cross-mapped to value streams and capabilities**. This relationship can be used to help to define success and measure progress during strategy execution in addition to measuring ongoing business performance and focusing improvement activities. **Objectives may be cross-mapped to initiatives** to provide valuable insights for strategic alignment.

These cross-mappings are typically made just enough, just in time, with the scope and level of detail driven by the immediate business needs. The cross-mappings may be created on an ongoing basis throughout the process of strategy translation. Or, a subset of domains, relationships, and content may be captured to support targeted alignment efforts. For instance, if the goal is to rationalize strategies, then content may be captured for the strategy domains along with value streams and capabilities. If the goal is to assess initiative alignment back to strategies, then the focus of content captured may be objectives, value streams, capabilities, and initiatives.

Role Interactions

Business architects and strategists (or business leaders and business experts) work together to create the relevant cross-mappings in the business architecture knowledgebase. Business architects often take the lead on documentation and review and iterate the results with strategists and business partners.

The roles of strategists and business architects are interlocking where strategists formulate strategy and business architects inform and translate strategy. However, introducing business architecture into the strategy process can create challenges in some organizations. For example, in the absence of business architects, strategists, leaders, or other roles may have taken on the responsibility for defining a set of high-level initiatives necessary to achieve the strategy. In cases such as these, the business architect role can at first seem like an unnecessary middleman. However, the change can be managed through relationship building and articulating the bigger picture vision of how business architecture will help the organization. In actuality, business architecture can help make the lives of strategists and leaders *easier* by providing new insights and allowing them to focus their time and talent on formulating strategy.

To start moving the strategy and business architecture collaboration into action, consider translating one strategy or select one alignment effort to assess together. Also consider identifying where strategy-related pain points or opportunities exist that business architecture could help with, such as communicating strategy, aligning leaders to a common direction, assessing strategic options, or addressing and preventing misaligned initiatives. These key pain points or opportunities can help to inform the priority for the initial collaborations as well.

Business Architecture Benefits

One of the most unique and compelling benefits of business architecture for strategy is that strategy content can be documented comprehensively in a reusable, shared knowledgebase. Strategy documentation often exists in fragmented presentations, documents, and tools across an organization, so business architecture not only helps to centralize this content, but also connects it with other architecture focal points such as capabilities and initiatives. This greatly expands the options for strategic options assessment, strategy translation, and strategic alignment.

Business architecture consistently decomposes and deconstructs strategy into its requisite components. Business architecture provides a repeatable and methodical approach to documenting strategy using a set of clearly defined components. This means that strategies can be more readily and consistently interpreted across an organization. It also creates apples to apples comparisons between strategies, goals, objectives, metrics, and courses of action for purposes of alignment and cohesiveness.

Business architecture ensures strategy is clearly articulated and communicated. The simple process of documenting strategy in a methodical way, along with the iterative refinement that occurs between strategists and business architects, helps ensure the clarity and measurability of business direction and outcomes. A well-defined and detailed strategy is the first step towards mitigating the diffusion that can occur as a strategy is consumed and interpreted throughout the layers of an organization.

Business architecture allows strategy to be collectively viewed through a customer and business value lens. By first defining the impacts to value streams and capabilities, the footprint of a strategy can be clearly understood and visualized holistically from a customer and business perspective. The comprehensive set of changes to the business and technology environment can then be addressed comprehensively, with more freedom for innovative thinking, and orchestrated in a coordinated way. Future state architecture views also help to build a common understanding of direction. This helps further mitigate strategy diffusion and allows every employee and partner to see where they fit in and contribute.

Business architecture makes strategy real through a prioritized and rationalized set of initiatives. With business architecture as the translator of strategy, resources can be allocated in the most effective way to initiatives that are intentionally scoped and sequenced, leveraging reusable solutions, with dependencies, coordination points, and stakeholders known up front. Business architecture also informs objective decision-making so that only initiatives aligned with strategic direction are prioritized and funded.

How does business architecture align with innovation?

On the surface it may seem that business architecture and its structure could constrain or slow down innovation. On the contrary, when leveraged correctly, business architecture makes innovation within an organization *more* expansive, impactful, and effective. Business architecture plays a role throughout the entire innovation life cycle to help generate, validate, disseminate, scale, and implement innovation ideas.

Domain Alignment

At the time of publication for this book, there is not currently an industry standard domain defined within the realm of innovation, though one could be created to capture **innovation ideas**. Relationships could be made to any business architecture domains, though the cross-mapping from **innovation idea to capability** would be one of the most useful since capabilities are the hub that connects to everything else. In fact, innovation ideas could even be tagged with the capabilities they enable to catalog them for future use within different business contexts and scenarios.

Other useful relationships may be created as well depending upon the business need. For example, **innovation ideas could be cross-mapped to the value stream stages or products** to which they directly contribute value. **Innovation ideas could also be cross-mapped to the objectives they help to enable**, or the **initiatives that are helping to realize them** at any stage from prototype to implementation.

Role Interactions

An ideal starting point for alignment is to identify where and how business architecture can be leveraged across the innovation life cycle. Then, innovation and business architecture team members can work together to identify the best ways to start using business architecture to support innovation activities. This may be based on where there are key opportunities or pain points or sponsor support.

Business Architecture Benefits

The framework of business architecture weaves innovation into the fabric of an organization. Business architecture not only provides direct benefits for generating, scaling, and leveraging ideas, but can even help to embed innovative thinking into an organization's ways of working. The additional visibility and credence can be especially useful for organizations that are trying to build a culture of continuous innovation.

Business architecture facilitates the generation of innovation ideas. Business architecture provides a high-level structure that can be used to methodically uncover new creative ideas. To illustrate, an organization's business model canvas can be used to reimagine how an organization delivers value. Or, capabilities, like Lego blocks, can be put together in different ways to generate new and unique value. In addition, business architects are excellent thinking partners and facilitators to help others innovate by using a componentized view of the business.

Business architecture facilitates the sharing and usage of innovation ideas. Countless ideas are generated through challenges and continuous innovation efforts, but unless they can be cataloged within a relevant context, it is difficult to locate and use them. Capabilities provide an ideal framework for organizing innovation ideas so they can be leveraged on an ongoing basis. For example, if a capability needs to be enhanced, the current set of innovation ideas could be consulted before generating new solution ideas. This concept can be extended to help match an organization's innovation needs to external partners as well. Suppose that, for example, an organization is looking to innovate around certain capabilities, they can seek out startups or other partners that are suited to fulfill them.

Business architecture assesses the viability and business impact of innovation ideas. The business architecture knowledgebase provides an efficient and comprehensive tool for assessing innovation ideas to quickly narrow the focus to only those ideas that are worthy of further investment. The knowledgebase can be consulted at different points, such as to assess the initial viability and impact of an idea and later to inform a final impact analysis and cost benefit analysis.

Business architecture uncovers additional usage scenarios for innovation ideas. Business architecture illuminates opportunities for leveraging innovation ideas beyond their original context, such as for other value streams, business units, products, or business scenarios. The expanded usage can even help to increase the support and funding for an innovation idea.

Business architecture informs priorities, timing, and relevant usage scenarios for innovation ideas. As ideas move into the experimentation stage, business architecture can help to identify focus areas where innovation is needed, either resulting from business priorities or known areas of improvement. It can even help to provide specificity and clarity on the problem to be solved or opportunity to be pursued. Business architecture can also help to objectively inform on how innovation ideas fit with the bigger picture of business priorities.

Business architecture facilitates the implementation of innovation ideas. Once an innovation idea is ready for commercialization and implementation, then it meets the sweet spot for business architecture to translate it into a coordinated, actionable set of initiatives to make it real at scale.

How does business architecture align with customer experience design?

Customer experience design is a holistic and strategic discipline that designs the experience of a customer across all touchpoints of an organization's brand. It may be considered part of the broader umbrella of Human-Centered Design, which encompasses not only experience design but other disciplines and practices such as service design, design thinking, and user experience design. Additionally, *business design* or *enterprise design* frameworks unite the design and architecture disciplines to create coherency of the human and organizational perspectives. Though the primary emphasis here is on customers, it is important to note that experience design can and should be leveraged to design partner and employee experiences as well.

Business architecture and customer experience design have a natural affinity. Business architecture already provides an outside-in perspective

Integrating with Other Teams and Disciplines | 141

by positioning around an external view of an organization's business eco-system, which puts the customer and value delivery at the center. However, customer experience design takes it much further. It brings the essential human perspective and empathy to the forefront to truly facilitate design from the customer perspective. It also allows business architecture to be viewed through the customer lens, which can make the architecture more familiar and relevant to other people. Business architecture helps to orchestrate the right business components at the right time to deliver customer experiences. It also helps with customer experience issue resolution and improvement, and informs and translates customer needs into action.

Domain Alignment

As part of experience design, a common set of evidence-based artifacts are developed, such as customer journey maps and customer personas. A customer journey reflects the experience from a customer's perspective as they perform steps to achieve a set of goals, along with their emotions, interactions, and touchpoints with an organization. A customer journey is comprised of stages and each stage may include specific physical or digital touchpoints in which the customer interacts with an organization. When we consider a specific customer segment or persona moving through a journey, it not only helps to create empathy but also ensures that the appropriate value and capabilities are delivered.

To create the formal alignment with business architecture, four domains within customer experience design serve as the focal point: **customer**, **customer journey**, **customer journey stage**, and **touchpoint**. The key linkage between customer experience design and business architecture is the **cross-mapping from a customer journey stage to one or more value stream stages**. Since capabilities are cross-mapped to the value stream stages they enable, **by extension a relationship is made from capabilities to the customer journey stages they enable**. Customers are represented as a category of stakeholders within the business architecture.

Figure 4.2 shows a simplified example of these relationships for a retail customer journey, where value streams and capabilities can be assembled to deliver a cohesive, consistent experience for customers.

Visit www.StrategyintoReality.com to download diagrams and other valuable resources.

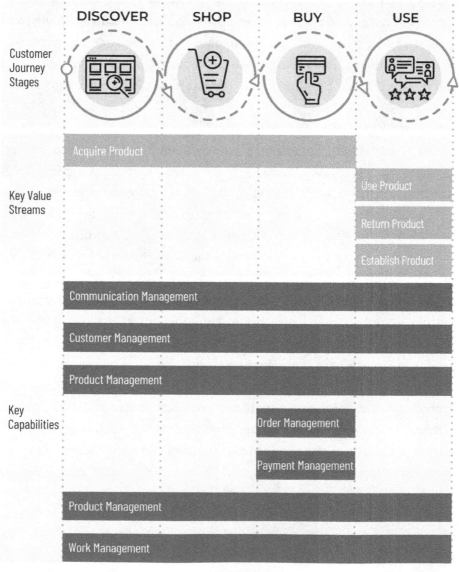

Figure 4.2: Alignment of Journeys, Value Streams, and Capabilities

Role Interactions

The discipline of customer experience design is mainly practiced by customer experience designers, while business architecture is mainly practiced by business architects. Customer experience designers and business architects exchange mutual benefit by working with each other, though some organizations blend design and architecture into one role. In cases such as these, it is important to stay true to the intentions, principles, and focus each discipline requires, even if a certain individual wears two hats.

Customer experience designers and business architects should work together to cross-map customer journeys and value streams and partner closely on efforts to design, improve, and implement the experiences that an organization delivers to its customers. Customer experience designers and business architects can also serve as advocates for each other to help people within the organization understand and appreciate the benefits of these valuable roles and disciplines.

Business Architecture Benefits

Business architecture and customer experience design are indeed mutually beneficial disciplines. Viewing the customer experience through the lens of business architecture can offer fresh new insights. Business architecture also helps to make the envisioned customer experiences real by translating them into action for people, process, and technology. On the other hand, customer experience design provides an invaluable view into customer needs and priorities and articulates a comprehensive vision of an organization's target customers and end-to-end customer experience. It can also identify new offerings and bring empathy into the design and innovation of products and related services and experiences.

Business architecture makes customer experience design artifacts actionable. Business architecture takes point-in-time customer experience design documents and converts them to living and breathing reusable assets by bringing them into the knowledgebase. Furthermore, business architecture connects customer experiences to information about the rest of the business and technology environment. This makes it possible to explore customer experiences from new angles and generate actionable insights.

Business architecture provides a top-down business perspective for planning customer-experience related improvements and initiatives. Business architecture provides a useful framework for planning customer experiences, automation, and digitalization. It can inform customer experience design plans with an understanding of what capabilities currently exist or are planned, and how well they are working. Business architecture can then be used to translate customer needs into logically structured initiatives that will deliver them, harmonized with related changes across the enterprise. The knowledgebase can also be used to assess the impact of any planned customer experience changes to customers and other stakeholders.

Business architecture supports shared decision-making, investment, and governance around the customer experience. The customer experience design sets the direction, but the business architecture provides the concrete focal points for decision-making and investment that transcend business silos. This allows business leaders across business units and products to come together with shared responsibility to set direction and invest in the capabilities that will deliver an integrated, end-to-end customer experience. Target architectures can also help leaders and their teams envision the future business and technology environment necessary to realize the customer experience vision. Target architectures and their corresponding strategic roadmaps also provide ideal structures for governing changes and measuring progress of customer experience enhancements from both a customer and business perspective.

Business architecture helps improve customer service-related experiences. A service (or product) is experienced by a customer within the context of a customer journey. Business architecture provides a focal point for targeting improvements because services can be traced to value streams and then to the capabilities that enable those services. Since capabilities connect to the business architecture and operating model domains, the potential root causes of a customer issue can be traced back to people, process, technology, or other perspectives, and then resolved accordingly.

Service design is a separate but related discipline from customer experience design. Service design takes a holistic view of an organization to design optimal service experiences for customers. One of the common supporting artifacts is a service blueprint, which shows the enabling components of a service, aligned with a customer journey, often for a specific scenario.

The key intersection between business architecture and service design is through the service being delivered to a customer, which is reflected in the product domain of business architecture. In addition, business architecture provides concrete, reusable perspectives that may be referenced on a service blueprint.

How does business architecture align with design thinking?

Design thinking is a methodology for creative problem solving. It applies human-centered techniques to solve problems in a creative and innovative way. It is a way of thinking and working and offers a robust set of methods. However, unlike the other teams referenced here, it is not a standalone discipline performed by a certain role with a set of domains to cross-map to.

Considering that design thinking is essentially an approach for creative problem solving, this means that an organization could leverage the technique at any time, within any context. *While design thinking and business architecture may have different intents and approaches, they co-exist and interact for mutual benefit.* For example, within a strategy execution context, design thinking could be particularly valuable to inform strategies in the Develop Strategy stage, to inform target state architectures in the Architect Changes stage, and to inform solution designs in the Execute Solutions stage.

Additionally, developing a strong competency in design thinking is highly beneficial for business architects in their roles.

How does business architecture align with organization design?

Organization design is a discipline defined as "The deliberate process of configuring structures, processes, reward systems, and people practices and policies to create an effective organization capable of achieving the business strategy."[12] The discipline is strategic, and its focus goes far beyond just defining the organizational structure.

There are different models for organization design such as Galbraith's Star Model, McKinsey's 7S Model, Weisbord's Six Box Model, Nadler and Tushman's Congruence Model, and the Burke-Litwin Model. For our purposes, we will anchor around the Star Model.[13] Each point on the Star Model represents a major component of organization design and they include: strategy, structure, processes, rewards, and people practices. The latter four components all support the strategy. When all points are in alignment an organization is most effective.

Business architecture and organization design share many of the same goals for organizations: intentional design, organizational alignment, and agility and adaptability. Organization design is concerned with aligning an organization's purpose and strategy with its operating model—and of course business architecture is the critical bridge between the two. As a result, tight partnership and integration between these two disciplines is essential and again, mutually beneficial.

Domain Alignment

The organization mapping technique within business architecture does not replace organization design. It is simply a representation of an organization's business units and their decomposition into sub-business units, along with their relationships to other capabilities and other domains. However, the organization domain (business units) within business architecture does provide an important architectural focal point for organization design that is maintained in the business architecture knowledgebase.

At the time of publication for this book, there are not any organization design domains defined in the BIZBOK® Guide. However, if we turn to the people component of the operating model then we might consider domains such as **role, skill, competency**, and others. For example, a **cross-mapping relationship between the business architecture stakeholder and role** could be valuable for a variety of analyses and usage scenarios. This could include assessing the impact of a change on specific roles to pinpointing additional detail from a people perspective for issue resolution or cost analysis.

As with any cross-mappings from business architecture domains to operating model domains, these relationships can become quite numerous and detailed, so as always, capture just enough, just in time to inform business decisions and needs.

Role Interactions

Organization designers may be part of the human resources department within an organization or part of a standalone discipline team, which may go by different names depending upon the team's scope and focus (e.g., organization design, organization effectiveness, organization development).

As mentioned, business architects and organization designers share many of the same goals, even if they approach them from different perspectives. *Both disciplines encourage intentional organization design.* They focus on the holistic design of an organization to deliver on its intended purpose and value most effectively. *Business architecture and organization design both ensure organizational alignment.* Strategies should align with value streams and capabilities (and other business architecture perspectives), which should drive and align with the operating model. Initiatives and investments should also align with strategy. *Both disciplines also seek to build an organization's agility and capacity to adapt to change.* Where organization design may have a concept of a *reconfigurable organization* to recombine skills, competencies, and resources in response to change, business architecture, and capabilities in particular, provide a modular view of common business components, which can be built once and reused in many different ways.

Business architects and organization designers partner to cross-map business architecture domains such as business units, stakeholders, value streams, capabilities, and objectives to any organization design domains, as business needs dictate. From a strategy execution context, the discipline of organization design has aspects that are both strategic as well as tactical related to the people component of the operating model. This means that business architects and organization designers need to work together especially closely upfront during strategy execution to inform and translate strategy, architect changes, and shape initiatives.

Business Architecture Benefits

Business architecture contributes unique value to each of the five major components of organization design within the Star Model.

Business architecture clarifies strategy for organization design. An organization's direction is the cornerstone of the organization design process. Business architecture drives clarity and measurability of business objectives and outcomes and translates strategy into the business capabilities necessary to enable it. Business architecture also ensures the alignment and cohesiveness of strategies, goals, objectives, metrics, and courses of action across an organization.

Business architecture informs organization structure decision-making and changes. Business architecture provides clarity and transparency about how an organization is structured, including views of internal business units and external partners, their relationships, and the products, value, and capabilities they deliver. Business architecture identifies opportunities for organizational improvement and redesign at a high-level. For example, it may uncover redundant capability enablement across business units, excessive committee or governance structures, or outsourcing opportunities. Business architecture is also ideal for comprehensively assessing the impact of potential organizational changes across the entire business and technology environment to support decision-making and communications.

Business architecture informs lateral mechanism design. Regardless of how well thought out an organization's structure, it will create some barriers to collaboration. These can be overcome by different lateral mechanisms such as interpersonal and technological networks, team and matrix relationships, lateral processes, and integrative roles.[14] Business architecture identifies where lateral mechanism are needed to bridge silos for information sharing, decision-making, collaboration, and reusable solutions. It also provides a shared, high-level framework to inform lateral mechanism design with natural areas of commonality and an end-to-end value delivery perspective.

Business architecture provides traceability for performance metrics. The design of metrics and reward and recognition systems influences the success of all other design components. Business architecture provides the traceability from the objectives and metrics of the *enterprise* to the objectives and metrics of *business units* to those used to measure the performance of *individuals*.

Business architecture informs people practices. Business architecture can inform staffing, selection, and development decisions related to the roles, skills, and competencies needed to deliver the organization's intended value and capabilities, in alignment with its purpose and strategy.

How does business architecture align with business process management and Lean Six Sigma?

Business architecture helps an organization to realize its business model, while processes help an organization to realize its operating model. These two very important disciplines work together to help an organization operate effectively and implement change—from the high-level perspective to the details.

Business architecture and business process professionals can be united around a view of end-to-end value creation. This provides an overarching framework for both disciplines and the ability to work across business silos to create cohesive experiences and effective operations. Business processes will also reflect the details of business management and operations at a much more granular level than business architecture.

The perspectives contained here on the interaction of business architecture and business process management have been informed by years of admirable collaboration between the business architecture and business process communities and will continue to evolve.[15]

Domain Alignment

We can use value streams as an anchor point between the business architecture and process disciplines. If we look at value stream stages through a business architecture lens, they are essentially a collection of capabilities. On the other hand, if we look at value stream stages through a process lens, they are essentially a collection of process activities (that may include subprocesses).

From a value stream perspective, processes—or more specifically the activities within them—implement a value stream stage. It is a many-to-many relationship, where **a process activity can implement many value stream stages**, and a **value stream stage can be implemented by many process activities**, even spanning across different processes. Capabilities of course enable value stream stages. It follows then that the processes aligned to value stream stages implement the capabilities that enable those stages. Again, it is a many-to-many relationship where **a process activity can implement multiple capabilities** and a **capability can be implemented by many process activities.** In fact, at a more granular level, a capability instance can be related to a process activity. Consider, a capability within a certain business unit context can be related to a process activity contained within a process that is relevant to that specific business unit. A similar cross-mapping approach applies to Lean value streams and the steps within them.

Organizations can have hundreds or thousands of detailed processes, so the scope and level of detail included in business architecture and business process cross-mapping efforts should be driven by clear business needs for the information. For example, while a more detailed set of relationships may be ideal to capture (and can be rolled up to a higher level), an initial business usage scenario for supporting enterprise impact analysis may just require relationships to be approximated between capabilities and processes.

Role Interactions

Business architects and process professionals partner on cross-mapping activities. Process professionals typically take the lead on creating and maintaining the relationships from processes to business architecture domains because of their familiarity with the processes.

While business architecture and process cross-mappings are typically created in support of specific business usage scenarios, they can provide valuable insights into process effectiveness and streamlining in general. For example, the alignment of processes to value streams can uncover redundancies, inconsistencies, or unnecessary variation across processes. Or, the alignment of capabilities to the business processes that operationally enact them can provide insights into necessary process improvements when a capability is underperforming.

Beyond the cross-mapping, business architects and process professionals collaborate on a broad spectrum of operational and change initiatives. For example, they may work together on anything from diagnosing the root causes of an enterprise issue to shaping the target state architecture for a transformation.

Business Architecture Benefits

The disciplines of business architecture and business process management are mutually beneficial and interlocking. Business architecture provides a framework for organizing, optimizing, streamlining, prioritizing, and leveraging processes holistically across an organization. On the other hand, process offers unique insights for business architecture, such as where end-to-end optimization is needed. In addition, business processes are where the real work is done to bring the business alive.

Business architecture provides a framework for process governance at an enterprise level. Value streams can be used as the framework to organize business processes within an enterprise level value context. Value streams and the stages within them can even inform the scope and focus of business process design. Business architecture also provides the shared business vocabulary and information concepts that can be used in process conversations and design.

Business architecture identifies areas for process improvement and collaboration. Business architecture can illuminate process redundancies, inconsistencies, or gaps. It can also identify new opportunities for teams to collaborate or share best practices across related processes. In addition, capability assessment ratings can help target where potential process improvements may be needed.

Business architecture guides process priorities. While continual process improvement may be ideal, organizations have a finite set of resources. Business architecture provides a top-down perspective to focus process efforts and investments on those which are the highest priority to the business. For example, if value streams and capabilities are aligned to key objectives, then any related process work is likely to be a higher priority. Or, processes aligned to a capability assessed as ineffective may also be a higher priority for investment.

How does business architecture align with event modeling?

Some organizations leverage an event modeling approach in addition to or instead of process modeling. An event-based approach can be beneficial in organizations with complex business environments, many knowledge workers, and unpredictable workflows. Work can be represented in a more flexible way compared to a process approach that defines prescribed paths. An event-based approach can lead to more flexible solutions and create greater transparency for the state of work at any time.

The BIZBOK® Guide highlights the value of business architecture to inform and provide the context for case management. Case management is a "method or practice of coordinating work by organizing all of the relevant pieces into one place—called a case."[16] For example, consider a legal case or healthcare case that brings together all related information and interactions for a customer.

Business architecture value streams provide the ideal framework for organizing the event-based flows of work between work queues, represented through an artifact which the BIZBOK® Guide refers to as a rules-based routing map. Value streams make an ideal organizing construct because they are focused on stakeholder value delivery and are flexible event-based frameworks themselves. Furthermore, like process maps, rules-based routing maps describe the additional "detail" that occurs within a value stream stage.

Event models or rules-based routing maps are part of the operating model, not business architecture. Business analysts and/or solution architects typically create them and align them with value streams, working in close partnership with business architects.

If an organization is not already using event modeling approaches, a good place to start is by trying them out for a small scope. For example, rules-based routing maps may be created to help with a new solution or solution redesign.

How does business architecture align with IT architecture?

Business architecture informs enterprise architecture scenarios and decision-making with business direction, priorities, language, and context. It can also help to make the lives of IT architects easier and allow them to focus more strategically on the IT architecture—versus trying to understand and rationalize business needs. The relationship between business and IT architecture and architects within the enterprise architecture umbrella is crucial to an organization's ability to implement strategy and operate effectively.

Domain Alignment

There are four key areas of linkage between the business and IT architectures, all contained within the application architecture and the data architecture domains. Direct relationships are not typically made between the business architecture and technical architecture. The linkages to infrastructure are typically made through the application architecture and data architecture.

First, **system applications are cross-mapped to the capabilities** that they automate. This provides a foundational understanding of how what the business does is automated. Shadow systems may also be captured as applications. This may include Excel spreadsheets or Access databases or even subscription software that are critical to the business but are beyond the IT department's line of sight. An application can automate many capabilities and a capability can be automated by many different applications. **The business unit domain may be used to further delineate the applications used by each business unit for a given capability**. For example, different business units or product areas may have the same capability but leverage different systems to automate it. Business information concepts can be tremendously helpful to help identify which capabilities that an application automates. For example, a sales system can be traced back to capabilities related to products, customers, agreements, and payments or a procurement system can be traced back to capabilities related to assets, partners, agreements, and payments.

Second, **software services are cross-mapped to the capabilities** that they automate. In fact, capabilities can and should be used to identify the inventory of reusable software services in the first place. Capabilities clearly illuminate where common business actions are performed across an organization. In addition, capabilities share key characteristics with software services in that they are bounded by the scope of one information concept, and they produce concrete outcomes. Capabilities also use or modify business information as software services use or modify data.

The BIZBOK® Guide does not recognize a domain of business service. In practice the business service domain is often used to represent a grouping of capabilities, typically more functional in nature. The cross-mapping of software services and capabilities provides a simple and elegant approach.

Third, **value streams put automation into the broader business context**. They show what capabilities are delivering stakeholder value along with the applications that are automating them. **Value streams frame service orchestration**, providing insights into which software services are used and when, and how information flows. **Value streams also frame workflow automation through their alignment with processes and/or event models.** They also guide user interface design.

Finally, **the information map informs the data architecture** with business information concepts and their relationships. This can inform any changes that need to occur to the existing data architecture from a business-driven perspective.

The scope and level of detail of business and IT architecture cross-mappings should be driven by the need for them to support specific business usage scenarios. This provides the best value back to the business, especially considering how many systems can exist in a large organization. For example, a subset of applications may be cross-mapped to capabilities within the scope of a transformation or the scope of analysis for application portfolio management. Furthermore, the best approach is to stay at a higher level of detail in the cross-mappings and decompose into lower levels of detail as specific needs dictate. For example, start by cross-mapping application systems to level 2 or even level 1 capabilities and then go to a finer grain of application and/or capability in the future.

Role Interactions

Business architects work closest with application architects and data architects to create business and IT architecture cross-mappings. *All archi-*

tects are united by the vision and value proposition for enterprise architecture within their organization. They continually work together on various initiatives and usage scenarios—and ensure the dots connect across all of them.

An architect is a professional who facilitates macro-level decision-making, design, and alignment of the business and technology environment to support an organization's goals and strategies. All architects should have a base understanding of architecture concepts and principles but specialize in their architecture domain: business, application, data, technical, security, or solution. Think: the medical profession where all physicians have a base set of knowledge and competencies and could help a person in need, but may specialize in areas such as family medicine, pediatrics, dermatology, or surgery. *All* architects should have a strong working knowledge of the business and the business architecture, not just the business architects. On the other hand, business architects should have a strong working knowledge of technology, which has never been more important than it is today in our digital world.

Successful architects think globally but act locally. They are not only concerned about their individual scope and scenarios, but they also think holistically and make sure that all the pieces fit together for an organization, both strategically and tactically.

Business Architecture Benefits

The fusion of the business and IT architectures helps to facilitate alignment between business and technology and ensures that architecture and technology decisions are business-driven. Business architecture frames technology discussions with a business lens. For example, instead of analyzing information at the system application level, it can be elevated to a conversation around capabilities. Business architecture also reflects business priorities. Value streams and capabilities inherently convey business priorities based on the objectives they are tied to as well as any metric ratings such as capability effectiveness or strategic importance. Any system applications or software services cross-mapped to these perspectives will inherit the business priorities. Business architecture also provides a shared business language and mental model that allows all parties to communicate, regardless of their business or technology perspectives.

Business architecture helps IT architects engage strategically. Business architecture provides the business vocabulary for IT architects to speak the language of the business. In addition, the positioning of business architecture upfront in the strategy execution life cycle helps to engage IT architecture early as well. Strategic IT architects work as valuable partners alongside strategic business architects to help inform business direction, which is especially important as the lines between business and technology continue to blend.

Business architecture drives IT architecture alignment and transformation. Business and IT architecture alignment is a state in which an organization's IT architecture fully supports its business architecture. The focal points for alignment are the applications, services, and data deployments in the IT architecture with the strategies and objectives, value streams, capabilities, and business information in the business architecture. Again, the technical architecture alignment occurs through the application and data architecture. Business and IT architecture alignment may be an aspirational state—and one that will continue to evolve with business and IT strategy—but it provides a vision to work towards. Business and IT architecture transformation is a means of achieving this alignment together. Business strategy, as translated through the business architecture, helps to inform the IT strategy alongside other technology-related inputs.

Business architecture is also a critical driver of the direction and investment priorities of IT architecture transformation. Business architecture drives changes to the IT architecture based on business direction and planned changes of any size, from creating a new software service to address a capability gap to supporting a reinvented business model. Business architecture also provides the business lens for other IT architecture transformation, from application rationalization to a shift towards a service-oriented architecture (SOA) or microservices architecture. Business architecture also facilitates business-driven approaches and roadmaps for IT architecture transformation. For example, the level of application technical debt and business misalignment aggregated by capability can guide whether targeted investments are needed to improve the IT architecture or whether a major architectural investment is needed to address the foundation. Capabilities can also guide on when IT architecture investments should be made based on business priority and the timing of other initiatives.

Business architecture drives technology selection and deployment. Business architecture plays a key role to define the business needs, priorities, and usage scenarios for potential technology solutions and vendors to address. It can also be used to perform impact analysis on the business and technology environment for various build or buy options.

Business architecture can also guide organizations as they make decisions, implement, adopt, and govern emerging technologies. This may include artificial intelligence (AI), blockchain, virtual reality, robotics, and others. For example, beyond guiding on business direction and usage scenarios, business architecture can ensure data is rationalized around a common business perspective, particularly important for use by emerging technologies such as AI. Business architecture can help uncover workforce implications related to emerging technologies and guide workforce planning and upskilling. Coupled with human-centered design, business architecture facilitates cohesive experiences and interactions between humans and technology. It is also an ideal framework to facilitate governance and risk management. For example, an algorithm can be tied to a source system, capability, and policy, which not only creates transparency but can be used to support the isolation and resolution of any issues that occur.

Business architecture puts IT metrics into a business context. Business architecture can be used to aggregate and frame IT metrics from a business perspective. For example, instead of measuring continuity at an individual system level, it can be measured at the capability level. Since a capability may be supported by many systems, an interruption to any of them counts against the capability's performance. This approach drives more holistic business ownership and investments and improves the overall outcomes for the customer and organization.

How does business architecture align with TOGAF® and EA Frameworks?

A variety of enterprise architecture frameworks exist, including The Open Group Architecture Framework (TOGAF®), the Zachman Framework™ and the Department of Defense/Ministry of Defense Architecture Framework (DoDAF/MODAF). While these frameworks do include the business architecture domain, they do not provide the same robust perspective on business architecture as described within the BIZBOK® Guide.

TOGAF® is one of the most used enterprise architecture frameworks within organizations. The business architecture perspectives within TOGAF® began aligning with the BIZBOK® Guide starting with TOGAF® version 9.2. The Open Group is a global consortium that enables business objectives through the advancement of technology standards and manages the TOGAF® standard and associated ecosystem of guides and resources. While TOGAF® does not fully align with the BIZBOK® Guide business architecture domains and concepts at this time, an admirable amount of collaboration and work has been completed to date by The Open Group and its members, which include the Business Architecture Guild® and employees of member companies. At the time of publication for this book, collaboration and alignment between the Business Architecture Guild® and The Open Group continues across various standards and initiatives.

Regardless of the enterprise architecture framework that an organization uses, the business architecture framework as described in the BIZ-BOK® Guide can be aligned with it. For example, the IT architecture domains may remain the same, but any business architecture domains are replaced by the ten domains and their relationships as defined in the BIZ-BOK® Guide metamodel. The ecosystem-wide and strategic philosophy and positioning for business architecture should also be adopted.

How does business architecture align with program and project management?

Business architecture's role in shaping initiatives as part strategy translation can be invaluable to program and project managers. Business architecture ensures that initiatives are defined with clear, mutually exclusive scopes, and anchored back to the specific business and IT architecture focal points that are changing. It helps to maximize resource utilization by scoping and sequencing initiatives in the most logical way from an enterprise perspective. Business architecture aligns initiatives to strategy, ensuring that the most important initiatives are prioritized at the right time. It harmonizes solution reuse and integration across initiatives and helps ensure the collective changes delivered across initiatives are consumable by individual stakeholders. Business architecture methodically identifies applicable considerations such as stakeholders, policies, risks, and any other aspects tied to capabilities. Business architecture also accelerates and improves requirements definition and even helps facilitate collaboration across different initiative roles.

All these benefits help to accelerate initiatives, head off common issues, and allow program and project managers to focus their precious time and unique talent on delivering initiatives successfully. Business architecture also gives program and project managers a common business language shared by all roles, business or technology.

Business architects create any initiative-related cross-mappings in the business architecture knowledgebase. This includes cross-mapping initiatives to objectives, the value streams and capability focal points that are being targeted for enhancement, and requirements.

Business architects can serve as invaluable consultants to program and project managers, especially related to the bigger picture business and architecture direction across initiatives. Where a large scope of work is being defined, such as in the case of a business transformation, business architects and program managers may even begin working together prior to initiatives. They may work in partnership, along with IT architects, to scope, shape, and estimate initiatives at a macro level.

The introduction of business architecture as a discipline can require a mindset shift for program and project managers, but in the end, it makes their jobs easier and improves the chances of initiative success. A good place to start is building relationships between business architecture, program and project management, and business analysis. Business architecture can be leveraged on one initiative to test and learn before scaling to others. Over time, the role and inputs of business architecture can be formally integrated into program and project methodologies, such as to reflect business architecture contributions within a charter or equivalent document.

How does business architecture align with business analysis?

Business architecture and business analysis are again two distinct but mutually beneficial disciplines. Business architecture and business analysis focus on different goals, work at different scopes and elevations, engage at different points during strategy execution, and produce different outputs. However, partnership is critical for an organization to move ideas into action.

Domain Alignment

Requirements may be represented as *ability to* statements at different levels, user stories, or in other formats. Regardless of an organization's approach, the most critical cross-mapping between business architecture and business analysis is between a **capability and a requirement**. This creates an alignment back to the business strategy and business needs, and facilitates the reuse of requirements. **Value streams are important to put capabilities and the changes needed to them within an overall context** of external or internal stakeholder value delivery.

Another valuable cross-mapping may be made to link a **requirement with the related stakeholder** in the business architecture. **Requirements may also be cross-mapped to the initiatives** of which they are part to complete the traceability from strategy to execution. These relationships can be used to support different analyses, including for dynamic replanning so that if business direction shifts, any applicable requirements can be paused.

Role Interactions

Business architects work at the enterprise level and upstream in strategy execution to translate direction into initiatives, scoped and framed by business architecture. Business analysts consume the business architecture changes related to their specific initiative(s), with the key inputs being capabilities and the value stream context for them, stakeholders, and rules-based routing maps if available.

Business analysts, in collaboration with business architects, translate business architecture-framed changes into a set of requirements for their initiative(s). Business analysts also take the lead on creating the cross-mappings from requirements to business architecture capabilities and stakeholders.

Business analysts should be conversant in an organization's business architecture. They play a critical role to carry forward the business architecture vocabulary and thinking into initiatives and can serve as valuable stewards. For example, business analysts may uncover gaps to be addressed in the business architecture.

Business Architecture Benefits

Business architecture helps to streamline, accelerate, standardize, and improve the outcomes of business analysis. Business analysts often perform heroics on initiatives to help ensure the goals and scope are clear, the right people are at the table, and all the appropriate dots are connected. Business architecture can be a breath of fresh air for business analysts, allowing them to focus on the true business analysis needs versus bridging gaps that should have been addressed early on.

Business architecture accelerates the creation and consistency of requirements. Business architecture clearly defines the scope of an initiative, which sets an unambiguous boundary for requirements. More importantly, business architecture ensures there are no gaps or overlaps in scope across initiatives, and that all dependencies, integration points, and stakeholders are known upfront.

Business architecture also accelerates the creation of requirements since the business architecture focal points and vocabulary can be used as building blocks to compose requirement statements. For example, a requirement of *As an Insured, I want to define my preferences to receive my communications according to my preferred method* would leverage and tie back to the business architecture stakeholder of Insured and the capability of Customer Preference Definition. Leveraging concrete business architecture focal points also ensures that requirements are written with consistent language and level of detail across business analysts and initiatives. It allows a clearer set of requirements acceptance criteria to be defined.

Finally, the very existence of a shared business vocabulary and framework can save business analysts countless hours reconciling business concepts and perspectives across stakeholders and business units.

Business architecture ensures requirements align back to business direction and priorities. The alignment of a requirement to a capability provides the link back to business strategy and priorities. This end-to-end traceability provides business context for why a given requirement exists. For example, if a requirement is targeting a capability that is not related to a business objective and/or that capability does not require improvements per its Business Effectiveness rating, the need for the requirement should be revisited.

Business architecture facilitates requirements reuse. Capabilities provide an ideal catalog for organizing requirements because they are based on a high-level, shared business context. Since the capabilities are reusable in the business architecture knowledgebase, when requirements are cross-mapped to them, they also become searchable and reusable—versus being archived with solution or initiative documentation. Organizations have saved days and weeks by being able to find and reuse existing requirements versus recreating the wheel.

How does business architecture align with organizational change management?

The discipline of business architecture is very much about change and business architects are change agents themselves. However, employees, customers, and partners need to be ready for and able to consume the changes that are planned. Organizational change management is a critical discipline that helps organizations prepare, equip, and support individuals to successfully adopt change. After all, organizations are made up individuals who each need to make their personal transitions.

Organizational change management should be treated as a strategic discipline, not as an afterthought or simply a communication and training effort that occurs at the end of an initiative. Change managers should be engaged early in strategy execution, ideally during the Develop Strategy stage when business direction is still being shaped. For example, change managers can inform on an organization's capacity for change, which can be valuable input for prioritizing business direction. Change managers and business architects partner closely, especially to assess the potential scope and impacts of change early on in the Architect Changes stage.

The organizational change management discipline does not have specific domains to connect to the business architecture. However, change managers consume business architecture to help assess change impacts and inform the change management strategy. For example, value streams and capabilities convey what is being changed and the scope of impact. Other domains such as products, policies, information, or initiatives may be used to assess impacts along with related discipline domains to highlight changes to jobs, organizational structure, processes, technology, or even the customer experience. Business units and stakeholders convey who will be impacted by the changes. In addition, capability changes may be aggregated across initiatives to help quantify how much change will be made to stakeholder groups collectively.

Traversing the Mapping Nuances

One of the common challenges that organizations encounter as they start developing their business architecture is what can be described as a confluence between representations from other disciplines and modeling techniques. Some of the commonly confused disciplines and techniques preceded the formalization of business architecture, some have coincided with it, and some emerged afterwards.

As it turns out though, the various spectrum of business representations and models that exist are rarely competing. Each typically has a unique form, function, and intent. Where models *can* become competing or overlapping, is when an underlying set of principles and best practices are not used to create them. For example, if a value stream looks like a customer journey, then the value stream was not likely modeled using mapping principles from the BIZBOK® Guide. Or, if a customer journey looks more like a process, it may not have been modeled using the principles or techniques that are established within the customer experience design discipline. Following clear and robust industry defined principles when creating any model will largely result in representations that are as they should be: of different scopes, different levels of detail, different notations and formats, different naming conventions, and different intents.

The best way to demonstrate how different models fit together—and potentially uncover any overlap—is to overlay or cross-map them together. Do not spend hours in meetings theorizing about how they are the same or different or which technique is better. The quickest way to get a pragmatic understanding of how models relate is to just jump in and create the cross-mappings. For example, cross-map value streams (and ideally stages within them) to the stages of the customer journeys they enable. Cross-map processes (and ideally the activities within them) to the value stream stages they enable. Cross-map business architecture value streams to Scaled Agile Framework® (SAFe) value streams or Lean value streams. The relationships and differences will be illuminated quickly so that you can help to educate others, or if applicable, take some actions to address any unintentional similarities or overlaps.

The key to staying sane is to *embrace the nuances in terminology and different levels of abstraction and develop your ability to traverse them.* Additionally, help others to see the spectrum of different techniques and levels of detail, so that they can embrace the nuances too and understand how each technique contributes a unique perspective. Try not to get zealous because, honestly, nobody wins in the battle of frameworks. In the end, everyone is trying to do what they think is right and what they know, so build bridges instead.

Look beyond the literal interpretation of the words for the meaning and intent. Business architecture does not have a corner on the English language (or any others), so pick your spots to enforce the terminology and framework. For example, if an executive is speaking broadly about developing a strategic capability (with a big C) to perform acquisitions effectively and consistently, embrace the broader intent of the word. However, if a group within the organization has developed a competing framework that includes a different set of capability groupings (with a small C) than the enterprise capability map, then that is an important issue to resolve. Or, within the course of daily conversation if people within a certain business unit refer to clients instead of customers as they may be called in the organization's capability map, that's just dialect. However, when conversations are had at the enterprise level about investments, solutions, issue resolution or other discussions, then the shared business vocabulary as defined in the business architecture should be used. Encourage precision in language when it matters to the outcomes.

What is the difference between value chains, value networks, and value streams?

Value chains, value networks, and value streams all fall within the realm of the business architecture discipline. However only value streams are a true architectural construct and domain captured within the business architecture knowledgebase and cross-mapped to other business perspectives. Both value chains and value networks are views that can be created for specific purposes, but they are not comprised of business architecture domains and they are not maintained in the business architecture knowledgebase (unless to store them as artifacts).

A **value chain**, originally developed by Harvard Business School professor, Michael Porter, is a one-page, enterprise-level view of an organization, which depicts the major activities necessary to deliver a valuable product or service to the market and support its operations. *It is not an architectural perspective and does not in any way replace business architecture value streams.* Furthermore, a value chain is not comprised of value streams, even if it may seem to be the case on the surface. However, a value chain can be a useful view for strategic conversations. For example, it may provide a reference point to help leaders make decisions around how the organization should engage in the industry value chain, with integration (i.e., when an organization performs multiple steps in the value chain) or modularity (i.e., a more plug and play approach). Some organizations also use value chains as an organizing construct for processes. (See next section on high-level processes.)

A **value network** shows the value exchange and interactions across multiple organizations. Each entity is represented along with the tangible (e.g., monetary exchange) and non-tangible (e.g., ideas and intelligence) value it exchanges with others, shown on lines between entities. A value network is a useful view to help people build a high-level understanding of an organization's business ecosystem. This may be helpful input for strategic conversations or even to establish the scope for business architecture mapping sessions.

Value streams are an end-to-end view of external or internal stakeholder value, and form the critical foundation of an organization's business architecture along with capabilities.

What is the difference between value streams and high-level processes?

The business architecture discipline represents end-to-end value creation through value streams. However, the business process management discipline also needs a value creation perspective to organize, guide decomposition, and anchor processes back to the broader end-to-end perspective. The contemporary process professional does not just work at a detailed process or workflow level, but also at a higher and more conceptual level to ensure cross-functional process performance, ownership, and governance.

Value streams in business architecture and high-level processes representing the conceptual perspective within business process management have often been thought of as distinct and different structures. However, over time, it is becoming clearer that both business architects and process practitioners share a much closer perspective on the creation of value. In fact, at a higher level of representation, value streams and high-level business processes can seem similar in many ways.

It is possible and ideal for both the business architecture and business process management disciplines within an organization to share the same value creation structure. Practically speaking, if an organization has already defined business architecture value streams, they may serve to provide both the business architecture value context to which capabilities are cross-mapped as well as the high-level, value-oriented process perspective. On the other hand, if an organization has already created high-level processes (or does not yet have a business architecture practice or knowledgebase), they can be modeled following the same principles and naming convention as value streams in the BIZBOK® Guide. This not only ensures that a viable representation of stakeholder value is produced, but also creates consistency in the modeling of high-level processes across organizations and practitioners where there are not strong standards in place today.

Providing business architecture and business process management with a shared value perspective as starting point can go a long way in bringing the two disciplines together and helping them to achieve the critical results they are both striving to deliver for the business.[17]

What is the difference between journeys, value streams, and processes?

On the surface, customer journeys, value streams, and processes may all seem like the same flows, but they differ in why they are created, when they are created, who creates them, and how they are created. Each representation is *fit for purpose*, so it is important to understand their intentions, where they apply within an enterprise context, and how they fit together.

Customer journeys design, deliver, and improve the experiences that customers (or partners or employees) have as they interact with the organization. **Value streams** are a core domain within the reusable business architecture knowledgebase and together with capabilities, they translate business strategies and customer journeys into the changes necessary to the business and IT environment, and then help to package those changes into a coordinated set of initiatives for execution. The actual changes are made to the operating model, including people, process, and technology during initiatives. **Business processes** are not only used to carry out the detailed changes resulting from strategies and other change initiatives, but they also promote continuous improvement to increase the efficiency of the internal operating environment.

Customer experience designers create customer journeys, business architects create value streams, and process professionals (and/or business analysts within an initiative context) create business processes. Within a strategy execution context, customer experience designers and business architects define any changes to customer journeys and business architecture upfront during the Architect Changes stage. Process professionals may be consulted as needed. Then, process professionals make any defined process additions or changes during the Execute Solutions stage.

This is an ideal allocation of responsibilities as it allows for each role to best leverage their strengths. It also separates out an external versus internal focus and varying levels of detail. In addition, it allows for each individual discipline (i.e., customer experience design, business architecture, and business process management) to be leveraged distinctly and entirely without forcing a blend.

Customer journeys, value streams, and processes together form a cohesive chain from the outside-in to the inside-out, and from high-level to detail. Value streams are the keystone between customer journeys and processes. Value stream stages cross-map to customer journey stages and processes (ideally at the activity level) cross-map to value stream stages. This traceability supports bi-directional impact analysis and traceability for targeting and implementing enhancements and change.

What is the difference between value streams in business architecture, Lean, and SAFe?

Each type of value stream is fit for purpose and again differs in why they are created, who creates them, and how they are created. Within the Scaled Agile Framework®, **SAFe value streams** are a primary construct used to organize and deliver value. SAFe defines operational value streams and development value streams. Operational value streams are closer to business architecture value streams. However, SAFe value streams are based on guidelines, which are widely interpreted in practice and are often scoped to represent entire life cycles. This means that multiple business architecture value streams may apply across one SAFe value stream. For example, three business architecture value streams may apply for one SAFe value stream related to loans: Execute Campaign (for the steps related to attracting loan customers), Establish Financial Agreement (for the steps related to applying for and receiving the loan), and Settle Financial Accounts (for the ongoing repayment of the loan). SAFe also connects the enabling systems directly to value stream steps versus the business architecture approach of connecting systems to capabilities and capabilities to value stream stages.

It is possible and ideal for principle-based, reusable business architecture value streams to be used within SAFe for an organization's operational value streams. However, this is not always feasible depending upon the size and needs of an organization. Regardless, business architecture value streams should be used as input to the definition of SAFe operational value streams. In cases where both exist, business architecture and SAFe value streams can be cross-mapped together to provide context and understanding as well as traceability.

Lean value streams are a part of the rigorous Lean discipline that focuses on removing or reducing waste within an organization. Lean value streams are used to help design and increase the efficiency of the internal operating environment. Where an organization typically has only 25+ high-level business architecture value streams, which are relatively static, it may have many Lean value streams to represent the necessary granularity. Lean value streams are more likely to evolve as the business evolves and because of targeted improvement activities. Business architecture value streams do not have a required notation and are typically represented simply as boxes and arrows. On the other hand, Lean value streams use a specific notation that helps to highlight and analyze key attributes such as how long an activity takes or the wait time between activities. Finally, the scope of business architecture and Lean value streams often differs. For example, the scope of business architecture value streams may extend past the scope of Lean value streams because of the requirement to deliver end-to-end stakeholder value.

Business architecture value streams and Lean value streams work well in conjunction with each other. The activities within a Lean value stream may be cross-mapped to the applicable stages within a business architecture value stream. Business architecture can be used as an organizing framework for Lean value streams and help to identify areas for alignment and best practice sharing, as well as inform Lean work priorities. Lean value streams can help inform business architecture with a more detailed understanding of the current state.

Business Architecture is the Gateway to Organizational Agility

Today's environment is driving organizations to adapt more quickly than ever before. There is a widespread movement within organizations to shift to more agile mindsets and ways of working. However, agility is not just for execution. Simply speeding up execution does not ensure we are doing the *right* things—in fact we could be doing more of the wrong things faster. Quite the contrary, agility is a concept that ripples from strategy to execution. Execution agility is just one piece of end-to-end organizational agility. The way our organizations strategize, architect, and implement change needs to further evolve from linear and relatively static to proactive, continuous, and flexible.

The relationship between architecture and agility is like the yin and yang, as inseparable and contradictory opposites. On the surface, business architecture may seem like an impediment to agility, something that is too structural, static, constraining, governing. *However, there is a powerful paradox here: business architecture is the gateway to agility.* When business architecture is adopted, positioned as a facilitator of effective strategy execution, and leveraged ubiquitously throughout an organization, it provides the foundation for an agile enterprise.

End-to-end organizational agility *and* delivery agility are critical. Business architecture and agile teams play different, complementary roles as it pertains to business change. Many of the strategy execution challenges that exist in organizations do not just go away by adopting an agile framework, especially in the case of large and complex change initiatives. Business architecture focuses on the business at a macro level and translates and aligns strategy. It creates a shared view of the future, and together with other disciplines, ensures that the business outcomes are achieved, and that organizational change occurs. Agile teams are the mechanism that take the direction and deliver the results.

Business architecture is a practical way to accelerate and enhance the outcomes within and across agile teams and tie their results back to the bigger picture.

How does business architecture and SAFe and agile terminology align?

One of the benefits of business architecture is the sharp clarity of its definitions, which are further supported by principles that produce mapping consistency. SAFe terms have definitions as well, though they can be interpreted more broadly in practice.

A good starting point for business architecture and SAFe collaboration is to align on terminology. Business architecture and SAFe use some of the same key terms differently, so it is important just to acknowledge this and clarify how each group defines them. This creates awareness so that all parties can correctly interpret the meaning of terms in different conversations based on the context.

Some of the most important terms to align upon include value stream, capability, customer, and product. Business architecture value streams are end-to-end views of external or internal stakeholder value delivery, used for a broad range of business usage scenarios. As discussed earlier, SAFe value streams are a construct used to organize and deliver value, and are of two types, operational and development, where the operational value streams are more like the business architecture value streams.

On the other hand, business architecture capabilities are the specific abilities of an organization that produce concrete outcomes. They persist in the knowledgebase and are reused across many different business scenarios. In SAFe, capabilities are defined as "higher-level solution behaviors that typically span multiple ARTs (Agile Release Trains),"[18] and are not viewed as a persistent component.

In business architecture, customers and products are always defined as external ecosystem concepts with no exception. Customers are the individuals or organizations that purchase or otherwise benefit from an organization's products or services. Business architecture represents internal employees or external partners as stakeholders but reserves the term customer only for the end customer who is ultimately being served. The term product is reserved to describe the goods or services that an organization offers externally in the market. On the other hand, in SAFe, customers can be external or internal as can products. In SAFe, products and solutions are intertwined, and the term product may sometimes be used to describe what might be interpreted as a capability or system grouping from the business architecture lens.

What unique value does business architecture bring to SAFe and agile approaches?

Business architecture and agile approaches both care about the delivery of value and the achievement of business outcomes, with improved time to market. Business architecture contributes unique value on both fronts to enhance SAFe and agile efforts. It also provides the underlying business framework.

Business architecture articulates the business framework. Business architecture provides *the* business framework for an organization, including value streams, capabilities, business units (which may include internal business units, agile teams, and partners), and products—and the cross-mappings to other domains. Furthermore, the business architecture framework creates a shared mindset around the end customer and value delivery as the ultimate goal. *The setup of an agile organization is key, and business architecture can provide invaluable input.* For example, business architecture value streams may potentially be used for SAFe operational value streams, or at least inform them. In addition, because of their reusable nature, capabilities can be used to scope Agile Release Trains.

Business architecture informs investment decisions. Business architecture-based impact assessments, anchored by capabilities, can inform decision-making at any point on whether to continue investing or stop the work. Business architecture helps identify the potential scope of work and complexity, as well as the right players to help shape the work ahead. Business architecture also pinpoints what parts of the organization will be impacted.

Business architecture informs agile team priorities. Business architecture helps to clarify, rationalize, and articulate strategies and objectives upfront that can be leveraged for strategic themes and budgets. *Most importantly, business architecture guides agile teams on business priorities to ensure the right work is done at the right time.* Work at any level, from epics to features to user stories, can be framed within the broader business context that business architecture provides. This allows agile teams to better align their work to the value streams and capabilities of the business. In addition, the ecosystem perspective of business architecture always keeps the ultimate focus in the right place: on the end customer and the business. Business architecture ensures that all aspects of an organization are considered beyond just the technology, including the people, the culture, the experiences, and the processes.

Business architecture connects the dots across agile teams. Using value streams and capabilities as focal points, business architecture connects the dots to identify opportunities for collaboration, integration, shared solutions, and dependency management across agile teams—as well as with other enterprise teams and initiatives. Business architects also create holistic views for leaders and other key stakeholders. For example, an aggregate view of a capability may be created to help executives see a comprehensive view of the change that is planned, what value will be delivered to customers and the business and when, and what impacts to the experiences or operations need to be managed.

With a clear understanding of business direction, priorities, and context—as well as a clear understanding of where to work with others—business architecture enables agile teams to be even more empowered and effective in the delivery of value and outcomes.

How do business architects work with agile product roles?

Agile product roles focus on iterative planning, development, and delivery of a product/solution. A product manager owns their strategy and roadmap, but business architects are the connectors to ensure alignment *across* strategies and roadmaps—and that ultimately the organization's broader strategic outcomes are achieved.

Business architects can be beneficial to agile product roles in several ways. First, business architects articulate and consult on the big picture view of business and architectural direction along with planned evolution over time. They also consult on the organization's business architecture, especially the business context around value streams. In addition, business architects can guide agile product roles on how to align outcomes across capabilities and value streams and ensure there is no duplication of effort. Business architects inform product roadmaps and backlogs with business priorities and gaps to ensure that the work is focused on the right things. They inform on high-level work scope, reusable solutions, and dependencies. Business architects also identify collaboration and integration points across agile teams and other enterprise efforts.

5

Maximizing the Business Architecture Team

Establishing a business architecture team within an organization is about more than just introducing a new discipline. At the core, it is about enabling a new vision for strategy execution and creating a new capability within an organization to enact change. As a result, how a business architecture team is introduced and structured is critical to its long-term success.

Once the decision has been made to create a formal business architecture team, even if just a team of one or two people to start, teams progress along a similar path and often seek answers to the same set of questions such as: *To whom should the business architecture team report? How do we distribute business architects across the organization? How many business architects do we need? What does a business architect do? How do we find great and develop business architects?* and *What is the career path for a business architect who masters the role?* While any approaches must be adapted to an organization's specific situation, needs and culture, there is a large body of experience that can be drawn from on how to establish a business architecture team most successfully.

While business architecture may be the thing we are creating and using, it is the *people* who make a business architecture practice. Shape your team with meticulous intention and attention, and invest in building competent practitioners. With a highly adept and motivated team—backed by active, courageous, and visionary leaders—all things are possible.

Structuring the Team for Success

There are three considerations when designing a business architecture team. The first is related to the **organizational structure**. This entails determining where the business architecture team will report and how key partnerships will be maintained (**positioning**), as well as how business architects will be distributed across the organization and how they will collaborate with each other (**distribution**).

The second design consideration is related to the **team**. This includes determining how diversity will be built into the team (**composition**), how many business architects will be needed (**size**), and how business architects will be discovered and developed (**sourcing**).

The last design consideration is related to the **role**. This includes establishing how the business architect role will be defined (**role definition**), which skills and abilities are needed in business architects (**competencies**), and the options that will exist for business architects to advance within the organization (**career path**).

Where should a business architecture team be positioned?

As stated earlier, with the evolution of contemporary business architecture practice, more and more business architecture teams are reporting to business leaders, which has directly contributed to their success. It gives business architects more access to and acceptance from the business. Business architecture teams often report to business leader who is responsible for strategy, transformation, innovation, and/or planning or a C-Level executive. Ideally, a business architecture team will report to a business leader that best aligns with the value proposition of business architecture for the organization. For example, if the focus of an organization's business architecture practice is enabling enterprise-wide business transformation, then the team should report to a leader within a strategy or transformation department. If the value proposition is entirely focused on cost or operational effectiveness, then a CFO or COO may be an ideal leader.

As a practical note, the business leaders referenced here are those who are ultimately accountable for the business architecture practice within the organization. However, there may be other leadership levels in between. For example, business architecture teams frequently report directly to a business architecture director or equivalent role.

Since business architecture is still part of the enterprise architecture umbrella, the business architecture and IT architecture leaders must be closely aligned, even if they report up to entirely different leadership chains. Having dual leadership for the enterprise architecture function (assuming the IT architects report to a single leader) can work surprisingly well when the business and IT architecture team leaders work together jointly on direction, plans, priorities, communications, knowledgebase, and practices. Close partnership at the leadership level will cascade down to the individual business and IT architects.

Another common option is for business architects to report to an enterprise architecture leader. This positioning leads to a more cohesive and effective enterprise architecture function. Enterprise architecture leaders frequently report within the IT department, but if they report to a leader within the business or a neutral area, this may help to increase the success for both business and enterprise architecture overall.

Regardless of where a business architecture team reports though, they can succeed by thinking, speaking, and acting *business* and building a business-owned business architecture in alignment with principles.

How should business architects be distributed across an organization?

With the overall anchor established for business architecture within the business or IT, the next key decision is how business architects will be distributed across an organization, especially as the team grows over time. There are a few common structures for business architecture teams: centralized, decentralized, or a hybrid. While the centralized and hybrid options tend to be the most effective, the decentralized option can also be effective if there is strong virtual coordination across all business architects.

Centralized, Hybrid, and Decentralized Team Structures

A **centralized team structure** facilitates closer business architect collaboration and support and keeps the structure simple. It is especially beneficial for new business architecture teams that are trying to build a strong and consistent foundation as well as more mature teams where it is advantageous to report one leader.

As a business architecture team grows and matures, it may shift from a centralized team structure to a **hybrid team structure**. In this case, some business architects report to a central leader while one or more business architects report to a leader within each business unit or domain. This not only allows for full coverage of business architecture demand across an organization, but it can greatly accelerate the integration and buy-in for business architecture within the individual business units.

In addition, a hybrid structure allows business architecture to support change initiatives with a greater scope and complexity because business architects can work together. For example, a business architect on the central team may take responsibility for architecting a horizontal domain related to a set of customer-facing capabilities that crosses business units while working with the appropriate business unit business architects to define the specifics within their area.

With a hybrid structure, the central business architecture team also serves as a Center of Excellence (COE) to facilitate, steward, and govern the business architecture knowledgebase and practice for all business architects. This includes establishing, socializing, and measuring the overall value proposition of business architecture for the organization; managing the knowledgebase; defining the role, education curriculum, methodology, and support structure for practitioners; governing the business architecture; and integrating with other disciplines and frameworks. The hybrid structure facilitates a cohesive virtual community that includes all business architects, business leaders and their team members, IT architects, and partnering roles from other disciplines and teams.

A **decentralized team structure** may be employed when there are structural or cultural constraints. For example, it may be used when architects must work across multiple legal entities or where there is a strong bias that business architects should report to business units.

Figure 5.1 shows a best practice hybrid business architecture team structure. The central team, inclusive of the CoE, reports to a business leader (Business Strategy and Transformation Head). Business architects may report to the central team or within individual business units. The central team builds key partnerships across business and technology.

Visit www.StrategyintoReality.com to download diagrams and other valuable resources.

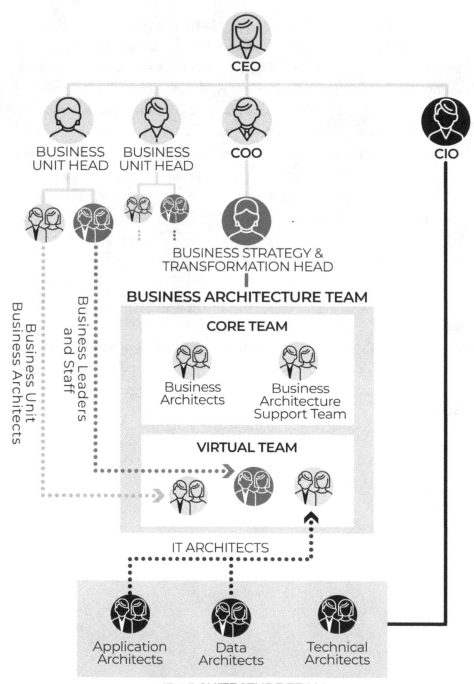

CEO

BUSINESS UNIT HEAD

BUSINESS UNIT HEAD

COO

CIO

BUSINESS STRATEGY & TRANSFORMATION HEAD

BUSINESS ARCHITECTURE TEAM

CORE TEAM

Business Architects

Business Architecture Support Team

VIRTUAL TEAM

Business Unit Business Architects

Business Leaders and Staff

IT ARCHITECTS

Application Architects

Data Architects

Technical Architects

IT ARCHITECTURE TEAM

Figure 5.1: A Best Practice Business Architecture Team Structure

The Two Immutable Principles of a Business Architecture Practice

Regardless of how business architects are distributed across an organization, a cohesive business architecture practice can thrive if the two immutable principles are followed: *there should be one shared business architecture for an organization and one shared business architecture methodology for practitioners.* This will facilitate an enterprise view and mindset and ensure that architects have a common education and frame of reference.

Business architecture teams have achieved incredible outcomes with entirely virtual coordination across business units and even across legal boundaries such as different operating companies. What is needed most is commitment and accountability, a desire to collaborate, and a vision for business architecture to serve the greater good that transcends organizational boundaries.

Other Business Architecture Team Deployment Options

The centralized, decentralized, and hybrid structures describe ways to distribute business architects as part of a dedicated business architecture practice. However, as an organization's needs and understanding of business architecture evolve, and as the practice matures and becomes more embedded, even more creative structures may emerge. Consider, business architects may be deployed as part of a multi-disciplinary design team. This emerging structure may either be formed temporarily, such as where teams are created to deliver a specific capability, or permanently such as in a digital or mobile area. This structure emphasizes the business architect's role as part of strategy execution and enterprise design and allows them to be more closely integrated into the business. However, this can make it more difficult to ensure cohesiveness and consistency of the business architecture function.

In addition, business architecture responsibilities may be deployed as part of multiple people's roles. This concept may co-exist with one of the other business architect distribution options. In this case, business architecture responsibilities are performed not just by business architects, but by people in other roles as they utilize and refine the business architecture as part of their jobs. This structure allows business architecture to scale, be adopted, and permeate across an organization, though again, it may be more difficult to ensure cohesiveness and consistency of the function.

What is the right size for a business architecture team?

Most business architecture teams start with one, two, or a few people and then scale up over time. As a team scales, determining the ideal size and managing fluctuations to meet business architecture demand becomes important to plan for. *The right size for a business architecture team is driven by the size of the organization and the amount of organizational change that is in-flight or planned, which may evolve over time.* Consequently, there are three key variables that when added together can help to approximate the ideal number of business architects needed at any point in time, especially if the intention is to scale across the enterprise.

The first variable is the **number of business architects required to support overall change initiatives and usage scenarios**. For example, business architects may be assigned to support strategic priorities, transformations, acquisitions, or other usage scenarios on a part-time or full-time basis.

The second variable is the **number of business architects required to support business domains**. A domain could be defined vertically such as by business unit or horizontally such as by groups of related capabilities that span business units. A business architect may be assigned to cover one or more business domain, depending upon the scope of change and usage scenarios. A business domain may even require the support of multiple business architects.

The third variable is the **number of business architects required to support the practice**. As a business architecture team grows, it requires additional capacity to maintain the knowledgebase, hire and develop business architects, facilitate governance processes, and socialize and integrate the practice. Many organizations assign a team member(s) to focus on these activities versus spreading the responsibility across all business architects. In addition, there may be a need for non-business architect resources as well such for graphic design or tool support.

How can business architect capacity be supplemented?

Business architecture teams can be challenged with not having enough business architect resources at certain points in time. For example, this may occur as they are beginning their business architecture journey but do not yet have buy-in for more resources. Or, as business architecture starts to gain traction, the demand for engagement may outweigh the business architect resources available. Then again, there may be a temporary need to surge in business architect capacity to support a large, enterprise-wide business change initiative. Regardless of the reason, organizations have employed various clever strategies to scale up their capacity during times of need. These include:

Share business architecture resources. One strategy is to share business architecture resources. Shift business architects from their current focus area to one where additional capacity is needed. Don't let organizational boundaries get in the way because this is a win-win scenario. The area that needs help will get it and the business architect who fills in will get new understanding, experiences, and exposure.

Create a rotational program. Another strategy is to borrow resources from within the organization. Create a program to offer short-term business architecture opportunities (full-time or part-time) to people within the organization. A rotational program may even be formalized. These opportunities can be valuable to those who are aspiring to the role (e.g., business analysts) or to others who would like the exposure and experience (e.g., a businessperson who wants to increase their problem-solving skills or a technology person who wants to learn about the business).

Outsource aspects of the role. An additional strategy is to outsource aspects of the business architect role to other people. Make it very easy for others to contribute to or use the business architecture wherever possible (e.g., for impact assessments or heatmapping). Provide guidelines to ensure consistency and indicate when a business architect should be engaged. On the other hand, support resources can be used to offload administrative or lower-level activities so that business architects can focus on the highest value aspects of the role and engaging with others.

Leverage external resources. Finally, leverage external resources to supplement capacity. Creating an internship program is a great way to develop others who could potentially work for the organization someday as well as get some extra help. Be realistic about what an intern can do, but they can minimally take on some of the basic work so that business architects can focus on value added activities.

External consultants can be leveraged as well and bringing them onboard can sometimes be easier than hiring a new employee, especially if consulting can be obtained from a different budget than headcount. They can also bring new best practices and ideas to help develop the internal team.

When bringing on external resources, consider requiring them to be trained on and even certified in the methodology you use. For example, if your organization is leveraging the BIZBOK® Guide, consultants should have the Certified Business Architect® certification. This will ensure you share the same vocabulary and mental model around business architecture and that they are already up to speed and can perform the role effectively within your environment.

Furthermore, set clear expectations for how consultants will use the organization's business architecture knowledgebase and how they will interact with the business architecture team. Some organizations even define these types of expectations in their Requests for Proposal (RFP). One of the most detrimental things that can happen is when an external firm comes into an organization and brings their own capability map and methods that undermine the credibility and traction of the internal business architecture team. *Leverage the knowledge and capacity of external consultants strategically but build your business architecture capability for the long-term.*

How should a business architecture team be composed?

At first, it may seem that a business architecture team should be composed of all-in-one business architects. Individuals who can build the knowledgebase, architect a business transformation, and work with executives to inform strategy with brilliant ideas. Individuals who have deep technology expertise including hands-on coding, have knowledge of the entire organization and industry, have worked with all disciplines across strategy execution, who are politically savvy, influential, great story tellers, and create visualizations that will knock your socks off. While these unicorns do exist, experience has shown that *diversity is what makes a business architecture team the most valuable and scalable.*

A team comprised of varied individuals performs better because it can deliver a broader range of business scenarios, build relationships with different types of people, and solve problems more comprehensively. Business architects are also happier because they can leverage their strengths and do what they enjoy. Creating a diverse business architecture team should be an intentional goal. *Build your business architecture practice as a function, not just a role.*

One key area of diversity is in the **levels of team member knowledge and experience**. Individuals may have varied backgrounds ranging in the depth and breadth of their business architecture experience. This also gives business architects a career path and alleviates hiring and compensation demands. Another area of diversity is in **business architect focus area**. Team members can concentrate on different usage scenarios, business domains, complementary disciplines (e.g., customer experience design, organizational change management, or strategy), and aspects of the practice to which they contribute. Having different concentrations across a business architecture team allows business architects to explore their areas of interest while simultaneously helping the practice to meet demand and develop relationships with a wide group of people. An organization's business architect role and level definitions are often crafted to reflect this variation in knowledge and experience and focus areas.

In addition, the **personalities or personas** may vary across team members. Business architects are naturally drawn to different aspects of the role. For example, some individuals are outgoing and enjoy facilitation and relationship-building, while others prefer the more introspective and analytical activities such as building and leveraging the knowledgebase for insights. Some business architects enjoy socializing business architecture and its benefits, while others would prefer to perform the role once buy-in is in place.

What Do Business Architects Do?

Business architects are business professionals who facilitate the development and usage of business architecture to enable effective strategy execution, decision-making, and macro-level design for their organization and the ecosystem in which it operates. *The business architect role is a business-focused and strategic role.*

Business architects have responsibilities related to the three key aspects of a business architecture practice. First and foremost, they facilitate the application of business architecture for business value. In support of this, they also build and maintain the business architecture knowledgebase, and provide input and assistance to the internal business architecture practice.

Business architects are not only architects, but also leaders, catalysts, and change agents. They often take responsibility for the business direction that they translate and see it through, serving as a guide and change leader to ensure understanding, alignment, delivery, and adoption.

How is the business architect role and career path defined?

At the time of publication for this book, an industry standard business architect job description does not exist. However, organizations define business architect roles that are often themed along the same lines. A common progression of roles starts with the **business architect**, followed by the **senior business architect**, followed by **lead business architect** that is the most experienced. Organizations may create multiple levels within each of these roles as well. These roles should be formalized through the human resources department for purposes of hiring, compensation, and performance management, as well as to give them credence within the organization.

When an organization is beginning to establish business architecture, they may formalize just one role. A good place to start is with the senior business architect role, which leaves room for growth and promotion. The lead business architect role may also be formalized first. Either way, it is important to ensure that the people within these roles are entirely qualified at that level because it establishes a precedence and speaks volumes to others in the organization about the abilities of a business architect at each level. As an organization matures around business architecture, additional roles and levels within roles will become more relevant. Some organizations may later add one more role for a **business architect fellow** or equivalent, which denotes additional levels of industry and thought leadership and contribution. Furthermore, some organizations will create a role for a **chief business architect** that is responsible for the entire scope of an organization's business architecture.

There is elegance in the logical progression of the business architect roles. They not only build a diverse team, but also make hiring more feasible and provide a clear development and career path for business architects. Business architects can learn the business, the discipline of business architecture, and other foundational skills as they progress towards the more experienced business architect roles.

Each business architect role includes some responsibilities related to each of the three key aspects of a business architecture practice, with the most emphasis on building and applying business architecture to usage scenarios. There are often some responsibilities related to supporting practice activities as well. In addition, business architect roles may vary by the scope of business architecture responsibility, focus areas, level of strategic involvement, and mentoring or management responsibility.

Scope of business architecture responsibility. As it pertains to scope of responsibility, a business architect may be responsible for architecting at the initiative level, the business unit or domain level, or across business units or domains, such as for a set of capabilities. Business architects, senior business architects, and lead business architects may be assigned to any of these scopes. If a chief business architect exists, he or she would be responsible for the scope of the entire enterprise.

Focus area. As discussed earlier, business architects may have different focus areas or usage scenarios upon which they concentrate. Senior business architects and lead business architects are typically assigned to lead the largest and most challenging strategic efforts across business units or the enterprise. *The most experienced business architects think strategically and architecturally to facilitate strategy execution and solve complex problems, leveraging business architecture as the foundation, blended seamlessly with many other approaches and abilities.*

Level of strategic involvement. Senior business architects and lead business architects typically have the highest level of involvement in strategic activities, such as informing strategy formulation or advising business and technology leaders. This is not only a function of experience, but also of reputation, respect, and relationships that are earned over time to have this very special role and seat at the table.

Mentoring and management responsibility. Additionally, business architects may have varying levels of mentoring and/or management responsibility. Mentoring and apprenticeship is key to developing a solid, consistent business architecture team. Business architects should intentionally mentor each other on an ongoing basis. The level of mentoring responsibility is greater for senior business architects and lead business architects, where senior business architects mentor business architects and lead business architects mentor senior (and all) business architects. From a management perspective, in most organizations business architects report to a non-business architect leader(s). However, there are cases where business architects report to more senior business architects.

Moreover, consider the appropriate positioning and organizational context when establishing the business architect role. The business architect role should be designated at a level high enough for those individuals to be respected and involved in strategic activities. In addition, the business and IT architect roles should have a level of parity. For example, the top business architect and IT architect roles should be at the same level, with neither higher than the other.

What does a business architecture practice director do?

Business architecture practice directors should have a solid understanding of business architecture and may even have been practitioners themselves. However, their responsibilities do differ from the day-to-day business architect role.

Business architecture practice directors lead the business architecture practice and manage the business architects and other resources who report to them. They work with leaders and the team to define the business architecture's value proposition for the organization and then lead the people and necessary activities to achieve it. They are accountable for building and managing all the components of a business architecture practice, including the knowledgebase and all the supporting infrastructure. They focus on the *marketecture* for the business architecture practice, continually socializing and building advocacy as well as identifying new opportunities for business architecture to engage throughout the organization. They ensure the business architect work force is appropriately skilled, staffed, allocated, and cared for.

Business architecture practice directors are very special people. In fact, they are arguably the most important and irreplaceable resource within the entire business architecture team. They are the leader, cheerleader, and rock for the practice. When executive leaders move on, the business architecture practice director carries the vision forward and ensures continuity. When there is turbulence from organizational change or politics, the business architecture practice director manages those dynamics and insulates the team so they can keep working productively. The team will rise to the business architecture practice director's vision, inspiration, expectations, and example.

A business architecture practice director may have sole responsibility for the business architecture practice, or their role may be combined with other practices or responsibilities. For example, an enterprise architecture leader will focus on the business and IT architecture practices. Or, a practice director may be responsible for another practice(s), such as strategy and architecture, or business architecture and process, or business architecture and business analysis or enterprise design including business architecture, customer experience design, service design, and potentially others.

What deliverables do business architects create?

The business architecture deliverables to be created depend on the specific usage scenario for which business architecture is being leveraged. A prescriptive set of business architecture deliverables does not exist for the discipline overall. *However, organizations should define key deliverables for relevant usage scenarios within their own internal playbooks.* For example, heatmaps of business direction and planned spend may be created to support project portfolio investment decision-making. Or, target architectures and strategic roadmaps may be created when translating a large change into action, such as a new strategy or transformation.

What is most important is not to focus on creating deliverables, but rather to focus on delivering value. In fact, embodying this value-first mindset versus a deliverable-focused one is what distinguishes successful business architecture teams from non-successful ones.

In Search of Greatness: How to Find or Be a Great Business Architect

With an understanding of what business architects do, the next consideration is what they need to be successful. What differentiates business architects and enables them to succeed lies in a specialized set of **knowledge**, **experience**, **abilities (competencies)**, and **characteristics** that define who they are and how they show up. Their success is also undoubtedly underpinned by their internal organizational conditions as well. For example, business architects need leader support, ongoing investment in their personal development, and resources to be effective, such as automated tools. When business architects are supported and successful, more business value can be delivered.

The business architect role is not just rewarding in its own right, but also provides a valuable jumping off point to transition into other roles, in any type or size of organization. Whether an individual chooses to keep advancing as an architect or pivot to another path, their time spent in the business architect role will be delightfully challenging and meaningful.

What competencies do business architects need?

Competencies are the knowledge, skills, abilities, or other characteristics that a business architect needs to perform the role effectively and advance their career to the next level. Competencies can be measured and observed. An individual may develop their competencies through formal education, work experience, mentoring, or a combination of sources. Competencies also form the basis for hiring criteria, education programs, and consistent, methodical performance assessment of business architects.

An organization should create and utilize a formal business architecture competency model, especially as the business architecture team grows. The business architecture competency model can be used alongside or combined with any existing organizational competency models to provide the business architecture-specific lens.

To create a competency model, first identify the applicable competencies and organize them into categories. Inspiration for competencies and categories may be drawn from Table 5.1 below, the BIZBOK® Guide, SFIA (Skills Framework for the Information Age), and other sources. Be discerning and limit the number of required competencies and categories to the absolute minimum or the model can become unwieldy and ineffective. Second, align the business architect roles with competency expectations. The competency expectations for each role may be indicated with a binary yes or no, or a formal scale with defined performance levels from 1 through 5. Some competency expectations may apply uniformly for all roles, while the expectations for others may increase for the more experienced business architect roles.

Table 5.1 reflects some key competencies for business architects, organized into three distinct categories. The first category, **business architecture mapping and architecting**, encompasses many of the essential competencies that set business architects apart. For example, it includes competencies for abstracting concepts, developing business architecture content and blueprints, and framing business situations through the architecture to provide context. It also includes the robust competencies of assessing and enhancing the business architecture (e.g., identifying streamlining or reuse opportunities or developing a target architecture for a strategy), as well as defining and sequencing initiatives.

The **cognitive** category includes competencies related to how business architects think. This includes big picture thinking and formal systems thinking, strategic thinking, design thinking, problem solving, and creative thinking.

Lastly, the **communication and relating** category describes the competencies necessary for communicating, collaborating, and influencing others. The **behavioral** sub-category includes competencies important for an individual to embody, including adaptability, emotional intelligence, accountability, humility, and candor. The **group dynamics** sub-category includes competencies for working with others including different aspects of communications, collaboration, facilitation, influence, leadership, and relationship building.

Visit www.StrategyintoReality.com to download diagrams and other valuable resources.

Competency Category	Description	Competencies
Business Architecture Mapping and Architecting Competencies	Representing and evolving the business architecture structure of an organization and its ecosystem.	**Strategic Thinking** ✓ Information rationalization, abstraction, analysis, and synthesis ✓ Business architecture mapping and blueprinting* ✓ Business context creation and framing* ✓ Business architecture analysis and enhancement* ✓ Initiative definition and roadmapping * Includes relationships to the operating model and related disciplines
Cognitive Competencies	Analyzing, designing, and problem solving in various business opportunity and challenge scenarios.	**Strategic Thinking** ✓ Systems thinking ✓ Design thinking ✓ Analytical thinking ✓ Problem solving ✓ Creativity and innovation

Competency Category	Description	Competencies
Communicating and Relating Competencies	Communicating, collaborating, and influencing others towards understanding and change.	**Behavioral** ✓ Adaptability ✓ Emotional intelligence ✓ Accountability ✓ Humility ✓ Candor **Group Dynamics** ✓ Written and verbal communication ✓ Visualization ✓ Storytelling ✓ Collaboration ✓ Facilitation ✓ Influence ✓ Leadership ✓ Relationship building

Table 5.1: Key Competencies for Business Architects

Beyond the competency expectations for each role, individual business architects may want to emphasize certain competencies over others to help them with their specific areas of focus and passion. For example, business architects who concentrate on the business architecture knowledgebase will especially want to hone their business architecture mapping and architecting competencies. Business architects who help to socialize business architecture and build organizational buy-in will need especially sharp communicating and relating competencies. Furthermore, when business architects are applying business architecture in any number of business scenarios, they will need to draw on all three categories of competencies.

Do business architects need to be subject matter experts?

A business architect is a specialized practitioner and is not intended to be a subject matter expert. They should, however, have access ongoing to and a close relationship with business subject matter experts. Part of what makes business architects so valuable is their unique and objective thought process and facilitation. In fact, business architects who are also subject matter experts in their focus area can become biased, overlook things, make assumptions, and miss opportunities to build collaborative engagement.

On the other hand, a business architect can certainly be more effective if they have strong knowledge of the industry and business domain in which they are working. This becomes especially important for informing and translating business direction. *This underscores the importance of an organization building its internal business architect capacity versus outsourcing it.*

In some organizations, business architects need to be recognized as subject matter experts to earn the credibility to perform in the role. Ultimately each organization needs to do what makes the best sense for its needs and dynamics, especially when introducing the business architecture discipline. However, once an individual moves into a business architect role, they should focus on performing the role full-time and work alongside other business subject matter experts as needed. When hiring business architects, remain open-minded on candidates because requiring depth in a specific domain of expertise can make recruiting an already sought-after resource even more challenging to find.

What does a great business architect need to know and do?

Beyond the development of specific competencies, there is knowledge and experience that is invaluable for business architects to have. *Business architects should chart their own course and do so with intention.* They should consider **what kind of business architect they want to be**—leadership-oriented, strategy-oriented, architecture- and design-oriented, technology-oriented, something else? They should consider what interests them and **where they want to develop complementary skills**. Do they want to cross-train in strategy, human-centered design, organization design, organizational change management, application or data architecture, something else? A successful business architect *majors* in business architecture, but *minors* in other disciplines and frameworks. Finally, they should consider **their ideal career path**—is business architecture a long-term career or part of a bigger journey?

As mentioned previously, the most adept business architects think strategically and architecturally to facilitate strategy execution and solve complex problems, leveraging business architecture as the foundation, blended seamlessly with many other approaches and abilities. *This means that great business architects continually develop and leverage a wide range of knowledge and experiences—much of it beyond the realm of business architecture.*

Key Areas of Knowledge for Business Architects

Here are a few key areas of knowledge for business architects, provided as an aspirational list to work towards over time—*not* a requirement for a business architect on day one. This list is just a starting point because individuals should always explore topics that are most relevant to their work and passions.

How business works. Business architects need to have a solid understanding of how organizations function and are structured. This is the type of knowledge that one would gain in business school.

Business models and strategy. Business architects can benefit greatly from studying how to structure and evolve business models and formulate strategies to win. This is essential to becoming a strategic trusted advisor and to effectively translating strategy. Business architects also need to continually stay on top of trends and evolution for the business landscape relevant to their organization.

How the organization executes strategy. Business architects should have solid working knowledge of how *their* organization works from strategy to execution. This minimally includes an understanding of the inner workings of the strategy development, investment, planning, and solution development processes.

Complementary disciplines. It is helpful for business architects to have a basic knowledge of every complementary discipline with which business architecture integrates. They may choose to develop deeper competency in some, but understanding the goals, domains, artifacts, and activities of each related discipline can go a long way to facilitate partnership and integration.

Technical mastery. Business architects should have some degree of technical mastery. This includes an understanding of how technology is designed, developed, and deployed. Knowledge of technology and its possibilities is not only essential for architecting, but also to guide the business on leveraging technology strategically.

Key Areas of Experience for Business Architects

Here are some of the top experiences to aspire to that make rock solid business architects. There is no substitute for doing, so these opportunities are worth seeking out or creating over time.

Build a business architecture baseline. First and foremost, business architects should build a business architecture baseline for the entire scope of an organization. This includes facilitating a cross-functional group of business representatives to create a capability map, a set of value streams, and cross-mapping the capabilities to value streams. Furthermore, business architects should *live with* and evolve the baseline they have created for a substantial amount of time to see how it is actually consumed by people and used for value. Over time, business architects should also gain experience in capturing the extended domains of business architecture and the domains from other disciplines and creating the relevant cross-mappings.

Architect a large change initiative. Business architects should participate in architecting a large change initiative from end-to-end. This is often a breakthrough point for business architects because it brings everything together, and it turns conceptual ideas into reality. They experience firsthand what it really means to take high-level business direction into execution, using business architecture to make the translation. They go deeper into the business operations and technology. They learn the interplay of their hard skills and soft skills, and how to work with executives and the ecosystem of other teams. They also learn what it means to lead and advocate for a significant organizational change.

Gain direct experience across strategy execution. It is not enough just to know how their organization works from strategy to execution, but business architects should gain direct experience with as much of it as possible. Using business architecture for portfolio management and initiative planning is one of the most valuable experiences to strive for. This is frequently an area of relevance and opportunity—and for which business architecture is well-suited.

Architect a smaller organization. Business architects can greatly benefit from architecting a new business or non-profit organization or helping one to scale. The strategic thinking, innovation, and urgency within a smaller organization puts an individual's business architecture skills to the test in a different way, especially if they work in a corporate environment. Creating a business model and business architecture for a smaller organization also makes the concepts more tangible where they can otherwise seem lofty and hard to relate to within a large corporate context.

Expand life experience. Beyond professional experiences, life experiences also make great business architects. While they may have nothing to do with business architecture, these experiences can challenge us in new ways, push our boundaries, broaden our perspectives, give us more confidence, help us learn patience, and make us better humans. So, take a sabbatical, go on a trek, or volunteer for a cause that stirs you. It all matters.

What education does a business architect require?

While a bachelor's degree is generally recognized as a minimum qualification for business architects (with an MBA or other master's degree as preferred or optional), a wide variety of concentrations have proven to be effective. Business architects can come from anywhere. Business architects have degrees in business, organization development, information technology, data science, engineering, science, math, history, psychology, performing arts, and too many others to mention.

Arguably though, **specialized academic programs** are needed for business architecture. This is especially important for the discipline to become recognized and established as a profession, like the medical or legal professions. Though awareness is increasing, there are currently a small number of universities that view business architecture as a strategic discipline and facilitator of strategy execution.[19]

Professional training is a cornerstone of a business architect's development—especially at this juncture while the discipline is emerging—to learn the theory and practice of business architecture from experienced professionals. For business architects, learning is an ongoing journey. It is best to start with training on the foundational concepts and then keep building upon them with more expansive and refined concepts, interaction with other disciplines, and complementary topics. Training should include both theory and hands-on application. **Business architecture community interaction** both within an organization as well as with the external global and local community is also essential for a business architect's ongoing learning and growth.

Business architecture education is not just for practitioners though. Executives should have a base understanding of the discipline and its value as should key partners from other disciplines such as strategy, planning, human-centered design, organization design, business process management, and business analysis.

Is business architecture certification important?

Certification alone does not make a great business architect, but it is an important part of their foundation. The level 1 Certified Business Architect® (CBA®) certification from the Business Architecture Guild® is based on the BIZBOK® Guide, making it the most business-oriented certification that is also based on an authoritative source and co-created by the global business architecture community. Additional business architecture certifications are available from other organizations. Some of those organizations view the CBA® as being a complementary certification for the business architecture specialization while others have created their own based on methodologies other than the globally agreed upon body of knowledge.

Benefits for individuals. Certification can help individual business architects solidify and demonstrate their business architecture knowledge. It can also serve as a differentiator to increase marketability for new job opportunities. Some organizations now require CBA® certification or strongly prefer it.

Benefits for organizations. Organizations can leverage business architecture certification to define job descriptions, evaluate candidates, and assess business architect performance more consistently. Certification is an effective way to ensure that all business architects on the team share a common frame of reference and to the same depth. It accelerates the time for a business architect to become productive and start delivering value. Some organizations set goals for business architecture team members to become certified and support them in their preparation. This support for employee development can even increase retention of valuable business architect resources.

Benefits for the discipline. From a global business architecture perspective, certification helps demonstrate the growth, strength, and relevancy of the discipline. The stronger the discipline becomes, the stronger the position of each individual business architect, so there is even an argument to becoming certified for the greater good.

What makes a business architect successful?

The success of a business architect lies not just in what they know and do, but in how they show up. Working in ways that are engaging, contemporary, and relevant help business architects get invited to the right strategic tables to deliver the value proposition for which business architecture is intended. Effective engagement also helps business architects perform in their roles, such as when facilitating people toward a common vision and understanding.

Below are a few characteristics that encapsulate how successful business architecture practitioners think and act.

Value-driven. Successful business architects focus on business value, outcomes, and results for their organizations and its customers. This means that the architecture, the models, the deliverables, the governance, and the other aspects of the practice are simply a means to the end—not an end in themselves.

Business-minded. Successful business architects emphasize the *business* in business architecture. They always frame conversations, opportunities, challenges, and solutions within the bigger-picture business context. They are respected as problem solvers and over time become trusted advisors.

Enterprise advocates. Successful business architects are champions for the enterprise. No one gave them the role, they just started doing it because they cared, and it was the right thing to do. They relentlessly seek to create more effective end-to-end strategy execution and facilitate cross-business unit collaboration. They are stewards of enterprise direction, decision making, resources, and common language.

Bridge builders. Successful business architects know that it takes an ecosystem of teams to translate strategy into action and run an organization successfully. While they perform unique responsibilities as business architects, they also build close partnerships with others because they realize their own success—and the success of the enterprise—depends on making *other people* successful.

Visualizers and storytellers. Successful business architects are masters at simplifying, visualizing, and explaining complex concepts and showing new connections. They leverage the power of visual techniques such as visual thinking, graphic recording, and graphic facilitation, to bring people together and incite action. They are storytellers and change agents for new ideas.

Interactive co-creators. Successful business architects are hands-on and interactive. They facilitate using tactile and engaging techniques. They co-create outcomes together with business stakeholders and partners. They bring fun to the work.

Iterative and adaptive. After the business architecture baseline is established, successful business architects build just enough business architecture, just in time to support the business scenario that they are focused on. They deliver results quickly and iteratively and adapt their approaches and outputs to the needs of each specific situation.

Business architecture teams should develop their own set of business architecture imperatives that describe how business architects think, act, and are perceived by others. Recognize team members when they exhibit these characteristics and hold them accountable when they do not. Use the imperatives to bring new team members up to speed. Show up with wow.

How do we find great business architects?

Experienced business architects are in high demand, and the fact that business architecture is still an emerging discipline makes the pool of practitioners even smaller. This means that finding great business architects can require some creativity. It also means that making great business architects is just as important. Invest in building a strong team of practitioners—and then hold onto your precious resources.

Here are a few places to find great business architects. It is wise to consider the entire range of sourcing options, which not only increases the available pool of talent but creates a more diverse business architecture team as well.

Hire a business architect. Business architects can be sourced externally or internally. For example, an experienced business architect can be hired who has either worked as a business architect within another organization or in a consulting role. An infusion of external expertise can help accelerate a business architecture practice and bring fresh ideas, even if it takes a new team member some time to learn the environment and build relationships.

Hire a business person from within the organization. Another option is to hire a business person from within the organization and train them on business architecture. The right person can come from any business unit or an area such as strategy, product, planning, or transformation, or even any related discipline, so stay open-minded. They will bring a strong business mindset to the business architect role, which is essential for success. Additionally, they can also help to create tighter integration with and adoption by the business due to their existing relationships and credibility.

Hire a technology person from within the organization. Yet another option is to hire a person from within the organization with a technology, architecture, or analyst background and train them on the business and the business architecture. They can bring a strong technological perspective to business conversations and help build strong ties with technology teams due to their existing relationships and credibility.

To identify **internal talent**, always keep an eye open for potential business architects throughout the organization. They are often readily identifiable through their unique characteristics. For example, they will be the person in the meeting who is asking *why* and who readily sees the patterns and connections.

To identify **external talent**, leverage professional sources such as LinkedIn as well as specialized job boards where available. Make sure to have honest conversations with candidates about their understanding of and experience with business architecture though, because a broad range of interpretation and practice still exists. However, one of the best ways to find star talent is through authentic networking and relationship-building at business architecture (or complementary) events and communities.

How do we develop great business architects?

We must empower business architects and unlock their unique talents. It starts with recognizing the value of the business architecture discipline and role, investing in practitioners, and allowing them to do their jobs. While business architects should take responsibility for driving their own careers, leaders should ensure they have the structures, resources, and conditions to be successful. Here are the essentials.

Support business architecture training. Support business architects in taking foundational business architecture training as soon as they move into the role and support additional training and coaching on an ongoing basis. In addition, support membership to professional organizations and community events throughout their career. Since business architecture is a new concept to many people, there can be some hesitancy to invest. However, an investment in good training and some hands-on external assistance in the beginning goes a long way to accelerate a business architect's career and the practice itself, versus the all-too-common alternative of requiring a new architect to learn by putting the pieces together through their own research project. This approach can also lead to a practice getting off track, which can be highly time consuming to fix later or even lead to the eventual failure of the team.

Formalize a training curriculum. As a business architecture team grows, create a formal education curriculum and learning paths. The curriculum may be comprised of formal training, sourced internally and/or externally, along with any number of informal resources including webinars, videos, podcasts, books, articles, and other resources. The content within the curriculum should directly support and align with the organization's business architecture competency model. This way business architects can identify applicable resources to address any of the competencies they would like to strengthen.

Formalize a mentoring program. Develop a robust culture of mentoring. Business architecture is best learned not just through training, but also mentoring and apprenticeship. Create a formal mentoring program where business architects mentor each other right from the start. This is critical to developing competent and consistent business architects. Mentoring approaches can include one-on-one relationships and group sharing sessions and may even include mentors outside of the business architecture team, such as business leaders who mentor business architects for business acumen. Incorporate mentoring work into development plans and track results.

Cultivate opportunities for leveraging business architecture. Business architects need opportunities to apply the concepts in practice, even if informally. There is of course no better way to learn—or prove out the discipline—than through action. Leaders are crucial to help identify or create these opportunities, especially in the beginning.

Formalize business architecture performance management. Be deliberate about development. If necessary, create an additional layer on top of an organization's performance management process. Create a business architect scorecard, directly based on the competency model. Business architects can create their own development plans to track goals, competency development areas, and progress. Development areas may be addressed by training, mentoring, and hands-on experience.

Facilitate community. Provide support for the business architecture community and facilitate collaboration. Community is absolutely essential for business architecture because the discipline is relatively new and continually expanding. In addition, the role can be demanding—intellectually, politically, and emotionally—especially for practitioners who work on their own in different areas of an organization. Providing community support includes the basics, such as communicating about the practice and helping to onboard new business architects as well as providing ongoing guidance related to methods and approaches. It also includes facilitating sharing and exchange around success stories, approaches, and examples as well as facilitating collaboration across architecture efforts. Business architects should also actively engage in their local and global communities wherever possible to learn, stay up to date, and give back.

Create conditions for business architect success. Even the most highly competent practitioners still need to have an effective environment to fully thrive. Hire the best people for the role, formally name them in the role, assign them responsibilities at a strategic and enterprise level, provide them the resources they need, and empower them to act. Particularly in the beginning of a new practice, actions speak louder than words. The people in the role and how they perform it will demonstrate to the organization what business architecture is and is not.

In addition, the role that the business architecture practice director and executive leaders play to advocate for business architecture and create demand cannot be understated. This includes helping others in the organization understand the vision for business architecture and strategy execution, building advocates and adoption, and identifying opportunities for business architecture to help, especially in the beginning.

What can business architects do after they have mastered the discipline?

Once a business architect has truly mastered the role and reached a high level of competency, there are many possible career path options they can pursue. A successful business architect can shift their career in the direction they desire, either making the business architect role a long-term career choice or a step in a larger journey.

Working as a business architect provides an opportunity to gain the knowledge, skills, and exposure that can be highly beneficial for advancement. A business architect acquires a solid understanding of their organization from end-to-end, including an awareness of how it creates value and how business direction is executed. They also have opportunities to accomplish significant and visible achievements by leading and architecting strategic efforts and serving as trusted advisors. Business architects also develop valuable relationships across an organization and knowledge of how to work within the culture.

The most straight forward path for a successful business architect is to **continue specializing in business architecture**. They may continue to advance their business architecture career within their own organization or move to another one for a new challenge. Some business architects may choose to continue architecting increasingly large and complex change initiatives while others may move into the business architecture practice director role so they can start or lead a practice.

Another possible path for a successful business architect is to **move into a business or technology leadership or practitioner role** within their organization or another one. Business architects have gone on to hold a wide variety of positions such as being leaders for a business unit, a product, a technology team, and many more. They have also moved into roles as leaders or practitioners within other functions or disciplines such as strategy, innovation, planning, human-centered design, design thinking, IT architecture, and others.

A successful business architect can also transition their skills and experience into a **completely different career**. For example, they could become a management consultant or work with a startup organization.

These paths are only a sample of what is possible. With all the options that are available and that can be invented, business architects should take ownership of their careers and be intentional about how they develop themselves. *And, no matter where a business architect decides to take their career and life path, the best thing they can do is to take their business architecture roots with them.* Sometimes it is the leader or practitioner in a non-business architect role who can be the best champion for the discipline when they advocate for and weave business architecture seamlessly into their area of responsibility.

6

Building an Internal Business Architecture Practice

Once business architecture gains enough traction and acceptance within an organization, it becomes important to formalize the practice. While applying business architecture to deliver value is top priority, building a solid practice provides the long-term ability to scale and meet the demand for business architecture across the organization—with quality and consistency.

The concept of a business architecture practice is simply a way to refer to the intentional collection of activities performed to achieve the defined mission for business architecture within an organization. This includes activities such as managing and governing the business architecture content, structuring and supporting the team, managing architecture methods and guidance, and facilitating organizational integration and change management. Formalizing business architecture is akin to establishing a new department within an organization. It also shares some characteristics with building a startup as well and it can be helpful to think about it in these terms. For example, formalizing a practice requires crafting the business architecture offering and matching it to the right audience and needs, creating demand and buy-in, and developing and scaling the team's ability to deliver—much like a startup—but just within the context of an existing organization.

When the business architecture team is small, formalization is not as urgent. Coordination is simpler and a small team does not draw as much attention from others. However, as business architecture's footprint expands in terms of team size and engagement in strategic efforts, there will be an increasing need to have sharp clarity on the purpose of business architecture to articulate to others. In addition, the team will need a clear structure for interactions and decision-making, consistent methods for leveraging business architecture, and effective processes for managing demand and supporting the work.

The act of formalizing a business architecture practice makes it real and gives it credibility. It provides a focal point for sponsorship, leadership, advocacy, and socialization as well as managing resources and funding. Formalization helps to centralize business architecture governance, center of excellence-related activities, and interactions with other teams. It also provides accountability for the measurement and achievement of business architecture results against the defined value proposition and success metrics.

One of the greatest mistakes that business architecture teams make is not formalizing their practice. However, the symptoms often do not manifest until much further down the road when they show up as team dissatisfaction, inconsistency, and an inability to meet the organization's growing demand for business architecture. However, a deliberate and practical approach to establishing and maturing a business architecture practice over time meets both the short-term and long-term needs. Build just enough practice infrastructure just in time to support the current opportunities to deliver business value—and grow into the vision for business architecture within the organization one step at a time.

A Practical Approach to Establish and Mature Business Architecture

Establishing a successful, sustainable business architecture practice is a journey that takes time, especially within large organizations. There are some factors that can accelerate the process though.

The first accelerator is **direct business architecture experience**. This may come in the form of an experienced business architecture practice director and/or experienced business architects on the team. It can also come in the form of an experienced external expert who can serve as a continual guide on the journey.

The second accelerator is **organizational readiness**. An organization that has or is developing a certain enterprise mindset, values, and culture is more likely to embrace business architecture. For example, when people start to focus more on cross-business unit coordination, enterprise optimization, and bigger picture thinking, then business architecture is more likely to be welcomed.

The third accelerator is **organizational impetus for business architecture**. An organization with a clear, strong driver for business architecture (e.g., a large transformation or urgent regulatory challenge) will be able to achieve more acceptance and pull for the discipline because people are more receptive to trying something different. This accelerator is the most powerful one because it creates strong purpose, momentum, and investment that business architecture can naturally come alongside and help to make successful.

What is the path to build a successful business architecture practice?

While there can be many ways to achieve an outcome, a highly practical and proven path has emerged for establishing and maturing a practice with great success. While some aspects are intentionally organic, *the approach works*—especially at this juncture of business architecture's global recognition.

The approach, shown in Figure 6.1, is comprised of two tracks, and is entirely guided by delivering business value, and then developing just enough practice infrastructure just in time to support it. The **first track** focuses on building and maintaining the knowledgebase as well as applying business architecture for value. The **second track** focuses on establishing, maturing, and socializing the business architecture practice. This approach allows business architecture teams to simultaneously build their business architecture while they are using it for value—or as it is often referred to: building the plane while flying.

Visit www.StrategyintoReality.com to download diagrams and other valuable resources.

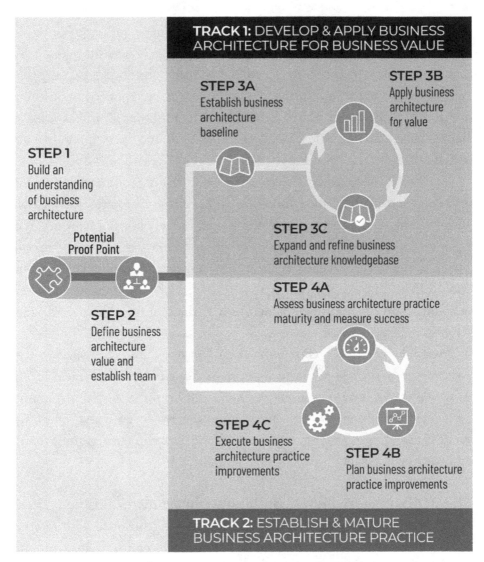

Figure 6.1: A Roadmap for Building a Business Architecture Practice

The Foundational Steps

The first two steps in the path provide the foundation for all subsequent ones. It is difficult to succeed when these steps are not executed well. In fact, the root causes of the challenges that mature business architecture teams often face can be traced back to a lack of understanding or clear articulation of value.

The path starts in **Step 1** with building an understanding of business architecture, including the scope of what it is and is not, how it can be used, and how it can be integrated into an organization. Some organizations need time to first prove the value and gain support for business architecture (the **proof point**) before moving onto Step 2. In this case, a light business architecture baseline may be built and then applied to an initial business usage scenario or two.

In **Step 2**, business architecture's value to the organization is defined and the team is established. Business architecture value must be clearly, simply, and consistently articulated to all stakeholders, including the business architecture team itself. It serves as a compass and guide for all business architecture decisions, from how to socialize to where the team should focus to the right people to hire. To establish the team, a charter is created, an organizational structure is defined and implemented, and team members are hired.

After the business architecture value and team are established in the first two steps, the rest of the path proceeds along two parallel tracks, both of which are important and related. At this point there should be organizational commitment to move forward in earnest—even if that commitment is just by one leader committing to one person focusing on business architecture full-time.

Track 1: Develop and Apply Business Architecture for Business Value

The first track is for developing and applying business architecture for business value. The loop within this track will continue indefinitely, though the applications for business architecture will likely grow in scope and complexity over time.

Within Track 1, **Step 3A** establishes the business architecture baseline including capabilities, value streams, and their cross-mapping. Of course, a greater scope of business architecture could be mapped up front, but this is not always feasible for some organizations for various reasons. Not to mention, putting the business architecture to real use will do more to test it and identify new needs than speculating about it from a theoretical mapping perspective.

Once the baseline is in place, it is quickly put into action in **Step 3B** to start providing business value, in alignment with the value proposition defined in Step 2. **Step 3C** continually refines the business architecture baseline and expands the business architecture content within the knowledgebase just enough, just in time. The expansion activities in Step 3C are typically prioritized based on the types of scenarios in which business architecture will be applied during Step 3B. *In other words, Step 3B for applying business architecture for value is the guiding light for the whole practice—it is the little cog that drives the entire machine.*

Track 2: Establish and Mature Business Architecture Practice

The second track is for establishing and maturing the business architecture practice. The loop in this track will also continue indefinitely, but once a practice reaches a state of desired maturity, the focus becomes more on continuous improvement versus large steps of advancement.

Within Track 2, there is a continual loop for maturing the business architecture practice that starts in **Step 4A** with an assessment of the current practice maturity and measurement of its success. Along with practice goal setting, this leads to **Step 4B**, which is where enhancements are planned for the practice over the next horizon. **Step 4C** implements those changes, which are measured again in Step 4A. This loop typically occurs as an annual planning process where the measurement, goal setting, and next horizon planning for the business architecture practice is done at the end of the year, and then practice enhancements are implemented during the following year. It is essential that the planned practice enhancements are aligned with how business architecture is being applied in Step 3B.

What are the components of a business architecture practice?

There are a finite set of components (i.e., activities to be performed) that are essential to any business architecture practice. They can be measured through a business architecture maturity model and serve as a checklist to be addressed over time as a practice grows. Each component should be considered during business architecture practice planning and roadmap development.

Business Architecture Components

The first set of components are related to an organization's business architecture itself. Every practice needs to create, organize, attribute, and cross-map the **business architecture content** for the organization. **Tools** are necessary to house the business architecture content and make it available for all business architects and consumers along with visualizations and analysis. Additional tools may be needed to support business architecture team needs, such as collaboration and facilitation.

Another necessary component is **governance**. This includes the governance structures, processes, and guidance (e.g., principles, standards, patterns, guidelines) to govern business architecture content from both a business perspective to set and align direction, as well as from an architectural perspective to ensure adherence to architectural guidance and direction. Finally, **architecture process, methods, and practices** provide the methodology that guides business architects on how to use business architecture consistently within the context of different business scenarios.

Business Architecture Practitioner Components

The second set of components are related to the business architecture practitioners and team. This includes the **team structure and roles**, which defines the business architect role(s), competencies, and team structure. Another component is **resources and staffing**, which develops the competency of business architects through training, mentoring, and performance management. It also includes staffing and assigning business architects appropriately across the organization to meet demand. The **education and mentoring** component establishes and manages formal and informal training and mentoring programs to build the competencies of business architects. This also includes customized training programs for executives and key partners within the organization. Finally, **community and support** provides business architects with the ongoing assistance they need in the role and facilitates communication and collaboration among the internal business architecture community.

Business Architecture Practice Components

The last set of components are related to the business architecture function. **Practice planning** includes the activities necessary to mature the practice as well as manage the team and work, just as any other department would require. The critical component of **organizational change management and adoption** ensures the business architecture discipline is understood, adopted, and funded across the organization, facilitated by intentional change management and relationship building activities. The **organizational alignment and integration** component integrates business architecture into all related functions, disciplines, processes, and frameworks across the organization. Finally, **measurement** keeps the business architecture team accountable to achieving the defined value proposition for the organization by measuring, tracking, and reporting on the business value delivered along with business architecture maturity.

What are the cornerstones that can accelerate a business architecture practice?

While every component is required at some point in time, there are four must-have artifacts that can drive the critical conversations that will accelerate the establishment of a business architecture practice. These artifacts include the charter, the role definition and team structure, the engagement model, and the practice roadmap. The business architecture team and its stakeholders are the consumers of these artifacts. These artifacts are always necessary and create essential clarity. They should ideally be created upfront as a new practice is being established, but they can always be created later, even for an established business architecture team. Of course, business architecture exists within the broader context of enterprise architecture, so these artifacts should be developed in partnership with other architecture disciplines.

Charter. The business architecture charter communicates the definition and intent of business architecture and the team. The very process of creating it can be a valuable way for a team to fully think through and come to consensus on the value they deliver to the organization and how they do it.

The charter is created through a series of conversations, the results of which are compiled into a document containing sections such as the definition of business architecture, the purpose and value of business architecture for the organization, measures of success, the scope of the team, the business architecture services offered by the team, principles, and the engagement model (another key artifact). The charter should be created during Step 2 of the roadmap defined in Figure 6.1.

Role definition and team structure. The role definition and team structure communicate the responsibilities and scope of business architects, as well as provide clarity on reporting relationships, decision-making, and team interactions. The role definition and team structure are typically created in partnership with the business architecture team, its leader(s), and a representative(s) from human resources. The results are documented through job descriptions and organizational diagrams, which are then formalized through human resources. The role definition and team structure should ideally be created during Step 2 of the roadmap defined in Figure 6.1 but may come later as part of the work in Track 2 when buy-in for the discipline has increased.

Engagement model. The business architecture engagement model communicates how the business architecture team will interact with other upstream and downstream teams. The engagement model is created collaboratively through conversations between the business architecture team and each partner team to confirm inputs and outputs, as well as any process or role adjustments needed on either side to ensure integration. The results are documented in an interaction diagram, which can take a variety of formats. This exercise not only creates clarity and efficiency for team interactions, but also helps to jump start relationships and can diffuse any concerns about the scope and role of business architecture. An initial engagement model should be created during Step 2 of the roadmap defined in Figure 6.1 but may be further detailed as part of the work in Track 2.

Practice roadmap. Lastly, the business architecture practice roadmap communicates an intentional plan for maturing the practice over time. The roadmap is defined primarily by the business architecture team, driven by the business architecture practice director. The practice work efforts are typically identified after performing an annual business architecture maturity assessment, which uncovers key gaps that need to be improved over the next year. Progress against the roadmap is reported to the accountable business architecture executive on a regular basis. The roadmap can also be used to justify resource needs and to align plans with other teams. A new business architecture practice roadmap is typically created every year during Step 4b of the roadmap defined in Figure 6.1. *More on the practice roadmap is discussed in the next section.*

How do we mature a business architecture practice within an organization?

The business architecture maturity assessment and business architecture practice roadmap are the two key tools that can help an organization to deliberately mature its practice over time. A **business architecture maturity assessment** measures the progress of an organization's business architecture practice against an objective business architecture maturity model standard. A **business architecture practice roadmap** reflects the specific enhancements to be made to achieve the target maturity levels for the next horizon.

A business architecture practice does not have to be mature before it can provide value to an organization. In fact, performing *any* business architecture activities can add value right from the start. For example, the collaborative sessions to establish an organization's capability map and business vocabulary can bring people together in new ways and give them new insights about the organization and what each other does. *However, as an organization's business architecture maturity increases, the value delivered most certainly increases.* This is a function of having more information in the business architecture knowledgebase, more skilled and recognized business architects, more involvement within the organization, and the ability to scale to meet all the demand for business architecture.

Assessing Business Architecture Maturity

The BIZBOK® Guide provides a Business Architecture Maturity Model® (BAMM®). Like other maturity models, the BAMM® includes a set of categories and levels. The categories cover the components described previously related to the business architecture, the practitioners and team, and the function. There are five levels of maturity in the BAMM®. As a practice progresses towards level 5, it becomes more strategic and embedded into the fabric of the organization.

Consider performing the maturity assessment towards the end of the year but with enough time to also put the practice enhancement roadmap in place before the next year begins. When getting started, it can be beneficial to have an independent expert do the first maturity assessment to help the team learn the tool and make sure to get an accurate baseline. From that point forward, the business architecture team can complete the assessment and engage a third-party expert periodically to make sure the results remain unbiased and aligned with the most recent thought. As a practice matures, the assessment can even be expanded to include the voice of partners (e.g., strategy team) and consumers (e.g., business leaders and representatives).

The Journey Towards Maturity Takes Time

When assessing business architecture maturity for each category, keep in mind that the *entire organization* is being assessed. For example, consider an organization with multiple different business units that operate disparately, each with their own capability map, role definition, and methods. No matter how mature any given business unit may be on its own, the overall maturity score for the organization would never exceed a level 2 (ad-hoc) because business architecture is meant to be practiced as an enterprise discipline.

As a result, the journey towards maturity can take time. A score of level 3 (reflecting definition, consistency, and standardization) or higher for any maturity category should be celebrated, considering the enterprise achievement that it signifies. It is important to be aggressive in setting maturity goals but also have realistic expectations on how quickly a large organization can feasibly advance.

Moving Into Action

In addition to the **current state maturity score**, two other scores can be defined for each category to inform planning. The first is a **long-term target maturity score**. Most organizations aim for a level 4 or 5 long-term maturity score across the categories. Not every organization targets a level 5 maturity for every category, but rather they balance their needs against the investment to achieve the target level of maturity. The second additional score is a **next horizon target maturity score**. This indicates the desired score for the next horizon, which is typically for the next year.

The gap between the current state maturity scores and next horizon maturity scores across the categories becomes the basis for the enhancement activities that are included on the business architecture practice roadmap. The business architecture practice roadmap should show the full picture, reflecting activities related to all three key aspects including developing business architecture, applying business architecture, and establishing, maturing, and socializing the practice. For communication purposes, the roadmap usually takes the form of a summarized visual, though a work plan may be created with more detailed activities if necessary.

Once the annual business architecture maturity assessment and business architecture practice roadmap are complete, they should be communicated to the business architecture executive leader(s) and any key stakeholders. This provides them with a snapshot of how the practice is progressing as well as the plans for advancement.

Whether an organization has a new business architecture practice or a mature one, assessing its business architecture maturity and creating an intentional practice roadmap is always one of the most relevant and valuable activities to perform.

How can business architecture be practiced consistently within an organization?

The starting point for building consistency in a business architecture practice is by defining a set of **business architecture services**. They are the mechanism through which business architecture can be applied to specific business scenarios *and* with consistent outcomes—no matter who performs them. These services provide a simple way to explain to others how business architecture can be used to help. Services also give people something concrete to ask for. For example, Investment Decision-Making Support may be a defined service that helps leaders visualize and analyze planned initiatives for alignment. Business architecture services also provide the anchor point and structure for a shared business architecture methodology.

As a business architecture team grows and the demand for business architecture services increases, at some point a defined **business architecture methodology—or playbook**—becomes highly valuable. The major factor that drives the need for a business architecture playbook is the number of business architects within an organization. The larger the team, the more important it becomes. However, a light-weight business architecture playbook can still help guide even a small team of practitioners.

The Value of a Business Architecture Playbook

A playbook allows a business architecture team to *scale faster*. It is an excellent tool for onboarding and training new business architects that join the team. It helps to facilitate team collaboration and best practice sharing on an ongoing basis. It also helps a business architecture team to *deliver better*. It ensures that business architects deliver business architecture services efficiently and consistently—and that those services also achieve the intended business outcomes. Consistency not only provides a uniform experience for business architecture consumers and partners, but also ensures that demand is created for the *discipline* of business architecture, not just specific individuals with special skillsets. In addition, the activity of creating a playbook can be quite valuable in and of itself. It brings the business architecture team together to really introspect on what they do, why, and how. It is also a great opportunity to initiate conversations with other teams to create clarity around responsibilities and interactions.

A business architecture playbook is a practitioner's guide on how to create, use, and govern business architecture within an organization. The emphasis is on *using* business architecture, though having at least an overview of other business architecture-related information all in one place can be helpful. Most importantly, a playbook should be *simple, focused on outcomes,* and *supported by significant collaboration and knowledge sharing* among practitioners. The playbook is usually stewarded by the central business architecture team or Center of Excellence but should be used by all business architects across an organization.

Creating a Business Architecture Playbook

To create a business architecture playbook, first define the purpose, scope, audience, structure, and format. Complete the general sections of the playbook, which may include sections such as About the Playbook, About the Business Architecture Team, The Business Architecture Knowledgebase, and Business Architecture Governance. Most importantly, define the Business Architecture Usage Scenarios section. This is the heart of the business architecture playbook, describing how to apply business architecture to different business scenarios, delivered through defined business architecture services. Each business usage scenario has its own sub-section, which may include an overview, key outcomes, inputs, activities, deliverables, and participants. The strategy execution perspective shown in Figure 1.2 can provide a valuable context to organize the business usage scenarios.

When the playbook is drafted, review it with the business architecture team and other key stakeholders. For example, it may be helpful to review with the IT architecture team (unless it was created jointly as an enterprise architecture playbook), the strategy team, and other key partners. The playbook does not need to be perfect. In fact, it is better to publish it, start using it, and continually refine and expand it iteratively based on use.

Business Architecture Governance

Business architecture governance is not an isolated, theoretical activity for architecture's sake. It is about something much bigger: *the organization itself.* An organization's business architecture represents how it is structured and how that structure will change as a result of strategic business direction. Business architecture governance then is a means to ensure an organization is designed to meet the organization's needs today and in the future.

As the role of business architecture and business architects expand within an organization, the need for governance also expands. Different aspects of governance can be put into place just in time when key milestones are reached. Most importantly though, *business architecture governance should exist to provide business value and ensure outcomes—not create unnecessary bureaucracy.*

What is business architecture governance and why is it needed?

While the concepts of enterprise architecture governance are well-defined—and of course business architecture is a part of this broader context—no formal definitions for business architecture governance currently exist with the specialization the discipline needs. The definitions that do exist tend to be focused on just one aspect. For example, some references to business architecture governance focus on the governance structure reflected through the team structure (see Chapter 5), while others focus on a process for managing changes to business architecture.

More holistically then, business architecture governance is the set of structures and processes to manage and control the creation and evolution of business architecture content aligned with business direction and architectural guidance and direction. It may also be expanded to ensure that a business architecture practice delivers its intended outcomes.

Business architecture governance requires defined structures, processes, and criteria. **Governance structures** define who will make decisions and have accountability. It may also include defining a new organizational structure(s) such as a governance committee. **Governance processes** define the activities for reviewing, approving, escalating, and communicating business architecture-related decisions. **Governance criteria** define the direction or guidance against which to make business architecture-related decisions. From a **business perspective**, the criteria used is **business direction**. From an **architectural perspective**, the criteria used is **architecture guidance** (e.g., principles, standards, patterns, and guidelines) as well as **architecture direction** (e.g., as defined in target architectures). Specific metrics may be captured to report on the results of governance processes, such as the percentage of initiatives or solutions compliant with architecture guidance.

What are the different aspects of business architecture governance?

It is important to recognize that there are multiple types of business architecture governance. An organization does not need to adopt all of them, and certainly not all at one time, but they may be considered as options.

Business architecture governance can be considered in two categories. First and most importantly, there is **governance of business architecture content**, which focuses on the creation and evolution of business architecture content. Second, there is **governance of the business architecture practice,** which focuses on the services and outcomes provided by the business architecture team. Table 6.1 shows these two categories with potential types of governance within each, along with additional description. Organizations may establish other types of business architecture governance as well, but these provide a place to start.

Visit www.StrategyintoReality.com to download diagrams and other valuable resources.

Type/Sub-Type	Purpose	Who Does It	When
Business Architecture Content Governance Creating and evolving business architecture content			
Knowledgebase/ Business Review	Review business architecture content against the business direction and environment to ensure correctness and completeness	Cross-functional business representatives	Upon creation or update of all business architecture domain content and cross-mappings
Knowledgebase/ Architectural Review	Review business architecture content against architecture guidance to ensure quality	Business architecture experts	

Type/Sub-Type	Purpose	Who Does It	When
Target Business Architecture/ Business Review	Review target business architecture against business direction to ensure business alignment	Cross-functional business representatives and leaders	During key checkpoints across strategy execution (Architect Changes and Plan Initiatives) as key deliverables are developed (e.g., target business architecture and strategic roadmap)
Target Business Architecture/ Architectural Review	Review target business architecture against architectural direction and guidance to ensure architectural integrity and alignment	Business architecture experts	
Business Architecture Practice Governance Delivering business architecture services and outcomes			
Practice Direction	Review business architecture team outcomes and results against purpose, value proposition, and success measures to ensure value and effectiveness	Business leaders and/ or architecture leaders	During periodic checkpoints, including annual business architecture maturity assessment and practice planning

Type/Sub-Type	Purpose	Who Does It	When
Business Architecture Service Delivery	Review a business architect's delivery of a business architecture service against intended outcomes and business architecture playbook to ensure consistency, quality, and alignment	Central business architecture team	Upon completion (or during periodic checkpoints) of a business architect's delivery of a business architecture service
Business Architecture Tools	Review business architecture content captured in repository against architecture and tool usage guidance to ensure consistency, completeness, and alignment	Central business architecture team	During periodic quality reviews of the repository

Table 6.1: Types of Business Architecture Governance

From a business architecture content perspective, **knowledgebase governance** is performed by both cross-functional business representatives and business architecture experts to ensure the base business architecture content in the knowledgebase is correct, complete, high quality, and aligned with business architecture guidance. This type of governance is relevant to any organization as soon as they publish their business architecture baseline.

When larger scale changes are necessary, **target business architecture governance** can be highly valuable. This type of governance is performed by both cross-functional business representatives and leaders as well as business architecture experts to ensure that a target business architecture is aligned with business and architectural direction (including other target architectures that may exist), and that it is designed with integrity and aligned with architecture guidance.

From a business architecture practice perspective, **practice direction governance** may be performed by business and/or architecture leaders to ensure that the business architecture team outcomes and results are delivering on the defined purpose, value proposition, and measures of success. This type of governance can help to facilitate business engagement and may be beneficial to establish just for that reason in cases where business architecture teams do not work closely with the business.

Business architecture service delivery governance may be performed by the central business architecture team to help make sure that the business architecture services provided by business architects are delivered with consistency, quality, and alignment with the team's business architecture methodology or playbook.

Finally, **business architecture tools governance** may be performed by the central business architecture team to make sure that the business architecture content captured within repository is consistent, complete (e.g., all necessary attributes and cross-mappings captured), and aligned with architecture and tool usage guidance. This is particularly important when multiple people are entering content into the repository.

The specifics of exactly who performs the governance activities from a business or architectural perspective varies based on an organization's situation and dynamics. For example, business reviews related to content are performed by businesspeople, typically at multiple levels within the organization, though the final approval usually comes from an individual executive or committee. Architectural reviews related to content are performed by architects, which could range from the central business architecture team to the top architect to an architecture board. Practice-related reviews are typically performed by people on the central business architecture team. However, they may involve others outside of the team, which could include a steering or advisory committee comprised of people with business or technology perspectives.

Business Architecture in the Bigger Picture of Governance

Beyond business architecture-specific governance, the discipline and artifacts can also be integrated into *other* governance processes, including anywhere across strategy execution. For example, investment requests may require an assessment of the capabilities being enhanced so that prioritization and investment decisions can include an aggregated perspective across the organization. Innovation ideas that reach a certain point of maturity may require a business architecture impact assessment to determine viability and alignment before moving forward. In addition, business architecture can be leveraged to provide a wide range of data-based checks on proposed initiatives, from customer experience impact to technical debt impact.

As always, business architecture should be considered within the broader context of enterprise architecture, and governance is no different. If an enterprise architecture or IT architecture team pre-dated an organization's business architecture practice, some governance mechanisms are likely already in place. Business architecture may be incorporated as an additional layer within these structures and processes. For example, if an architecture review board already exists to assess initiatives and solutions, business architecture may be incorporated by adding some business-specific evaluations and engaging business architects in the review process.

Should ownership for capabilities be established?

While the concept of capability ownership is often discussed, it is not always clearly understood. Capability ownership typically relates to establishing business leader ownership and accountability for business architecture knowledgebase governance and/or target business architecture governance, as described previously. While this approach has worked for some organizations, it is often best to let the business architecture mature for some time, along with the peoples' comfort with it. Resist the urge to implement this type of governance too soon, otherwise it can end up reinforcing the current silos (or creating new ones) and implementing governance for the sake of governance. Below are a few key considerations that can help guide if or when capability ownership is established within an organization.

Start with why. *Define a clear purpose and goal for what will be achieved with capability ownership.* It can be an effective lever to engage executives and drive change, especially when implemented at the right time.

Ensure the capability map is stable. Establish capability ownership only after the capability map is solid. This means that the capability map has not only been created by a cross-functional group of business representatives, but that it has been in *use* for enough time to validate and refine it. If the capability map needs to change significantly, it will be disruptive to the capability owners—or worse, the existence of defined ownership may deter necessary changes from being made to a capability map.

Draw the boundaries that are best for the enterprise. Consider the reality of how capabilities need to be owned, managed, directed, and invested in—which might require a different way of thinking than status quo. For example, it should not be assumed that business ownership will fall neatly with each business leader owning a level 1 capability. Ownership might be more relevant for a set of capabilities, such as those which are customer-facing. Or, ownership may require more than one business leader. For example, a customer leadership committee may own and be accountable for the direction of those customer-facing capabilities.

Consider the value stream perspective. This does not imply that every organization must have value stream owners as well, but the end-to-end value perspective should always be considered when making capability-related decisions.

From a practical perspective, capability ownership can be established incrementally. Assign owners to the highest priority capabilities first, gain some experience with the process, and then continue assigning ownership for the remaining capabilities in the future. Additionally, the same goals may be achieved through the broader perspective of target business architecture governance instead.

How should business architecture governance be put into place?

Historically, enterprise architecture governance has sometimes been perceived as an unnecessary layer of bureaucracy because the benefits to the business have been poorly communicated. This is an important lesson to take to heart when designing business architecture governance. The establishment of business architecture governance should be approached practically and incrementally, focused only on activities that provide business value.

Introduce governance with key milestones. Each aspect of business architecture governance should be introduced over time as key milestones are reached, making them relevant. Do not just establish governance because it is a step in a methodology or because it seems that other organizations are doing it. For example, introduce knowledgebase governance when version 1.0 of the business architecture baseline is published or introduce business architecture tool governance when an automated tool is put into place. Introduce target business architecture governance with the first large change initiative that leverages business architecture.

Govern what is important. For example, focus on governing target architectures and strategic roadmaps, not every detailed deliverable. Furthermore, focus business architecture service delivery governance on the outcomes achieved, not whether a practitioner followed a prescriptive set of steps.

Keep it as light as reasonable. Keep governance processes light and potentially informal until the organization matures. Lighter governance will encourage more people to participate, and facilitate learning and evolution, especially in the beginning. Increase the rigor of governance over time when it is needed to support increased business architecture maturity.

Measuring Success and Building Adoption

Even as business architecture understanding and adoption is increasing globally, there are still some burning questions that just about everyone seeks to answer: *How do we measure the success of business architecture within an organization? If an organization invests in a business architecture practice, what is the return on investment (ROI)? What quantifiable proof exists demonstrating the value that organizations have achieved with business architecture?*

As much as we are desperately seeking to quantify and prove the value of business architecture, measuring success is one of the areas that business architecture teams focus on the least due to a lack of bandwidth and some of the challenges in doing so. Business architecture also provides a type of competitive advantage, so there can be a reluctance to share information publicly as well. On the other hand, everyone is looking for the magical data from *other* organizations to help make a case for business architecture in their own organization. So, the bad news: at present, only minimal quantifiable data about business architecture success is mainstream and publicly available. The good news: you are not missing anything.

The path forward then is for organizations to create their *own proof* and better yet, share it back with the global community to help build the collective case for business architecture. While quantifying the results of business architecture can be challenging, a consistent, simple, and practical approach to measuring its quantitative and qualitative impact can make this activity a realistic one, even with limited resources. The key is to build a cohesive *collection* of information and assets that work together and can be leveraged for educating and socializing. This may include tangible metrics and dashboards, success stories and anecdotes, and other engaging socialization materials such as videos and infographics.

Capturing this information from the very beginning can pay off greatly, even if just to track one or two metrics along with a success story for each business architecture engagement. The collective set of stories and data can help to create organizational awareness and adoption and increase the usage of business architecture. It can also help to secure funding and resources, not just for the business architecture team, but also for business leaders and their teams to participate in business architecture-related activities and make them a priority.

How do we measure business architecture success?

Business architecture success can be considered in two broad categories. First and most importantly, business architecture success can be measured by its **value to the organization**. These metrics are the ones that people most care about. They reflect the contribution of business architecture to what matters to the organization, such as revenue, customer satisfaction, or cost savings. Second, business architecture success can be measured by the **maturity of the practice**. These metrics reflect the maturity of business architecture based on formal maturity scores and other progress indicators, such as those demonstrating the degree of integration and scale. They are primarily useful for business architecture executive leaders and practitioners to demonstrate advancement to their stakeholders. They can also target areas of practice improvement.

Measuring Business Architecture Value Has Its Challenges

While measuring the maturity of a business architecture practice is relatively straightforward, measuring its value has some challenges. For example, some business architecture results are intangible. Benefits such as building a common understanding, creating clarity, and informing decisions are difficult to quantify. Business architecture can also lead to the avoidance of negative results such as preventing a misaligned investment or heading off a compliance issue. It can be difficult to measure all the things that did *not* happen. In addition, the discrete results attributable to business architecture can be hard to isolate, since it is one discipline among many working together across the ecosystem of strategy execution. Additionally, business architecture results can create unwanted visibility for some people. For example, while a leader may appreciate that business architecture helped to illuminate a strategic misalignment or redundant solutions, they may not want these results broadcasted widely to others.

Options For Measuring Business Architecture Success

One of the million-dollar questions is, what metrics should be used to measure business architecture success? Other than return on business architecture investment, there is not a one-size-fits-all answer because every organization and practice is different. The driver for selecting the right business architecture metrics is an organization's defined value proposition for business architecture. For example, a business architecture team that is focused on transformation may measure contribution to customer satisfaction or time to market, where a team that is focused on efficiency may measure contribution to cost savings.

The options for measuring business architecture value and maturity are endless. Table 6.2 provides a sample of simple measurement ideas for each category, for purposes of illustration and inspiration.

Visit www.StrategyintoReality.com to download diagrams and other valuable resources.

Category	Sample Measurement Ideas
Business Architecture Value to the Organization	✓ Stakeholder Satisfaction Score (derived from surveys of internal stakeholders who consume business architecture)
	✓ Revenue Generated
	✓ Customer Satisfaction Increased
	✓ Cost Saved
	✓ Cost Avoided
	✓ Risks Identified
	✓ Compliance Issues Identified
	✓ Cost of Fines Avoided
	✓ Innovation Ideas Submitted
	✓ Processes Optimized
	✓ Duplicate Applications Reduced
	✓ Shared Solutions Identified (by capability)
	✓ Integration Points/Dependencies Identified
	✓ Initiative Scope Changes Reduced
	✓ Requirements Definition Time Reduced
	✓ Solution Defects Reduced

Category	Sample Measurement Ideas
Maturity of the Business Architecture Practice	✓ Business Architecture Maturity Score (overall and by category) ✓ Strategic Priority/Strategic Initiative Engagements ✓ Business Domains Staffed with a Business Architect ✓ Initiatives Leveraging Architecture Guidance ✓ Business Architects Hired ✓ Business Architects Trained ✓ Business Architects Certified ✓ Quantity of Business Architecture Content Mapped (by domain) ✓ Teams Integrated With ✓ Stakeholder Communication Deliveries ✓ Stakeholder Level of Buy-In

Table 6.2: Sample Business Architecture Measurement Ideas

A Practical Approach to Measurement

Due to some of the challenges mentioned previously, taking a practical approach to business architecture measurement will improve success and reduce frustration. Aim to capture both measurable and non-measurable results. There is often a strong desire for quantifiable metrics, but qualitative information can provide just as much value and help to tell the story. Capture short success stories as well as quotes and anecdotes that describe how business architecture was used in various scenarios and the value it provided. These methods are particularly helpful for capturing the intangible value of business architecture such as the benefits of having a common language.

In addition, keep the business architecture metrics and reporting simple to start. Resist the urge to create a long list of complex metrics to report on. Select just a few simple metrics and start measuring them. Additional metrics and more complex ones may be added later. In the beginning, measuring business architecture results is most easily done with simple measures like counts. The information may even need to be collected manually in the beginning. It is better to start capturing and reporting on a baseline of information versus delaying the activity to pursue more complex approaches.

Finally, *start measuring results from the beginning*. This will prove to be valuable for purposes of history and building buy-in, even if it is only for two or three metrics along with a set of documented success stories.

Can we measure the return on business architecture investment?

There sometimes exists a perception that business architecture is "expensive" because it introduces new costs that did not exist before. However, this perception is short-sighted, and so tracking the return on business architecture investment can help to reframe the misunderstanding within the bigger picture and a longer-term perspective. Quite the contrary, if we tracked the results delivered by a business architecture team that practices the discipline effectively, their ROI would far exceed the investment. Consider the organizational cost and time that would be saved, the misaligned decisions or investments that would not happen, or the risks, issues, or mistakes that would be avoided.

It is important to keep in mind that ROI is just one metric that can help to socialize the value and impact of business architecture within an organization. In addition, success stories and other qualitative approaches can be just as useful as the numbers. Successful business architecture teams leverage each of these pieces, along with good organizational change management practices, and bring them together into a deliberate plan for continually socializing business architecture and its value.

However, **return on business architecture investment** (coined here as **ROBAI**) is a tangible and familiar measure that does speak to people. Tracking the ROI of a business architecture practice gives the team transparency and accountability for the value they deliver to the organization. In addition, communicating the ROI of a business architecture practice can help to build support for the discipline within an organization. To take it a step further, the collective sharing of ROBAI across organizations can help strengthen the case for the business architecture discipline worldwide.

Calculating Return on Business Architecture Investment

Calculating ROBAI is not difficult but obtaining the business architecture benefit and cost data requires some effort. Here is a method for determining ROBAI, which can be expressed as a ratio or percentage.

If the formula for Return on Investment (ROI) is:

ROI = (Current Value of Investment - Cost of Investment) / Cost of Investment

Then the formula for Return on Business Architecture Investment (ROBAI) is:

ROBAI = (Business Architecture Benefits - Business Architecture Costs) / Business Architecture Costs

Business architecture benefits are the summation of results from the metrics an organization has chosen that best monetizes their value proposition. These benefit numbers may need to be calculated manually and in partnership with the people to whom the benefits were provided—just to make sure they agree on how they are accounted for. Here are four example benefits categories.

Strategic Value Contribution. These metrics quantify business architecture contribution to business measures such as revenue or customer experience improvement.

Strategy Execution Performance Improvement. These metrics quantify business architecture contribution to end-to-end strategy execution and may be reflected in measures such as cost or time saved during the process. For example, with business architecture input, time may be saved defining requirements.

Operational Performance Improvement. These metrics quantify business architecture contribution to efficiency or simplification efforts and may also include preventing or reducing risk or compliance issues. They may be reflected in measures such as cost, time, or risk reduction or avoidance.

Business Effectiveness Improvement. These metrics quantify business architecture contribution to the daily course of doing business and may be reflected in measures such as cost or time saved. For example, the presence of a well-defined business architecture can save time on an ongoing basis by enabling effective communication and onboarding for both internal and external resources.

Business architecture costs are the summation of what an organization spends to create, maintain, use, and govern their business architecture and supporting practice. This could include categories such as **Team Compensation**, **Team Training and Resources**, and **Tools**.

Consider the following scenario: a dedicated, five-person business architecture team in its third year could feasibly have a Business Architecture Benefit/Cost Ratio of 3.33:1 and a Return on Business Architecture Investment of 233%. This is derived from a total business architecture benefit amount of 2.5 million USD across the four benefits categories and a total business architecture cost amount of 750,000 USD for people, training, and tool costs.

What is the best way to socialize business architecture in an organization?

At this point in time, socializing business architecture within an organization is arguably the top challenge that business architecture teams have worldwide. Data from surveys and gatherings continually substantiate this with the top challenges cited relating to business architecture understanding and buy-in as well as a related challenge for integration of business architecture with other teams. While there are not yet any easy routes to the top of this mountain, there is a set of practical tips, best practices, secrets, and hacks for business architecture socialization that work, based on the collective wisdom of business architecture practitioners around the world.

For the socialization techniques to work well though, an organization must have a clear, simple, relevant, and consistent value proposition for business architecture. This is the foundation. Remember the secret: this is not about the business architecture, this is about the business. Talk to just about any successful business architecture leader or practitioner and you'll find there is one common key to success, regardless of geography, industry, or organization: *demonstrate business value—don't sell business architecture.* When building a case for business architecture, first outline the opportunities or challenges that exist, including why they are so important to address now and the implications of not acting. Once the opportunity has been established, then articulate how business architecture can be a part of the solution.

The formula for success is to (1) deliver the business architecture value proposition through repeatable services, (2) achieve the intended outcomes of those services and create happy stakeholders, (3) tell the story, and (4) repeat. Keep delivering and keep telling the story. Even if there was a lack of initial buy-in, value delivery can overcome it. Rarely (other than politics) will any leader ever say, "please stop providing these benefits that are helping us to improve and advance the business so much." The results achieved with business architecture will convey more about what it can do than words ever could. In addition, remember the other key mantras: *lead with value and build the business architecture and practice as you go. Build strong partnerships. Position business architecture as a business-focused and strategic discipline. Show up with wow.* Here are a few tips and practices that can help.

Leverage other people. Make sure to leverage other people. Create ownership, peer pressure, and coalitions. Leverage advocates and success stories from both within and outside of the organization. For example, share business architecture case studies and success stories from other organizations and leverage external experts. Or, form a collaborative working relationship with other companies, especially those in non-competitive industries, and share stories and best practices. The exchange can be a one-time event or a formalized, ongoing relationship. Share your own success stories within the organization and ask internal advocates to endorse them and share a quote of support.

Build bridges through hiring. Be intentional with hiring to build bridges and address any gaps within the practice. For example, create a steering committee of business and technology leaders to guide direction and help advocate for business architecture. Engage leaders to mentor business architecture practitioners. They will inevitably develop a stake in the success of business architecture. In addition, hire people from the business area, discipline, or team that requires some bridge building. Or, hire an external resource who will be respected internally. Offer a rotational position on the business architecture team. The individuals who participate will gain a greater understanding of and stake in business architecture success and create additional exposure across the organization.

Make communications compelling. Engaging and polished visuals, designs, and tools help to get peoples' attention and respect so they are more likely to hear the important messages. For example, business architecture teams have used presentations, videos, animations, infographics, posters, dedicated rooms or areas to take people through "wall walks," interactive websites, mobile applications, and more. Consider enlisting some colleagues with marketing, communication, and design talents to help tell the story.

Weave into the business. One of the most effective ways to socialize business architecture is to weave it into the fabric of the organization. Remember that the best leaders and advocates do not necessarily need to have an official business architecture role to make a significant impact. For example, when a key supporter moves into a new role, do not be disheartened, but rather celebrate that there will be an advocate within another part of the organization. Furthermore, one of the most powerful amplifiers of business architecture can happen when a business architect moves into another role within the organization and leverages the discipline as part of their new job or function. In addition, when communicating with executives, learn their strengths, concerns, and mindset and speak in *their* language.

Business Architecture Socialization: When and Who

The question of when to socialize business architecture depends on the situation and organizational dynamics. Some business architecture teams build buy-in quickly and share with executives at the C-Level and wider audiences throughout the organizations relatively early in their journey. However, most teams socialize within a smaller sphere of the organization and then socialize more widely once they have proven successes to share and the ability to scale.

The business architecture practice director—and their executive leaders—should drive and play an active role in socialization. Other business architecture team members may have socialization responsibilities, either formally or informally, as part of their role as well. However, *every* business architect should be comfortable with describing the discipline and its value to at least some extent. This does not mean that the business architecture team must do it alone though. Other advocates within the organization need to catch the vision and help co-own it, tell the story about it, galvanize it, and drive it into action in partnership with the business architecture team.

While most people sign up for business architecture without realizing that it also comes with a heavy dose of *marketecture* and *politecture*, the opportunity to introduce business architecture to an organization and make a difference with it is incredibly rewarding. This is a journey that requires passion, patience, and persistence. Embrace the challenges and enjoy each lightbulb moment and breakthrough that comes along the way towards a new mindset and ways of working.

7

Shaping the Future of Business Architecture

Business architecture is increasingly practiced by organizations on six continents, across all industries, in all sectors, and of all sizes. More practitioners are pursuing business architecture as a career and pushing the role to new heights. There is an established body of knowledge, certification, and an accredited training program, as well as events and communities all over the world, supported by a growing market of professional associations, research analysts, and organizations that offer related services and tools.

The body of evidence around business architecture's value is mounting as it shared through success stories during events, among community members, and through various publications—even if these stories and tangible results are not yet in mainstream distribution. Positive trends are clear and increasing. More organizations are positioning business architecture upfront in strategy execution and leveraging the discipline for strategic business usage scenarios. More business architecture teams are reporting within the business. Business architecture teams are starting to architect across organizational boundaries.

Business architecture has likely *not* yet crossed the chasm[20] between early adopters and early majority on the innovation curve. However, there is an increasingly optimistic sentiment among practitioners that with the growing traction, including recognition by research analysts and universities, that we might be getting close.

Crystal Ball: A Glimpse Into the Future of Business Architecture

The business architecture discipline is continually evolving, so knowing where it is headed can help to guide practitioners' career choices and organizations' business architecture journeys. The potential of the discipline is vast and still relatively untapped. However, with a foundation in place and more organizations practicing it every day, business architecture can truly become the strategic and valuable discipline that we have always envisioned.

The next phase ahead will hopefully bring more practical usage, more professionalization of the discipline, and more adoption of business architecture into the mainstream. And, hopefully business architecture will cross that chasm.

What does the future hold for the business architecture discipline and role?

Based on the current state of business architecture state and growing trends, here are a few predictions for how the discipline and role will unfold over the next horizon.

Based on Trends, Very Likely

Prediction #1: Business architecture adoption and advancement continues at an increased pace globally. There will continue to be more organizations using business architecture, more demand for business architecture practitioners, more adoption by executives, academic institutions, and business literature, more formalization of the discipline, and more expansion of the market. The internal business architecture practices within organizations will continue to mature. For those organizations who are investing in business architecture today, the collective maturity level is likely between a mid-level 2 and a low to mid-level 3 for a significant majority. There are organizations who are currently at a business architecture maturity level of 4 or 5, but many more organizations are on the journey now and will be the leaders of tomorrow. With more business architecture maturity, more value to organizations will follow.

Prediction #2: Organizations increasingly leverage business architecture for strategic purposes and position business architecture teams to work upfront in the strategy execution life cycle. Business architects will become a focal point for strategy translation and prioritization, as well as key leaders in business transformations. To achieve this, established business architecture teams may need to shift left (upstream) in strategy execution to work closer with leaders and strategy teams, where new teams will be positioned there from the beginning. The trend of business architecture teams reporting to a leader within the business will likely continue and increase. Business architecture will become embedded into the fabric of organizations and just the way business is done. Those who adopted the discipline earlier on will enjoy competitive advantage.

Based on Trends, Reasonably Likely

Prediction #3: The focus of the business architect role continues to shift from developing the business architecture knowledgebase to architecting the business. With the continued availability and maturation of reference models and advances in technology, creating the business architecture knowledgebase can be greatly accelerated. In the future, this may even commoditize some of the mapping skills needed by a business architect. This means that business architects can focus where the real value lies— architecting the business and applying the knowledgebase in support of various business scenarios.

Prediction #4: The business architect role continues to elevate. Based on the strategic focus and usage described in Predictions 2 and 3, the business architect role will continue to increase in the responsibility and respect it receives, the talent it draws, and its desirability as a career. This means that business architects should steer their career towards practicing the discipline strategically, developing complementary value-added skills, and focusing on architecting, not just modeling.

Based on Evidence, but Somewhat Futuristic

Prediction #5: Business architecture is deployed in new ways across organizations. As the needs of organizations evolve and as business architecture matures, the function and role may be deployed in new ways. For example, business architects may work as part of cross-functional design teams or aspects of business architecture may become part of multiple peoples' roles. For the most part, organizations have defined a pure business architect role, which integrates with other roles and disciplines. However, some practitioners may play a more blended, interdisciplinary role (e.g., human-centered design and business architecture) including more blending across the enterprise architecture domains. All or a portion of the business architect role may be democratized through the usage of business architecture by many people in different roles and for different scenarios across an organization. More aspects of creating and using business architecture are likely to be automated as well.

Prediction #6: Business architects work across organizational boundaries. Business architects will work together across organizational boundaries to achieve common goals. Whether to coordinate with partners more effectively or facilitate cross-organizational ventures or ecosystem design, this type of collaboration will likely increase in our highly connected world. In fact, it will be essential to tackle some of the major opportunities and challenges that lie ahead.

Based on Evidence, but More Aspirational

Prediction #7: Architecture (business and technology) becomes a true profession. As business and enterprise architecture industry organizations come together, a true architecture profession will emerge. A common architecture foundation with specializations by architecture domain will be adopted, along with all the hallmarks of a profession such as a code of ethics.

Prediction #8: Business architecture and architectural thinking is leveraged in all organizations. Business architecture will be practiced in all sizes and types of organizations—for profit, non-profit, and governmental. In addition, organizations will leverage business blueprints and structured architectural thinking throughout the entire life cycle from startup, to scaling, to transforming and operating effectively.

Prediction #9: Architects use their talents for good. By nature, architects are passionate people who strive to make a difference. Business architects will share their rare talents to help non-profit organizations, non-governmental organizations, social enterprises, and other social impact organizations to achieve their missions.

What are the possibilities for business architecture as a profession?

The concept of business architecture has undoubtedly proven itself as a valid discipline and career path. Becoming a full-fledged profession like medicine, accounting, or law though, comes with a rigorous set of requirements. For example, a profession must have a defined value to society, defined boundaries of the discipline, a discrete body of knowledge for the discipline, formal education and certification, professional bodies with a regulatory role, a defined competency model, a defined career path, and a universal, enforceable code of ethics.

While business architecture meets some of the requirements for a profession when viewed exclusively through the business architecture lens with the formalization done by the Business Architecture Guild®, it still has a way to go. The same assessment looks a bit different when viewed through the lens of other professional organizations focused on enterprise architecture.

What is needed is a way to unify all architects as part of one profession but allow for the different specialties to exist in their fullness. In the case of business architecture, this also includes recognizing that some aspects of the discipline blend into strategic management and go beyond the pure business architect role or enterprise architecture context.

The road ahead to a unified enterprise architecture profession is doable, but the vision requires serious commitment, collaboration, and action. Architecture can provide an entirely unique and important value to society—and professionalizing would increase its recognition and success. How much *more* successful could business and technology architects be *together* as a force for change and good?

What is required to take the business architecture discipline to the next level?

By all measures, business architecture is here and here to stay. It is, however, at a key inflection point. While an incredible amount of growth and formalization has occurred and should be celebrated, the next frontier must focus on achieving and sharing more practical results, socializing with a much broader group of people, and building architecture as a profession. The value, adoption, and relevance of business architecture in the future depends on how we decide to leverage and scale the foundation we have built so far.

There are a few key focus areas ahead, all intertwined. First, business architecture must continue to deliver relevant value to organizations, with success stories and case studies communicated widely. Second, business architecture must be integrated into the fabric of organizations alongside all disciplines and teams from strategy to execution. Third, the business architecture discipline must be further professionalized, including formal definition of the business architect role, competency model, education, and career path. Lastly, business architecture understanding, credibility, and adoption must become mainstream.

What this means is that for business architecture to truly succeed, it will take all of us working together. This includes business architecture practitioners, executive leaders and business architecture advocates within organizations, human resources managers within organizations and human resources professional organizations, universities, business/enterprise architecture and related industry professional organizations, and the entire ecosystem of partners and advocates.

Organizations can contribute by using business architecture and then sharing stories and quantifiable data back with the global business architecture community. They can also help shape the future of the business architecture discipline and business architect role by informing on the evolving needs of business.

Hiring managers within organizations and **human resources professional organizations** can learn about and recognize the business architect role and its unique value to organizations. They can also inform the formalization of the role, competency model, and career path for business architects.

Universities can incorporate strategy execution and business architecture concepts into the business school curriculum and a wide range of other master's programs, such as enterprise risk management and entrepreneurship. Universities can also offer specific academic programs to support the business architecture discipline and career path. Universities can bring the full rigor of academia to further expand the concepts as well as play a significant role in conducting research, especially to facilitate collaboration between industry and academia.

The **industry professional organizations** that have led the way in formalizing the business architecture discipline deserve a lot of credit for how much has been done in a short time and done well. These organizations will need to continue the pace or increase it to keep up with—and keep ahead of—practitioners' needs and the new momentum that the discipline is experiencing. Industry professional organizations can formalize the role, competency model, and career path for business architects and work together to create a common foundation for a true architecture profession (with specializations by domain). They can provide mechanisms for sharing success stories globally and ensure their distribution beyond the business architecture community to publications and forums for executives, academia, business, human resources, and related disciplines. Industry professional organizations can continue to provide online and in-person events for business architects and other key stakeholders to come together and collaborate. They can also educate broadly on the vision for strategy execution and the role that business architecture can play.

Finally, **other ecosystem players such as training and tool providers**, can accelerate business architecture learning and knowledgebase development. They can continue creating resources and tools, which help business architects get up to speed quickly and make their lives easier. This includes accelerating business architecture knowledgebase development and maintenance as much as possible. In addition, tool providers can continue to meet the growing need to make business architecture consumable and engaging to all audiences.

What If? Leveraging Business Architecture to Make a Difference

Business architecture is an enabler for organizations that are seeking to contribute directly or indirectly to the social good. Non-profit organizations, non-governmental organizations, and social enterprises may leverage business architecture to achieve and scale their missions to the greatest extent possible—while being a good steward of their resources. For-profit companies may leverage business architecture to operate more sustainably and ethically, and as the lines between purpose and profit blend, use business as a force for good.

Zooming out to the bigger global picture, the unique structure and mindset of business architecture can help facilitate collaboration and design for opportunities and challenges that may otherwise seem out of reach. For example, the discipline can be leveraged to design sustainable ecosystems or even bring individuals and organizations together around common goals for the global good.

However, organizations are made of individuals. Nations are made of individuals. Ultimately, everything comes down to personal impact, and the ripple effect from one individual is incalculable. We can all help bring business architecture to the table to support organizations that are making a social impact. We can also introduce the thinking and discipline into conversations in any organization on sustainability and contributing to the greater good. Furthermore, business architects are uniquely positioned to contribute through their role. For example, business architects can—and do—provide pro bono assistance to help mission-driven organizations. In addition, if a code of ethics were adopted for the architecture profession, each business architect could also play a role in ensuring that organizations are designed sustainably and ethically.

A few ideas for leveraging business architecture for the greater good are shared here, and hopefully they will inspire many more. Some of these ideas may seem lofty or futuristic, but the evolution of business and technology is not slowing nor are our some of the greatest challenges of our time going away. We need holistic solutions and thinkers to rise to meet these challenges. Business architecture and business architects are well-suited to catalyze, drive, and architect change.

How can business architecture help an organization to become more sustainable?

According to the United Nations Environment Programme (UNEP), sustainability (or sustainable development) is defined as "Meeting the needs of the present without compromising the ability of future generations to meet their own needs." While the concept of sustainability has over time been continually recrafted through different messaging and emphases, it is still rooted in the consideration and balance of three very important perspectives: social, environment, and economics.

An organization should commit to all three components to help address the needs of society, aim to protect the environment, and focus on providing the best standard of living while remaining competitive in a world market. Organizations can measure their performance and value more holistically using the Triple Bottom Line, which includes not just financials but also social and environmental metrics to understand the full cost and benefits of doing business.

Why Sustainability Matters Within and Across Organizations

Sustainability is important for *all* organizations. It is a mindset and way of working. Sustainability should not be an afterthought or a set of isolated or superficial programs—but rather embedded in the DNA of how an organization thinks, acts, and operates. Beyond creating a better world, operating sustainably provides notable benefits to organizations, including for-profit businesses.

Customers and employees increasingly care about working with or for responsible organizations. As a result, operating responsibly and being a company that creates social impact can ultimately lead to attracting and retaining customers and employees. Of course, a good public reputation and trust can significantly enhance an organization's brand, but there are also more tactical benefits of operating responsibly. This may include increasing supply chain reliability, reducing costs, and ensuring compliance with regulations or UN Global Compact principles. Furthermore, taking a market-based approach to solving problems means that organizations can benefit from new product and market opportunities.

Sustainability concepts also apply *across* organizations. For example, the players within business ecosystems should not only consider the sustainability of their own individual organizations, but also for the collective ecosystem, its interactions, and its impacts. Countries, cities, industries, and many other systems all need to consider sustainability holistically as well. When designing systems, an overarching principle is to create a *closed loop system.* Taking a page from nature, this is the concept of the continuous flow of materials and energy through a system, which nature elegantly does with no waste. (For example, compare the regenerative cycle that happens in a forest with our linear processes of cutting down trees, turning them into wood pulp, making paper, using paper, and sending much of it to a landfill.) This concept is now often referred to as the *circular economy.* Shifting from our primarily linear model of business to closed loop systems can create sweeping changes to an organization. It requires designing or reimagining business models, strategies, and potentially entire ecosystems.

How Business Architecture Facilities and Embeds Sustainability

Since business architecture provides a set of business blueprints that represent an entire organization at a high level, it is a perfect framework for measuring, improving, and infusing sustainability into the right conversations and the very fabric of the organization. Below are a few examples of how it can be leveraged to help organizations with their sustainability journeys.

Target sustainability performance improvements. Business architecture helps organizations measure, target, and improve sustainability performance. To facilitate improvements, organizations need a framework to assess, analyze, monitor, and communicate sustainability performance. An organization's business architecture is an already agreed upon framework representing its entire scope, so another new one does not need to be created. Sustainability metrics and considerations can be tied to capabilities (and value streams) to ensure that measurement is framed and communicated within shared business context and priorities. For example, an Asset Management capability within a corporate vehicle context may have traditional metrics such as Average Utilization of Fleet Vehicles, but environmental and social metrics could be captured as well, such as Total Carbon Dioxide Emissions from Fleet Vehicles or Average Efficiency of Fleet Vehicles. Sustainability improvement opportunities can be identified at a high level by targeting capabilities and value streams, and then other teams such as business process management or Lean teams can focus in on the details to remove inefficiencies or waste.

Identify sustainability opportunities. Business architecture identifies new business opportunities and risks. New sustainability-related opportunities can be identified through the lens of business models, value streams, capabilities, or other architecture-based innovation. For example, an opportunity may be identified to convert a product offering into a service (and facilitate the sharing economy). Or, an opportunity may be identified to reuse an asset in new ways where it would otherwise be disposed. On the other hand, business architecture can help identify sustainability-related risks. For example, capabilities could be analyzed to identify those which are most at risk of climate change impacts or other environmental or social impacts.

Keep sustainability top of mind. Sustainability is hard to manage well in silos, so business architecture helps connect the dots and facilitate the right conversations at the right times. Business architecture provides the scaffolding to help make connections, especially using capabilities and value streams. For example, if an organization has sustainability metrics and considerations tied to each capability, and if all initiatives are framed by the value streams and capabilities impacted, then it becomes a natural trigger to review the potential sustainability impacts when assessing initiatives. This can help ensure that initiatives do not negatively impact sustainability—and that they can also take advantage of any opportunities to create a positive sustainability benefit as well.

Realize sustainability strategies. Business architecture translates sustainability strategies into execution. Translating strategies into coordinated action across an organization is at the heart of what business architecture does. Many organizations initially create targeted sustainability strategies to help them transform towards their sustainability visions and goals. Business architecture can be a key enabler to make them a reality.

However, once the transforming is done, sustainability should be fully embedded in every aspect of how the organization does business, not a standalone strategy or program.

Architect sustainable ecosystems. Whether designing a business ecosystem, an industrial ecosystem, or a broader set of entities forming a closed loop system, the business architecture perspectives and underlying principles are readily extensible to an entire ecosystem. The tools are there as is the integration with other disciplines, so what is needed most is the mindset shift from organization to ecosystem. For example, value networks and value streams may be used as key connectors across organizational boundaries, and even provide a framework for anchoring material and energy flows.

Guide the sustainability journey. Business architects can also be invaluable thinking partners to help organizations on their sustainability journeys. They are well-suited because they see the whole picture, how the pieces relate, and how decisions will play out long-term. Business architects are excellent dot connectors between ideas, people, and initiatives. They also work within the space of possibility and can balance many different concerns. For example, they can help to assess the needs and impacts across stakeholders including customers, employees, partners, the community, the environment, and governance bodies. They are also leaders and change agents—and are wired to care.

How can business architecture be leveraged to build a better world?

Setting our sights even higher, business architecture can be leveraged to bring individuals and organizations together to help us achieve our global goals. We will leverage the United Nations (UN) Sustainable Development Goals (SDGs) as a focal point.

There are 17 SDGs, applicable to all countries, that set bold global goals to help us move beyond traditional indicators such as GDP growth and per capita income to a broader set of objectives such as well-being, social fairness, and environmental sustainability. While every UN member state should use the SDGs for framing their agendas and political policies, the responsibility and potential for meeting these goals also lies with every individual and organization. This includes governments, non-profit organizations, and even for-profit businesses, which can be a powerful mechanism for change.

In our connected world, achieving the SDGs is important to all of us. The goals not only ensure that everyone's basic rights are met, but they also help to create stable and successful nations with economic growth, social trust, fairness, equality, and sustainability. Stable and successful nations in turn create a strong global market for us all. *Business architecture makes the achievement of the UN SDGs actionable, measurable, visible, and possible—within and across organizations.*

Business Architecture Helps Organizations Contribute to SDGs

Business architecture helps organizations contribute to SDG achievement. An organization can contribute to the SDGs either by operating responsibly and/or by directly contributing to the cause. For example, if the people within an organization would like to make an impact to SDG #13 (Take urgent action to combat climate change and its impacts), they can improve the environmentally sustainability of their products and service and operations. They could also decide to contribute directly to the cause by donating to climate action efforts or leveraging their brand to help create awareness.

Where should an organization start? First, key leaders within an organization should become versed in the SDGs and identify the one(s) that are most relevant to what the organization does or cares about. Relevance is highly important because it aligns motivation with action. Once the SDG(s) are selected, the next step is to set internal objectives and metrics to help the organization achieve the desired level of contribution. Then, high-level courses of action are defined to specify how the contribution will be achieved, through different aspects of responsible operation, direct contribution, or both. Once the direction is defined, it flows into the organization's normal strategy execution processes to be translated into action.

Since business architecture is both a critical enabler of strategy execution and an enterprise-wide business framework for analysis and decision-making, it can help organizations with their SDG contributions in several important ways. For example, business architecture can **inform decision-makers** by providing the potential impacts to the business and technology environment based on certain SDG-related objectives or courses of action. In addition, business architecture can **make the SDGs visible, measurable, and actionable** by capturing traceability in the business architecture knowledgebase from the targeted SDGs to the supporting internal objectives, metrics, and courses of action, to the impacted value streams and capabilities, and eventually the planned initiatives. Certainly, business architecture can help to **translate internal SDG-related objectives and courses of action** into a coordinated set of initiatives across the organization by leveraging value streams and capabilities to target changes needed, define reusable business components, use resources effectively, and **align SDG efforts** with existing initiatives. Finally, business architecture **provides transparency** on the achievement of planned SDG impacts, by measuring the performance within a value stream, capability, and initiative context.

Business Architecture Helps Organizations Collaborate Around SDGs

Business architecture also helps facilitate cross-organizational coordination for SDG achievement. Thinking on an even bigger scale, business architecture can help organizations work together to accelerate and scale the collective ability to meet the SDGs. What if we could leverage the full power of global collaboration to match those who have needs with those who have solutions, to share best practices and resources, and to connect all the key players including communities, governments, non-governmental organizations, non-profit organizations, businesses, startup ecosystems, and even individual contributors?

Business architecture can help to match people, organizations, and initiatives with needs to the global collective of people and solutions that can help meet those needs, within an SDG context. Brilliant methods and solutions have been created for everything from agriculture to healthcare to energy to banking that can be applied in additional locations, contexts, and scenarios beyond where they have been used today—especially for the benefit of emerging nations. Business architecture, with value streams and capabilities as the centerpiece, is a great connector for any scope of focus, large or small.

For example, consider SDG #4 (Ensure inclusive and equitable quality education and promote lifelong learning opportunities for all). To achieve this SDG globally, it will require some educational systems to be created where they do not exist and will require reformation or enhancement in others. However, we know that capabilities such as Learning Content Management and Learner (Constituent) Management are critical for educational systems anywhere. Utilizing a holistic capability map such as the Government Reference Model from the Business Architecture Guild®, which represents a comprehensive view of societal functions, we can catalog the people and solutions around the world who offer the desired capabilities and then match them to the governments, non-governmental organizations, non-profit organizations, and initiatives who need to leverage them to deliver or transform education around the world. Capabilities can essentially become the Rosetta stone for matching needs to solutions and resources.

This powerful global catalog shifts us away from local approaches where every educational system must recreate the wheel through point-to-point interactions to learn best practices and discover the people and solutions that will best meet their needs. Instead, it allows us to leverage the global community, technology, and best practices, and even facilitates cross-government and educational system collaboration around a common mental model. It can also help us shift away from siloed approaches that focus on individual responsibilities to an end-to-end focus on delivering outcomes together.

There is power in stepping into the bold realm of possibility and asking *what if?* Our ability to create change simply lies within our will to do it.

CALL TO ACTION

The power of clear intent translated into organized effort *can* change the world. Business architecture is the golden thread that connects all the pieces across an organization's entire business and technology environment and turns strategy into reality—making the seemingly impossible possible.

We have new mindsets to embrace and new muscles to build. Strategy execution—with transparency, collaboration, ownership, and account-ability from end-to-end—is a critical capability that every single organization needs to develop. Those that do will build the agility and resilience to survive and thrive into the future.

So, this is our call to action. It's a call for bold leadership, vision, and collaboration—and a commitment to something greater than ourselves. Let's come together and start a movement to formalize and practice *strategy to reality*, for the benefit of our organizations and world.

I invite you to continue this journey at **www.StrategyintoReality.com** where you will find an **online companion** to this book including down-loadable diagrams and examples that correspond to the topics through-out. The companion website is available just for readers of this book and includes additional valuable resources and references that offer immersive content. You will also find opportunities to join the global conversation on *strategy to reality*, and launch or accelerate the journey for your organization. See you at the summit, my friend.

ABOUT THE AUTHOR

Whynde Kuehn is recognized globally as a highly sought-after business architecture pioneer and thought leader deeply rooted in delivering measurable business results. As a boots-on-the-ground leader, Whynde has worked with an extensive array of organizations, including Fortune 500 and global enterprises, governmental and non-profit organizations, social enterprises, startups, and cross-sector initiatives. She has helped numerous companies improve their strategy execution ability to make highly informed decisions with the help of well-honed strategic toolsets that harmoniously move big ideas into action across business units, products, and regions.

One of Whynde's most recognized competencies is her ability to assist executives and their teams in cultivating their business architecture practices. She has a distinguished track record in successful team building worldwide. As a long-time educator and community builder, Whynde has also helped countless individuals develop their careers and accelerate their business architecture mastery. With vast experience in enterprise transformation and strategic planning, including leading large-scale transformations and her own business architecture team, Whynde walks her talk. She consults and works alongside strategy execution leaders, change makers, and business architects to create holistic solutions by leveraging business architecture as the keystone. The result: clear, purposeful actions and well-organized efforts with simple, practical, and repeatable approaches that yield transformational change.

Whynde is the creator of a dedicated online platform and community that helps professionals master the art and science of business architecture. She is also the co-founder of a not-for-profit business architecture professional association that has helped advance and formalize the discipline across the globe. Whynde is exceptionally passionate about assisting mission-driven organizations in succeeding and scaling through the application of solid business approaches. Likewise, she routinely inspires corporate entities to use business as a force for good. With a focus on Africa and emerging nations, Whynde has spent years assisting public and private partners in hands-on efforts to drive dreams into action through operating effectively, and creating systemic, sustainable change. Whynde lives with her husband in Norway, where she proudly brings her bold New York spirit, Wisconsin heart, and global ambition for adventure and possibility.

Whynde can be found at:
LinkedIn: linkedin.com/in/whynde-kuehn/
Instagram: instagram.com/strategytoreality/
Website: strategyintoreality.com

ENDNOTES

1   Adapted from the original definition of business architecture in the BIZBOK® Guide by the Business Architecture Guild®, which was "A blueprint of the enterprise that provides a common understanding of the organization and is used to align strategic objectives and tactical demands."

2   This definition of business architecture is currently used in the BIZBOK® Guide. It was ratified in January 2017 by FEAPO Member Organizations, including the Business Architecture Guild®.

3   Rick Kash and David Calhoun, *How Companies Win*: *Profiting from Demand-Driven Business Models* (New York, New York: Harper Collins, October 12, 2010).

4   Robert S. Kaplan and David P. Norton, "The Office of Strategic Management," *Harvard Business Review*, October 2005.

5   Ibid.

6   Whynde Kuehn and Pete Cafarchio, "Business Architect Strengths Study," March 3, 2020, https://bizarchmastery.com/business-architect-strengths-study-brief.

7   Dennis Gaughan, Yefim Natis, Gene Alvarez, Mark O'Neill, "Future of Applications: Delivering the Composable Enterprise," *Gartner*, February 11, 2020.

8   Jeanne Ross, "Architect Your Company for Agility," *MIT Sloan Management Review*, January 10, 2018, https://sloanreview.mit.edu/article/architect-your-company-for-agility/.

9   Alexander Osterwalder and Yves Pigneur, *Business Model Generation*: *A*

Handbook for Visionaries, Game Changers, and Challengers (Hoboken, New Jersey: John Wiley & Sons, Inc., 2010).

10   See Figure 2-1 within Jeanne W. Ross, Peter Weill, and David C. Robertson, *Enterprise Architecture as Strategy: Creating a Foundation for Business* (Boston, Massachusetts: Harvard Business School Publishing, 2006).

11   Andrew Campbell, Mikel Gutierrez, and Mark Lancelott, *Operating Model Canvas* (Van Haren Publishing, 2017).

12   Jay Galbraith, Diane Downey, Amy Kates, *Designing Dynamic Organizations: A Hands-on Guide for Leaders at All Levels* (New York, New York: AMACOM, 2002).

13   Ibid.

14   Ibid.

15   This section is informed by perspectives in the following white papers: Business Architecture Guild®, *Business Architecture and BPM: Differentiation and Reconciliation*, October 2014, https://cdn.ymaws.com/www. businessarchitectureguild.org/resource/resmgr/docs/batobpmalignment-positionpape.pdf and Business Architecture Guild®, *Similar Yet Different: Value Streams and Business Processes: The Business Architecture Perspective,* December 2019, https://cdn.ymaws.com/www.businessarchitectureguild. org/resource/resmgr/public_resources/bpm_paper_final_dec2019.pdf.

16   Keith D. Swenson and Nathaniel Palmer, *Taming the Unpredictable: Real World Adaptive Case Management: Case Studies and Practical Guidance* (Lighthouse Point, FL: Future Strategies, 2011).

17   This section is informed by perspectives in Business Architecture Guild®, *Similar Yet Different: Value Streams and Business Processes: The Business Architecture Perspective,* December 2019, https://cdn.ymaws.com/www. businessarchitectureguild.org/resource/resmgr/public_resources/bpm_paper_final_dec2019.pdf.

18   "Features and Capabilities," Scaled Agile Framework®, accessed September 7, 2021, https://www.scaledagileframework.com/features-and-capabilities/?_ga=2.207074323.1212395932.1628822807-2128532161.1628650528.

19   See The Pennsylvania State University, University Park, Pennsylvania, https://www.worldcampus.psu.edu/degrees-and-certificates/business-ar-

chitecture-certificate/overview.

20   The chasm as defined by Geoffrey Moore, *Crossing the Chasm* (New York, NY: HarperCollins Publishers, 2014).

A free ebook edition
is available with the
purchase of this book.

To claim your free ebook edition:

1. Visit MorganJamesBOGO.com
2. Sign your name CLEARLY in the space
3. Complete the form and submit a photo of the entire copyright page
4. You or your friend can download the ebook to your preferred device

Morgan James BOGO™

A **FREE** ebook edition is available for you or a friend with the purchase of this print book.

CLEARLY SIGN YOUR NAME ABOVE

Instructions to claim your free ebook edition:
1. Visit MorganJamesBOGO.com
2. Sign your name CLEARLY in the space above
3. Complete the form and submit a photo of this entire page
4. You or your friend can download the ebook to your preferred device

Print & Digital Together Forever.

Snap a photo

Free ebook

Read anywhere